DisOrientations

THE MAX KADE RESEARCH INSTITUTE SERIES:
GERMANS BEYOND EUROPE

Series Editor
Daniel Purdy

Founding Editor
A. Gregg Roeber

The Max Kade Research Institute Series is an outlet for
scholarship that examines the history and culture of
German-speaking communities in America and across the
globe from the early modern period to the present. Books
in this series examine the movements of the German-
speaking diaspora as influenced by forces such as migration,
colonization, war, research, religious missions, or trade. This
series explores the historical and cultural depictions of the
international networks that connect these communities,
as well as linguistic relations between German and other
languages within European global networks.

This series is a project of the Max Kade Research Institute
located on Penn State's campus. It was founded in 1993
thanks to a grant from the Max Kade Foundation, New York.

DisOrientations

GERMAN-TURKISH CULTURAL CONTACT
IN TRANSLATION, 1811–1946

The Pennsylvania State University Press
University Park, Pennsylvania

Kristin Dickinson

An earlier version of chapter six appeared as "Intervening in the
Humanist Legacy: Sabahattin Ali's Kleist Translations," *Turkish-
German Studies Yearbook* 8 (Spring 2017).

Library of Congress Cataloging-in-Publication Data

Names: Dickinson, Kristin, 1981– author.
Title: DisOrientations : German-Turkish cultural contact in
    translation, 1811–1946 / Kristin Dickinson.
Other titles: Max Kade German-American Research Institute
    series.
Description: University Park, Pennsylvania : The Pennsylvania
    State University Press, [2021] | Series: Max Kade Research
    Institute series: Germans beyond Europe | Includes
    bibliographical references and index.
Summary: "Explores the German-Turkish literary-cultural
    relationship from 1811 to 1946, focusing on literary translation
    as a complex mode of cultural, political, and linguistic
    orientation"—Provided by publisher.
Identifiers: LCCN 2021010374 | ISBN 9780271089843 (cloth)
Subjects: LCSH: Turkish literature—19th century—Translations
    into German—History and criticism. | Turkish literature—
    20th century—Translations into German—History and
    criticism. | German literature—Translations into Turkish—
    History and criticism. | Turkey—Relations—Germany. |
    Germany—Relations—Turkey.
Classification: LCC PL209 .D53 2021 | DDC 894/.35—dc23
LC record available at https://lccn.loc.gov/2021010374

The Pennsylvania State University Press is a member of the
Association of University Presses.

It is the policy of The Pennsylvania State University Press to
use acid-free paper. Publications on uncoated stock satisfy the
minimum requirements of American National Standard for
Information Sciences—Permanence of Paper for Printed Library
Material, ANSI Z39.48–1992.

For Tuncay

Contents

Acknowledgments

This book has benefitted from the generous support of numerous institutions, colleagues, and dear friends. I conducted research for chapters one, two, and five as a fellow with the Social Science Research Council. I later researched and wrote chapters three and four as a fellow at the International Research Center for Cultural Studies (IFK) in Vienna, Austria. The University of Michigan generously provided funding for a manuscript workshop. I am especially grateful for the detailed feedback I received at this workshop from Leslie Adelson and Azade Seyhan. Their thorough and thoughtful comments have shaped and strengthened this book, just as their scholarship has served as an important source of inspiration for my own. I would also like to thank the many people I have worked with at Pennsylvania State University Press to bring this book to fruition, including Daniel Purdy, Kathryn Bourque Yahner, Laura Reed-Morrisson, Maddie Caso, Alex Ramos, and Leyla Aksu.

Numerous colleagues at the University of Michigan have also read and commented on different sections of this book over the past five years, including Maya Barzilai, Gottfried Hagen, Julia Hell, Fred Amrine, Helmut Puff, Kerstin Barndt, Silke-Maria Weineck, Peter McIsaac, Scott Spector, Tyler Whitney, and Kira Thurman. Yopie Prins and Scotti Parrish provided valuable feedback on my book proposal. Special thanks go to Andreas Gailus for his detailed comments at different stages of the writing process. And I am particularly grateful to Johannes von Moltke for his advice on questions of structure and theoretical framing. Damani Partridge and Kira Thurman also offered much-needed moral support and encouragement at different stages of this project.

Thought-provoking conversations with graduate students at the University of Michigan have contributed to the lines of thought I develop in this book in more ways than one. It has been a pleasure working with Duygu Ergun, Matthew Liberti, Ali Bolcakan, Elizabeth McNeill, Özlem

Karuç, Marina Mayorski, Veronica Williamson, Lauren Beck, Rhiannon Muncaster, Onyx Henry, and Berkay Uluç. Duygu Ergun in particular has provided invaluable support as my research assistant over the past several years.

I want to thank Deniz Göktürk for her pioneering scholarship in the fields of Turkish German studies and migration studies and for encouraging me to pursue interdisciplinary lines of thought from the earliest stages of this project's inception. Kader Konuk's research has similarly been instrumental to my own, and I am grateful for our productive exchanges over the years. Randall Halle's friendship and support have accompanied me through all stages of my career. I have cherished our many conversations in Turkey, Germany, Spain, and cities across the United States, and I look forward to many more. Sibel Erol infected me early on with her contagious enthusiasm for Turkish literature. And Thomas Hahn has encouraged my intellectual curiosity over the course of many years.

I have always admired David Gramling's scholarship and activism; this book has benefitted greatly from his suggestions, just as I have benefitted from our many exchanges and collaborations over the years. Pondering the future of Transnational German Studies with Ela Gezen and Priscilla Layne has also been an immensely productive experience. I thank them both for their friendship and inspiring interdisciplinary scholarship.

Cotranslating with Zeynep Seviner was an incredibly generative experience that also informed chapter five of this book. Etienne Charrière has also indulged me in ongoing conversations about translation, transliteration, and translingual communities in the late Ottoman Empire. He provided valuable feedback on my introduction, as well as chapters four and five. William Stroebel has been an important interlocuter and friend, and I thank him for his comments on my introduction in particular. I am grateful also to Jason Vivrette for his continued friendship, good humor, and willingness to entertain my questions on the etymologies of words.

This book benefitted immensely from the copyediting skills of Vanessa Larson. Working with her on this manuscript has reminded me of our past collaborations and how much I value her friendship and curiosity. I am also delighted to have befriended Johanna Schuster-Craig, with whom I regularly share thoughts, plants, and book materials. She has generously read numerous sections of this book. Robin Ellis and Annika Orich are two dear friends and colleagues without whom I would never have come this far; our regular conversations have sustained me in ways I cannot count.

From the day I first met Megan Ewing, I knew she would be a friend for life. I thank her dearly for sharing in all my joys and fears as if they were her own. I am also deeply grateful for the friendship of Radhika Dewan Fliegel, whose compassion and generosity never cease to amaze me.

This book is indebted to the continued support of my parents, Kathleen and Edward Dickinson. They gave me a pen and paper and encouraged me to write at a young age and always made me feel that I could accomplish anything I put my mind to. I would not be where I am today without them.

My daughter, Leyla, lights up my life with her creativity, curiosity, and kindness. Her commitments to creating a more equitable and just world inspire me every single day. My darling son, Tarık, fills the room with his infectious laughter. I thank him for reminding me when it is time to just take a break and play. Finally, I cannot express enough gratitude to Tuncay for his endless love and support. He has seen this project through from start to finish, all the while reminding me of what is most important in life. This book is dedicated to him and the many years, laughs, and languages we have shared.

Introduction
Translational Orientations

Having squandered his inheritance on expensive European items, Bihruz Bey, the protagonist of Recaizade Mahmut Ekrem's *The Carriage Affair* (*Araba Sevdası*, 1896), regularly puts himself on display in the promenade of a local park. It is here that he falls head over heels for Periveş Hanım, due not to her character but rather to the luxurious landau carriage in which he first spots her. Determined to present Periveş with a declaration of his love, Bihruz sets out to compose a letter worthy of the status he imagines she represents. Yet the series of misinterpretations and botched translations that he strings together from French source texts is matched only by the falsity of his assumptions: the woman is a prostitute and the carriage is rented.

In a crowning touch, Bihruz decides to append to his letter a verse of poetry. While certain that the Ottoman Turkish language is not suitable for this genre, Bihruz knows that Turkish women admire the work of a certain Vâsıf.[1] Yet after selecting what he deems an appropriate verse, Bihruz realizes he cannot decipher it on his own. Unwilling to admit defeat, he turns to an Ottoman Turkish dictionary once gifted to him by his father. Covered in dust and tearing at the seams, the "Redhouse" that Bihruz unearths from the messy depths of a drawer is in a state of clear neglect. Yet Bihruz immediately vows to rebind and prominently display the dictionary upon recognizing its author—Sir James Redhouse—as a well-known British Orientalist. Transformed in Bihruz's eyes into an omniscient source of knowledge on the Ottoman Turkish language, this dictionary suddenly takes on a more prominent role in the story line. Placing all of his trust in this book, Bihruz believes it to be more credible than his well-educated Turkish colleagues, only to discover in the end that the joke was on him. Due to his lack of education, Bihruz misreads the Perso-Arabic script of the Ottoman Turkish poem. Refabricating the verse in question, he refers to the blonde object of his affection as a "swarthy youth."

Written on the heels of political, economic, and educational reforms aimed at modernizing the Ottoman Empire, *Carriage* tells the tragicomic story of a *züppe*, or insufficiently Westernized Ottoman dandy: in his attempt to emulate European culture, Bihruz proves only his mediocre training in French, his equally poor knowledge of Ottoman Turkish, and his general disdain for Ottoman culture.[2] While this novel now forms a cornerstone of modern Turkish literature, *Carriage* faced heavy criticism in the twentieth century. In his landmark study, *A History of Nineteenth-Century Turkish Literature* (*XIX. Asır Türk Edebiyatı Tarihi*, 1949), for example, Ahmet Hamdi Tanpınar (1901–1962) describes *Carriage* as devoid of interiority. Interpreting Bihruz's mortgaged carriage—rather than Bihruz himself—as its protagonist, Tanpınar deemed the novel to be a "book of rootless shadows" populated by characters without a sustained presence.[3] Marked by transcience and artificialty, Tanpınar likened the novel to a joke.[4]

While Tanpınar viewed *Carriage* as the story of a specific generation—and thus understood its efficacy as limited to the critique of a passing era—he did not simply brush this work aside.[5] On the contrary, he identified *Carriage* as the first work of Turkish literature worthy of being considered in the category of the novel.[6] Thus even in his critique, Tanpınar recognized something foundational in *Carriage*, a recognition paradoxically corroborating his earlier declaration that Turks still did not have a novel of their own.[7] In essays such as "Our Novel" ("Bizde Roman I," 1936) and "Toward a National Literature" ("Millî Bir Edebiyata Doğru," 1940), Tanpınar expressed the "lack" of an authentically Turkish literature that could serve as the expression of a national self.[8] As a novel without an explicit center, *Carriage* only exacerbated this sense of lack.

Pointing to the novel as a genre borrowed from the West, Tanpınar underscored the need for a novel that could encapsulate the "totality" of Turkish experience.[9] Following an extensive period of Europeanization, he argued for the need to "return to ourselves, our own lives, our own past, and our own riches."[10] This, he believed, required not a rejection of Western art forms such as the novel but rather a synthesis of Turkish values and European ideals.[11] *Carriage* was, on the contrary, a novel that refused this kind of synthesis. If, for Tanpınar, Turkish literary history was marked by a lack, *Carriage* is a novel that flaunts this lack. Whereas Tanpınar longed for an authentically Turkish self, *Carriage* refused to render its characters with the interiority necessary to achieve this goal. And unlike Tanpınar, who viewed the creation of fully fleshed-out characters with complex inner thoughts and feelings as a prerequisite for cultural authenticity, *Carriage* upended the premise of authenticity itself.

The tension between these two positions has often been described in terms of belatedness.[12] Inspired by European models that preceded it, the Turkish novel in particular has been treated as a belated art form. This accusation is often tied to the fact that the genre of the novel in the Ottoman Turkish literary realm was in large part inspired by translations from French. The modern Turkish novel is thus linked to an understanding of translation as an art form that follows an "original" in both space and time. Like the character of Bihruz, the Turkish novel was doomed to merely mimic its European counterpart.[13]

This book seeks to reframe such conversations on Turkish literature and culture around the concept of orientation, as opposed to notions of interiority, authenticity, or belatedness. While Tanpınar did not use this term explicitly, the stakes of orientation were clearly an urgent theoretical concern for him. Registering both a deep sense of loss and an anxiety about the future, his novels reflect the "psychological dilemma" of a people whose identity had undergone profound transformations in the face of rapid societal changes across the late nineteenth and early twentieth centuries.[14] While Tanpınar was by no means a backward-looking fundamentalist, he responded by asserting the need to "return" to a collective "Turkish" self after decades of Westernizing reforms. He thus perceived a dissolution of Turkishness in the Ottoman Empire and modern Turkey's historic reorientation toward Europe. Despite his recurrent emphasis on interiority, Tanpınar presents us with a mode of orientation that is dependent on a fixed external referent (the "West"), which perpetuates the very dependency of Turkish culture it seeks to overcome.

By maintaining the "West" as a stable external referent, Tanpınar's need to "return" to a preconceived and collective Turkish self inverts phenomenological definitions of orientation, which describe this concept as starting with and affirming the individual self. In his focus on lived experience, for example, Edmund Husserl describes the body as "the zero point of orientation, the bearer of the here and now."[15] It is only from "here"—our bodily position in space and time—that, for Husserl, an external "there" may later emerge. This external point of reference toward which we orient ourselves serves in turn to solidify the interiority of the self.

Taking up the example of *Carriage*—together with its rendition into German in 2014—I argue here for an alternative model of *translational* orientation. Whereas Husserl assumes the self-as-body as the starting point and anchor for all subsequent acts of orientation, Tanpınar seeks to find orientation in a *return* to the self. Despite their differences, both of these models thus rest on the assumption of, or desire for, an intact self. In contrast, the concept of translational orientation refutes the idea of a clear starting point, or of a (national) consciousness that could exist outside of, or prior to, the play of language. Language—and in particular language in translation—is always relational, linking meaning to movement and displacement. Whereas Tanpınar longed for the return to an authentic Turkish identity, the concept of translational orientation underscores the multiple processes of translation at work in a novel like *Carriage*, and thus also in the production of "Turkishness" in the first place.[16]

Reading *Carriage* with Tanpınar under the sign of belatedness would uphold an understanding of orientation as a unidirectional affair: such a reading would suggest that modern Turkish literature was fundamentally altered in its reorientation toward Western European models in the late nineteenth century, whereas European literature remained intact in the exchange. Taking up the German–(Ottoman) Turkish relationship in particular, this book instead insists on an understanding of orientation as an omnidirectional encounter. In the words of Sara Ahmed, "orientations involve at least a two-way approach."[17] When we orient ourselves toward someone or something, we are also approached by that person or object. When we touch something, we are also touched. As a site of contact, orientation thus does not always affirm one's perceived bodily position but rather harbors a disorienting potential that may destabilize the boundaries of self and other, interiority and exteriority.[18]

This disorienting potential is inscribed in the very term "orientation," which is semantically linked to the word "Orient." Grimm's dictionary, for example, presents the concept of self-orientation as a *problem* rooted in the relationship of "West" to "East": "(in the absence of the compass needle) to try to find the excess—namely, the East—of one's familiar worldly location."[19] Orientation emerges, in this definition, as a process of turning toward an implied "East" that is nevertheless impossible to locate with accuracy. As the unknown excess of an implied West, the imprecise location of the Orient also implies the instability of the Western self who requires it as an external referent for self-definition. A critical approach to orientation, I argue, involves a similar rethinking of the relationship between Turkish and German, East and West.

Considering literary translations between German and (Ottoman) Turkish as one mode of textual, linguistic, and cultural encounter, this book builds on the work of Ahmed and others to argue that there is no zero-point of orientation, no clearly defined "here" and "there," and, by analogy, no original and translation that stand in opposition. While translation scholars have long recognized the paucity of theoretical frameworks based on binarisms, pointing to the need for "middle grounds, alternative possibilities, [and] positions of both/and,"[20] readers and scholars alike still often utilize the terms "source" and "target" as relatively stable categories through which we can refer to texts and languages.[21] Within this logic, translations are also generally assumed to travel in one direction: from source to target, and from past to present. This assumption prevails despite a sustained scholarly emphasis on translation as a dynamic and contested site of power relations, and as a creative rather than a merely mimetic act.[22]

We can see these assumptions of stasis—as Karen Emmerich has shown—in how scholars continue to treat "originals" as "categorically richer texts than translations."[23] But "originals" are also fluid texts formed through multiple mediating processes of editing, manuscript preparation, serial publication, and so on. By grappling with and extending the extant levels of variance within a given text, translation constitutes a creative act with the power to forge new textual reconfigurations.[24] The original thus serves neither as a static point of orientation nor as confirmation of originality.

In 2014, the first translation of *Carriage* into any language worldwide demonstrated precisely this, by projecting the questions of orientation so central to this novel into new linguistic, temporal, cultural, and geographic realms. *Leidenschaft in Çamlıca* (*A Passion in Çamlıca*), which formed part of the "Classics" series by the German publisher Literaturca, appeared in a very different historical moment from that of the novel's inception. While only a limited number of Ottoman Turkish texts had been translated into German by 1896, *Leidenschaft* participates in a contemporary uptick in translation activity from both Ottoman and modern Turkish literature into German. For comparison, a meager 260 translations were undertaken prior to 1989, whereas 750 books were translated between 1990 and 2010 alone. Together with newer and older publishing houses seeking to challenge cliché-laden representations of the Turkish cultural landscape—including Binooki, Manzara, Dağyeli, Babel, Ararat, Express-Edition, Rotbuch, and

Verlag am Galgenberg—Literaturca aims to bring a more diverse array of (Ottoman) Turkish texts in translation to the German literary scene.

These cumulative efforts have been bolstered by several key events: In 2005, the Turkish government established an extensive subvention program (TEDA) to support the translation of Turkish literature abroad, including 280 translations into German.[25] From 2005 to 2010, the Robert Bosch Foundation funded the Turkish Library, a high-quality twenty-volume translation series published with Unionsverlag.[26] Within this period, Orhan Pamuk received the Nobel Prize in Literature in 2006, bringing new attention to Turkish literature worldwide. Turkey's 2008 appearance as guest of honor at the Frankfurt Book Fair then led to both a record number of translations from Turkish into German and a yearlong series of cultural events across Germany.[27]

From within this contemporary context, what can a publication like *Leidenschaft* tell us about German–(Ottoman) Turkish cultural relations of the *past*? Bihruz's conception of Europe is shaped by France, and his main source of knowledge about the Ottoman Turkish language is a dictionary first produced by the British Orientalist Sir James Redhouse in 1861. In short, German language and culture are seemingly absent from the scene. But does *Carriage* simply corroborate an apparent lack of German–(Ottoman) Turkish cultural relations in the nineteenth century? Reading this novel in translation fundamentally alters the way we approach this question. It leads us, on the contrary, to read about such a presumed lack through the lens of the German language, 118 years after the fact. By enacting an unexpected site of encounter in the present through its very form (the German language), *Leidenschaft* also sensitizes us to other possible sites of connection in the past. This is to say it leads us to reconsider the importance of a German–(Ottoman) Turkish relationship where we might otherwise presume it to be absent.

Against this background, the relationship of *Carriage* to *Leidenschaft* serves as a springboard from which to take a long view of the German–(Ottoman) Turkish relationship in order to address the main premise of this book: the manner in which diverse translations between German and (Ottoman) Turkish have operated across time frames, political contexts, and literary traditions to serve as geopolitical and chronopolitical forces of orientation in their own right. As with the other diverse case studies addressed in this book, the example of *Leidenschaft* underscores multiple modes of directionality at work in the process of translation. While

Leidenschaft follows *Carriage* temporally in standardized calendrical time, for example, this translation does not reassert an "originary" quality of the Turkish novel. On the contrary, the German language highlights in new ways the manner in which a novel like *Carriage* negotiates the very terms of originality. In doing so, it also redirects the questions of orientation inherent both to Ekrem's novel and to this book.

Carriage contrasts *alaturca* and *alafranga* lifestyles, which represent an orientation toward traditional "Eastern" (Turkish) and "Western" (European) tastes and mannerisms, respectively. Yet while clearly exposing the farcical character of Bihruz's *alafranga* tendencies, the novel does not uphold some authentically Turkish alternative or provide an example of a successfully modernized character. *Carriage* instead exposes as the backdrop for Bihruz's follies a fundamentally shifting cultural terrain marked through and through by processes of translation.

Given the historical significance of translation as an Orientalist mode of knowledge production, *Leidenschaft* transfers the questions of origins and originality so central to *Carriage* into a new register. Even before the unification of Germany in 1871, German was an important language of scholarly Orientalism. Reading *Carriage* in German thus prompts us to examine the general role Orientalism played in asserting the difference between Orient and Occident, as well as the concept of an authentically Turkish character in the first place. This highlights in turn the links between a more general Western process of self-orientation vis-à-vis the East and the institutionalized practice of scholarly Orientalism. It furthermore invites us to analyze the specific role that German Orientalism played vis-à-vis its French and British counterparts in the late Ottoman Empire, as well as changes in the German–(Ottoman) Turkish relationship over time. Reading *Leidenschaft* with attention to these issues creates a productive tension between the diverse modes of mediation inherent to the Ottoman Turkish novel and the Orientalist fixation of an "Eastern" other in both space and time.

Opening up these diverse implications requires attention not only to the work of translation in the moment of its undertaking but also to the effects of translation across longer spans of time. In other words, reading *Leidenschaft* in 2014 may bring us back to issues inherent to *Carriage*'s inception, while also projecting us forward into potential reconfigurations of the German-Turkish relationship in the future. This approach attends to the transtemporal movements of translation, which "cross and connect times on different, yet 'jumping scales,'"[28] thereby allowing us to trace intersections across nonsynchronous histories. It is furthermore tied to the concept of orientation as a mode of situating oneself not only in space but also in time.

As Ahmed cogently argues, orienting oneself in time involves engagement with multiple temporalities. While orientation in the present often entails a process of looking backward, it can also propel us forward into the future: "The hope of changing directions is always that we do not know where some paths may take us: risking departure from the straight and narrow, makes new futures possible, which might involve going astray, [or] getting lost."[29] Similarly, this book examines the myriad ways in which a German–(Ottoman) Turkish translational relationship has "run astray" from the dominant historical and discursive narratives of Orientalism and modernization from which they emerged. In its sweeping view of the German–(Ottoman) Turkish literary-cultural relationship from 1811 to 1946, this book also looks forward to the as-yet-uncharted futures of fields like Turkish German, translation, and world literary studies. It does so by examining the omnidirectional and transtemporal movements of translations, which harbor the productively disorienting potential to reconfigure the relationships of "original" to "translation," "past" to "present," "West" to "East," and "German" to "Turkish."

TRANSLATIONAL REORIENTATIONS

At the time of *Carriage*'s composition, translation activity played a central role in the reorientation of Ottoman Turkish literature away from the long-standing influence of Persian and Arabic and toward new European cultural influences. Linked to questions of modernization and Westernization, and thus also imitation, authenticity, and originality, debates on the relative purpose and value of translations from European source texts were hotly debated in the public sphere.

The significance of translation for the project of Ottoman modernization dates to the early nineteenth century. Some of the first translations from European (predominantly French) source texts were undertaken for political purposes within the context of the Translation Chamber (*Tercüme Odası*), which was created in 1821 and fully established as a department of the Sublime Porte in 1833. In addition to teaching French, Arabic, Persian, general history, and math, the Translation Chamber trained its Muslim students as translators of official documents.[30] As an important center for the education of young bureaucrats who often went on to serve as diplomats in European capitals,[31] the Translation Chamber is but one example of how the institutions of civil bureaucracy helped produce members of a new intelligentsia that were active in both political and literary spheres.

The Translation Chamber took on increased importance in the 1840s, following the 1839 Edict of Gülhane, which ushered in the Tanzimat, or the "reorganization" era of the Ottoman Empire (1839–76).[32] During this period, a series of state-sponsored modernizing reforms modeled largely on European practices were initiated in the military, administrative, legal, and educational realms.[33] Translations of Western European source texts played a formative role in this wide-ranging attempt to revitalize Ottoman society, forming a basis for the sociopolitical importance of translation activity in the late Ottoman Empire and the modern Republic of Turkey.

In the literary realm, İbrahim Şinasi (1826–1871) undertook the first ever translations from a European language into Ottoman Turkish in 1859; his renditions of classical French poetry by Racine, Lamartine, La Fontaine, Gilbert, and Fénelon set the stage for the dominant role French literature would play in the field of late nineteenth-century Ottoman Turkish literature.[34] In this same year, Yusuf Kâmil Paşa (1808–1876) translated François Fénelon's *The Adventures of Telemachus* (*Les Aventures de Télémaque*, 1699) and Münif Efendi (1830–1910) translated a collection of philosophical texts by Fénelon, Fontenelle, and Voltaire.

Following a long and rich history of translations from Arabic and Persian, these first translations from French initiated an important paradigm shift in the Ottoman Turkish literary realm. Victoria Holbrook describes this period as nothing short of a "radical shift of semiotic orientation," during which characteristically Ottoman forms of literary criticism slowly gave way to the European-inspired genres of the novel, the journalistic essay, philological literary history, modern drama, literary criticism, and the anthology.[35] On the one hand, this introduction of new genres via processes of translation was incredibly generative: it contributed to the dissemination of new political and cultural ideals, affected new forms of literary experimentation, and contributed to the assertion of a modern Turkish literary voice.[36] On the other hand, the reorientation of Ottoman Turkish literature toward Western European models also produced crippling anxieties. The translation of European literature into Ottoman Turkish was linked to the presumed one-way movement of modernity from West to East. And like the growing body of European literature in translation, the Turkish experience of modernity was plagued by questions of secondariness and belatedness. Compounding these issues, cultural elites feared the erosion of a specifically Turkish cultural and religious identity in the face of modernization.

In the literary realm, these anxieties often coalesced around the figure of the dandy. Early examples of dandy figures—such as Felâtun Bey in Ahmet Mithat's *Felâtun Bey and Râkım Efendi* (*Felâtun Bey ile Râkım Efendi*, 1875)—appeared alongside counterexamples of "properly" modernized characters capable of forging a successful synthesis of Eastern and Western influences.[37] Such counterexamples served as a clear and confident voice from within the novel that could mock the dandy as a "false other."[38] In her brilliant analysis, Nurdan Gürbilek notes that any such confident voice is missing in *Carriage*, whether in the form of a character or an omniscient narrator. Shifting between third-person singular and first-person plural, the narration of *Carriage* wavers. At times, the narrator's authorial voice becomes indistinguishable from Bihruz's. "It is this faltering voice," Gürbilek argues, "that makes *The Carriage Affair* a novel going out of order, a novel in which the writer loses its voice among voices and texts other than his own."[39]

Of the many voices and texts that appear in *Carriage*, several serve as source texts for an act of translation that forms the core of the novel. In an attempt to compose a love letter, Bihruz turns to French Romanticism for inspiration. Yet because he is unable to comprehend his literary sources, he produces nothing more than a string of mistranslations. At its core, then, we might say that *Carriage* is about the failure of translation on both linguistic and cultural levels.[40] This is poignantly reflected in Bihruz's speech, which is shot through with superfluous French expressions, to the extent that he is at times unintelligible to family and friends. Placed in parentheses in the Perso-Arabic script of the Ottoman Turkish text,[41] these French terms are generally italicized in the myriad intralingual translations of the novel into modern Turkish. In each instance, French serves as a force of linguistic and cultural intrusion, as a sign of Bihruz's excessiveness, and as an indicator of his failure to communicate effectively.

In an iconic scene, Bihruz turns to the lyric poet Vâsıf to augment his already ludicrous love letter. Yet while relatively accessible in terms of form and content, Vâsıf's poetry remains indecipherable for Bihruz. Exasperated, he retorts aloud, "Çince mi bunlar? *Kel drol dö langaj*" ("Is this Chinese? *Quel drôle de langage*").[42] In this brief aside, Bihruz expresses his alienation from the Perso-Arabic script, which—through the comparison to Chinese—is coded as illegible and incomprehensible. He then openly belittles the "bizarre" Ottoman Turkish language, expressing an internalized sense of inferiority toward French *in French*.

The Ottoman Empire was never colonized; Bihruz's remarks are rather generated from within a process of modernization and societal reorientation actively undertaken by the empire. Yet his comments clearly exhibit an internalization of philological Orientalist rhetoric. While lauding the development of Turkish nationalism at the turn to the twentieth century, various Orientalist scholars dismissed the elevated rhetorical style of Ottoman divan poetry—which had served as the main literary genre since the fourteenth century—as outdated or difficult.[43] Bihruz's comments reveal how this Orientalist worldview permeated the thought of Ottoman Turkish cultural elites until it ultimately came to bear on their perception of the Perso-Arabic script itself.

As with myriad other French phrases in the novel, translator Beatrix Caner renders this entire scene into German: "Ist das auf Chinesisch geschrieben? Was für eine lächerliche Sprache."[44] (Is this written in Chinese? What a ridiculous language.) The implications of this shift loom large: Overwriting the French, the German language serves as a powerful medium of temporal reorientation, in that it asserts the strength and persistence of a German-Turkish literary-cultural relationship in the present. At the same time, the translation belies German anxieties of the late nineteenth century, when Germany vied with France and Britain for economic influence in the late Ottoman Empire through projects such as the Berlin-Baghdad Railway. Bihruz criticizes the Ottoman Turkish language *in German*, even as the content of the novel continues to detail his obsession with French. As such, the phrase "was für eine lächerliche Sprache" imagines the *potential* power of German as a dominant cultural influence in the late Ottoman Empire that could rival French. This tension itself then inadvertently recalls German authors' own sense of inferiority toward French classicism well into the nineteenth century, bringing yet another perspective to the concept of belatedness.

French classicism served as both a literary model and a hegemonic force for German authors throughout the eighteenth century. The resulting desire to establish a strong German literary and cultural identity that could counter French classicism was compounded by the Napoleonic Wars and the German battle against French "imperialism."[45] In the absence of a politically unified nation-state, German intellectuals imagined themselves as part of a *Kulturnation*, or a cultural union, sustained through recourse to a common language and literature. Projects such as Joachim Heinrich Campe's *Dictionary of the German Language* (*Wörterbuch der deutschen Sprache*, 1807) and Jacob Grimm's German lexicon (*Deutsches Wörterbuch*, 1854), which sought to record and preserve linguistic tradition, were central to a projection of the German language as a unifying force. An imagined national literature further served as critical preparation for the eventual political unification and economic integration of the individual principalities under a common German state in 1871.[46]

Translation played a central role in the early nineteenth-century assertion of a German *Kulturnation*. During this time period, authors undertook an unprecedented amount of translations from European and "Oriental" literatures, as well as biblical and classical texts. Their paradoxical investment in the transformative power of translation to exert a specifically *German* identity took recourse to an earlier precedent: Luther's Bible (1522). Establishing a common literary language through the act of translation, Luther's translational style was deemed an important expansion of the German language. Consequentially, many late eighteenth- and early nineteenth-century scholars saw him as both a reformer and a creator of language. Antoine Berman discusses, in particular, the importance of Luther's translations for the German concept of *Bildung*. German national self-awareness, he argues, developed not only through contact with the foreign but also by *passing through* the foreign in translation. Translation thus engendered a process of alienation that ultimately led to self-understanding.[47]

Around 1800, translation took on an increasingly important role, paving the way for the fields of philology, comparative grammar, textual criticism, and hermeneutics. The emergence of diverse theories of translation—as a journey abroad (Herder), as a form of enhancement (Schlegel), and as mode of rewriting (Hölderlin)—marked a paradigm shift from an early eighteenth-century emphasis on questions of fidelity to early Romantic conceptions of the translator as a creative genius.

As early as 1768, Johann Gottfried Herder quoted Thomas Abbt's idea that the job of a genuine translator is more than the simple transmission of foreign content. Rather, Herder elevates the translator to the rank of a classic author, who must be "a creative genius, in order to satisfy both the original and his own language."[48] Johann Heinrich Voss's translations of the *Odyssey* (1781) and the *Iliad* (1793) paved the way for the kind of translation Herder envisioned, establishing a new stage in German translation theory and practice. In addition to paying close attention to the syntax and word order of Greek, he also reproduced a very close approximation of Greek hexameter in German. While Friedrich Gottfried Klopstock had previously introduced Greek forms into German, even he was highly critical of Voss's style, arguing that Voss's translation of the *Iliad* "had done violence to the idiom of the Germans, and had sacrificed it to the Greeks."[49] Despite this initial criticism, Voss's close attention to form revealed a new flexibility in the German language that had previously been thought impossible, and by 1798 his translations had indeed come to be regarded as classics. Johann Wolfgang von Goethe in particular praised Voss's translations for their versatility and rhythmic quality, revealing important shifts in style and taste that were already occurring in the 1780s.

The translation of *Carriage* into German raises a number of issues central to this historical background. Reading this novel from the present affords a long view of German and (Ottoman) Turkish translational (re)orientations that predate *Carriage*'s first publication. Can a German historical understanding of translation as a creative act of cultural rejuvenation provide a counterforce to the anxiety of belatedness that pervades a novel like *Carriage*? The act of reading *Carriage* through the lens of the German language enacts a translational encounter that brings two nonsynchronous histories together and foregrounds the inherently comparative nature of both (Ottoman) Turkish and German literary histories.[50]

The contemporary context of *Leidenschaft*'s publication in 2014 also serves as a counterpoint to the novel's historical backdrop. *Carriage* was written at a time when Ottoman Turkish authors viewed their own work as "belated" and during which European source texts were translated into Ottoman Turkish in increasing numbers. Over a century later, we might understand "belatedness" as a quality of the German translation rather than the novel itself. Furthermore, *Leidenschaft* is one of an increasing number of Turkish literary texts being translated into German and other languages worldwide. While Turkish still remains a relatively "minor" literature on the global scene,[51] the twenty-first century has seen a reversal of directionality in German-Turkish translational flows. This is significant, in that German—alongside French and Latin—has historically formed the Eurocentric core of fields like comparative literature.[52]

All of these factors suggest the need to do away with linear models of comparison, which perpetuate scales of development. By figuring one group's present as another group's future, linearity fuels the same anxieties found at the core of the figure of the dandy. Reading *Carriage* in German prompts us instead to think omnidirectionally: Whereas *Carriage* portrays a one-way European (and in particular French) influence on the figure of Bihruz,

Leidenschaft brings a triad of relations (Turkish-French, German-Turkish, German-French) into contact, thus troubling the very dichotomy of orientations depicted through the terms *alafranga* and *alaturca*. Finally, the introduction of German—as a language of nineteenth-century scholarly Orientalism—into the narrative of *Carriage* highlights the geopolitical implications of translation as a historically powerful mode of orientation, *dis*orientation, and *re*orientation.

ORIENT-ORIENTATION-ORIENTALISM

The verb "to orient" is etymologically linked to the imagined space of "the Orient" as that which lies to the East. Derived from the meaning of Orient, as the (Eastern) horizon over which the sun rises, the verb "to orient" evokes both a general directionality and the more specific idea of "turn[ing] toward the east."[53] The "East" could of course denote any number of horizons. It is through Euclidean geometry, and its assertion of Greenwich as the prime meridian, that the practice of orienting oneself connotes "participat[ion] in a longer history in which certain 'directions' are 'given to' certain places: . . . *the* East, *the* West, and so on."[54]

This specific manner in which "East" and "West" have acquired status as global directions is also central to Edward Said's theory of Orientalism. Without denying its status as an actual place, Said emphasizes the "man-made" quality of an "Orient" imagined to be geographically, culturally, and historically distinct from the "Occident."[55] As a complex system of knowledge produced by Western scholars and statesmen, Orientalism represents, and thereby also contains, the Orient. Maintained through the self-projected positional superiority of the Westerner,[56] Orientalism enforces the Orientalist as the zero-point of orientation. The power of Orientalists to fixate the "East" in their orientation toward it is then reinforced by the expansive reach of European colonialism. It is no coincidence that the most rapid advancements in Orientalist institutions and scholarship corresponded with the period of unparalleled European expansion from 1815 to 1914; during this time period, European colonial domination grew from covering 35 percent of the inhabited Earth to nearly 85 percent.[57]

The effects of Orientalism on the Ottoman subject are explicitly broached in *Carriage* through the introduction of an Ottoman Turkish dictionary (*Lügat-ı Osmâniyye*) in which Bihruz searches for a key word from Vâsıf's verse. Hidden away in the depths of a drawer in the women's section of the house, this dictionary has clearly not been used in years. Yet Bihruz places newfound trust in this book upon recognizing its author as the British Orientalist Sir James Redhouse. Upholding the dictionary as an omniscient source of knowledge, Bihruz asserts that there is nothing the "Redhouse" does not know, to which his well-educated colleague Naîm Efendi[58] offers the tongue-in-cheek retort that "his excellency Redhouse" must be mistaken.[59]

In the end, the joke is on Bihruz. Mixing up the diacritical markings of the Perso-Arabic script, he misreads *çerde* (جرده, dark complexion) as *cerde* (جرده), which he discovers in the dictionary to mean "yellow horse." Assuming this word refers to a "blonde," he thus accidentally describes the object of his affection as "swarthy."[60] Comically poignant, Bihruz's interactions with Naîm Efendi and other colleagues involve an extensive back and forth in which they debate which letter is represented on the page. Does the word in question (*çerde*) begin with a *jīm* with one dot or three? Is it of Arabic or Persian origin?[61]

This portrayal of reading as a demanding process of decipherment points to important debates in the realm of language reform at the time of *Carriage*'s publication. One aspect of these multifaceted debates focused on the supposed inadequacy of the Perso-Arabic script to represent the sounds of Ottoman Turkish. Among other factors, reformers emphasized that the Perso-Arabic script contains more vowels and fewer consonants than Ottoman Turkish and that the Persian and Arabic writing systems do not write short vowels on the page. As a result, one combination of consonants in Ottoman Turkish could have multiple meanings depending on its (unwritten) vowels; alternatively, one word could be spelled with different combinations of consonants. In response, figures such as Mehmed Münif Paşa (1828–1910) and Mirzâ Feth'ali Ahûndzâde (1812–1878) put forth different proposals to modify the Perso-Arabic script. Through the introduction of vowel signs and new diacritical markers, these reformers aimed to produce a more phonetic writing system that could eradicate the orthographic ambiguities of Ottoman Turkish.

In her pioneering work on Turkish literary modernity, Nergis Ertürk shows how such proposals dovetailed with the Turkish "discovery of [a] native vernacular" during the world historical communications revolution of the nineteenth century.[62] During this period of intensified translation and textual dissemination, the Ottoman Turkish language was "freed" from the recitative power of authorial presence through its mass distribution in new print media. In this context, Ertürk reads the history of late nineteenth- and early twentieth-century linguistic modernization—which focused on phoneticizing and simplifying the Ottoman Turkish language by rendering it more essentially "Turkish"—as a process of first setting, and then violently defending, limits to the inherent omnidirectionality of Turkish writing. While on the surface, language reforms supported simplification and legibility, they also sought to contain the ambiguities of the (Ottoman) Turkish language. This process entailed producing a national language that heralded its essential selfsameness through the denial of its translative origins. Within this context, *Carriage* registers the tensions and effects of the communications revolution, which incidentally also served as one condition of possibility for it as a novel.[63]

Bihruz and his colleagues' inability to read the script of Ottoman Turkish furthermore pokes fun at the positivist master narrative of Orientalism, which described the hybridities of Ottoman Turkish and its main literary genre of divan poetry as excessively difficult and therefore inaccessible. This narrative emphasized not only that Ottoman Turkish was written in the Perso-Arabic script but also the manner in which it had incorporated vocabulary and grammatical structures from each of these languages. It further highlighted Ottoman Turkish literature's absorption of diverse poetic conventions from Persian, which had in turn absorbed and appropriated Arabic over the centuries.

Emphasizing the fluid nature in which these different traditions come together in Ottoman Turkish literature, contemporary scholars underscore the existence of an Ottoman interculture.[64] This concept seeks to overturn the lingering authority of an Orientalist approach steeped in nineteenth-century philological tradition. Driven by the search for historical origins, philologically minded Orientalists attempted to sort out the "Arabic," "Persian," and "Turkish" components of Ottoman Turkish literature and to foreground only that which was seen as exclusively "Turkish" as authentic or original. In the process, numerous aspects of Ottoman Turkish literary style were deemed to have been appropriated or borrowed from "foreign" (i.e., Arabic and Persian) traditions that were actually integral to it. In short, "Orientalist technique partitioned the body of Ottoman literature into components whose origins lay outside of it, whether geographically or in time."[65] As a result, Ottoman Turkish literature was generally deemed unoriginal in its own right.

These are the grounds on which the English Orientalist Elias John Wilkinson Gibb—who had dedicated the better portion of his life to researching a six-volume anthology on Ottoman Turkish literature—could declare the Ottoman Turks to be a "singularly uninventive people" in all matters pertaining to literature. Dividing the history of Ottoman Turkish literature into "old" and "new" schools, he declared the first to be modeled on the classics of Persia and the second on those of modern Europe—particularly France.[66] It is perhaps no surprise that he denied both schools any trace of "true genius." Compounding its implied difficulty, this supposed lack of originality led to a general consensus that Ottoman Turkish literature was inherently untranslatable, even as certain works *were* translated into Orientalist languages such as English, French, and German.

Inspired by Western European literary and political forms, pioneering Ottoman Turkish authors of the late nineteenth century also portrayed Ottoman divan poetry as lacking in innovation. While these authors broke new ground in terms of literary experimentation, their criticisms of the Ottoman divan tradition exhibited an internalization of Orientalist rhetoric fixated on the concepts of origins and originality. Bihruz's disparaging view of Ottoman Turkish as unfit for the genre of poetry is an excellent example of this, as are his colleagues' attempts to parse out the potentially non-Turkic (i.e., Arabic and Persian) origins of the word *çerde*. Yet the scene adds an additional layer of complexity when these colleagues suggest *çerde* might actually be a French cognate. Across the span of multiple pages, they then offer an increasingly absurd string of potential interpretations, including "to rock a cradle" (*berse/bercer*), "lullaby" (*bersöz/berceau*), "a woman's cape" (*bert/berthe*), "parsley" and/or "Roquefort cheese" (*persiye/parsillé*).

This scene stretches the translatability of *çerde* to a breaking point; meaning is lost in an endless chain of speculations. But why, I ask, must this process of deciphering the Perso-Arabic script of Ottoman Turkish morph into a world of French cognates? If, however comically, *Carriage* does partake in the trope of untranslatability, this scene underscores the central role European Orientalist scholarship played in the production of such rhetoric in the first place.

At the time of *Carriage*'s publication, the implied untranslatability of Ottoman divan poetry was tied to a new Eurocentric understanding of originality that was retrospectively applied to an Ottoman literary realm with more flexible understandings of both originality and translation. The Ottoman Turkish term *terceme* loosely corresponds to the English term "translation," but it also encapsulates a diverse array of practices, such as *tedkik* (investigation), *taklid* (imitation), *tanzir* (emulation), and *nazire* (parallel or competitive writing). *Terceme* thus does not uphold the same concept of unmediated originality that its more modern equivalents *tercüme* and *çeviri* suggest.[67]

To demonstrate this, Saliha Paker shows, in particular, how the connotations of the term *telif* have changed over time. In its contemporary usage *telif* is associated with original authorship and thus stands in opposition to an understanding of interlingual translation as a secondary or uninventive practice. Yet the processes of *te'lif* and *terceme* were closely interconnected until at least the second half of the nineteenth century.[68] Changes in the meaning of each word can be traced to a new conception of originality (*özgünlük*), which first entered Ottoman Turkish discourse as a literary term around precisely this time.[69] Paker highlights here the important role played by intellectual Namık Kemal (1840–1888), who was strongly influenced by European Romanticism and its conception of the author as genius. While Kemal did not explicitly use the word *özgünlük*, he employed a host of other words pointing toward this concept in his writing, such as *has* (peculiar to), *mahsus* (on purpose, intentionally), and *benzemezlik* (dissimilarity). According to Paker, Kemal thus translated into Turkish the terms of originality, which he attributed in turn to European literature as a model for a new and progressive Ottoman literature.[70]

Due to the intertwined nature of the literary realm with the cultural and institutional reforms of the Tanzimat era, and more generally with agitations for political reform thereafter, this new emphasis on originality also had important repercussions for the development of Turkish nationalism. Diverse intellectuals began to assert an essentially Turkic identity separate from the other ethnicities of the empire in the late nineteenth and early twentieth centuries. Yet this Turkish nationalism was largely spurred on by forces from outside the empire. Two of the most important influences on the movement were translations of foundational works from the Orientalist discipline of Turkology and newly disseminated writings by Turkic intellectuals from Russia. These translative origins of Turkish nationalism necessarily undermined the new emphasis on unmediated originality, which led Turkish intellectuals to seek out and foreground essential forms of Turkishness in the realms of literature, language, and culture.[71]

This tension comes to the fore in a novel like *Carriage*: often described as the founding text of modern Turkish literature, *Carriage* in no way emphasizes an essentially "Turkish" voice. Rather, the competing, wavering, and faltering voices of the novel highlight what Mahmut Mutman terms the "deterritorialization of language"[72] in the late nineteenth century.

Amid the multiplicity of languages in the empire (including Turkish, Greek, Armenian, Kurdish, and Arabic), the gradually eroding dichotomy of high (courtly) and low (common) registers of the Ottoman Turkish language, the communications revolution and its ushering in of a new public sphere via print media such as newspapers and books, and the proliferation of translations from European languages and literary schools, *Carriage* renders onto the page the impossibility of "establish[ing] a homogenous and stable referential world" outside of itself.[73] Yet as Ertürk shows, *Carriage* does not merely perform the failure of representation.[74] The novel also registers the very processes of "vernacularization and translational exchangeability as conditions of its own possibility."[75] As such, it also signals the multiple "origins" of the Ottoman Turkish novel in a language marked through and through by processes of translation.

Within this historical context, it is important to note that *Carriage* does not portray untranslatability as a *quality* inherent to divan poetry itself but rather as a *mode* that emerges from Bihruz's lack of education. Bihruz's inability to translate does not demonstrate the authenticity of Vâsıf's verse as an "original" source text.[76] By thematizing translation, the novel highlights the manner in which Bihruz has himself been fundamentally altered through his encounter with European—and in particular French—culture. Through this presentation of its main character as fundamentally mediated, the novel also reflects on its own generic form, which entered into Ottoman Turkish literature via literary translations. On multiple levels, then, *Carriage* suggests that in the throes of literary-cultural modernization processes conditioned by the empire's self-orientation toward Western European influences, there is no original "self" to return to in the aftermath of translation.

ORIENTALISM AND WORLD LITERATURE

Despite its significance for a modern Turkish literary canon, its engagement with European literature, and its thematization of translational processes, *Carriage* remained untranslated until 2014. As a result, it had virtually no European reception across the twentieth century. This simple fact would again seem to support a by now commonplace narrative regarding the manner in which literatures of the so-called periphery have been "interfered with" by source literatures from a geopolitical "center" that essentially ignores them.[77] Yet if we care to look closer, we might uncover a different story: namely, the manner in which the enterprise of world literature was built around the philological practice of European Orientalism and its search for national origins. Like the hybrid character of Ottoman divan poetry—an entire tradition that Recaizade Mahmut Ekrem (1817–1914) himself helped to overwrite—a novel like *Carriage* also fell by the world-literary wayside owing to its refusal to conform to the basic premises of philology.

As the discipline of Orientalism shows, Western culture did not simply ignore writings from the so-called periphery. Rather, at the time of *Carriage*'s publication, German scholarly Orientalists did take an interest in other pioneering authors—such as Namık Kemal and Halide Edip Adıvar (1884–1964)—who were more clearly recognizable as forerunners to a national Turkish literature. German Orientalists by and large embraced texts that conformed to their own historical presumptions about nation building. In other words, Orientalists' search for an authentic "Turkish" literature was shaped by their own cultural fantasy regarding Germany's emergence as a *Kulturnation* a century prior.

Many translations undertaken into German in the early twentieth century also served as an important mode of political orientation, which upheld Germany's self-presentation as a "neutral" partner for the Ottoman Empire. While lauding new developments in contemporary Turkish literature, for example, Orientalist Otto Hachtmann rejected the possibility that German literature might serve as a model for Turkish authors. This, he argued, could only lead to a third "literary imprisonment," following Ottoman Turkish literature's enslavement to Persian and then French models.[78] Self-righteous statements such as Hachtmann's—which played up Germany's presumed lack of colonial interest in Ottoman territories—conveniently ignore the kind of economic influence Germany exerted over the Ottoman Empire and its significance for Germany's self-positioning vis-à-vis France and Britain during the era of German colonialism (1884–1919). The Berlin-Baghdad Railway in particular, which Germany began constructing in 1903, served as a mode of access to regions that had not yet been colonized by other European powers.

While Hachtmann wrote from the specific perspective of the German-Ottoman military alliance during World War I, his comments are steeped in a much longer trajectory of German Orientalist scholarship that asserted its supposed innocence vis-à-vis its British and French counterparts. This narrative would much later be picked up and perpetuated in Edward Said's *Orientalism* (1978). Understood as "a Western style for dominating, restructuring, and having authority over the Orient," which was exercised through academia, literature, and the corporate institutions of colonialism,[79] Said famously did not address German Orientalist scholars in his path-breaking study. The "German Orient," he writes, "was almost exclusively a scholarly, or at least a classical, Orient: it was made the subject of lyrics, fanta-sies, and even novels, but it was never actual, the way Egypt and Syria were actual for Chateaubriand, Lane, Lamartine, Burton, Disraeli, or Nerval."[80]

In contrast to France and Britain—which form the core of Said's study—Germany had neither colonies nor a nation-state in the early nineteenth century. Via this exclusion, one implication of *Orientalism* is that in the absence of "actual" contact with the Orient, German Orientalist literature and scholarship was less insidious than that of its French or British counter-parts. Barring the fact that German-speaking lands—most notably Prussia and the Hapsburg Empire—*did* have diverse forms of direct contact with the Ottoman Empire,[81] many German Orientalists of the early nineteenth century adopted a similar position to Said. By upholding the belief that they were engaged in the study and translation of Oriental languages and literatures, and not the colonization and subjugation of Oriental peoples, Germans maintained a moralizing self-image.

Such assumptions were bolstered by the burgeoning realm of trans-lations and translation theory in the German context, which incidentally also picked up on tropes of orientation. Friedrich Schleiermacher's 1813 essay "On the Different Methods of Translating" ("Ueber die verschiedenen Methoden des Uebersezens"), for example, clearly depicts translation as a directionally motivated undertaking. In Schleiermacher's account, the translator positions a text within a new cultural context by figuratively *moving* the reader or author. For the translator who truly wishes to bring together these two persons, he argues, there are only two possibilities: "Either the translator leaves the author in peace as much as possible and moves the reader toward him; or he leaves the reader in peace as much as possible and moves the writer toward him."[82] These methods are now commonly referred to as foreignization and domestication, respectively.[83] In the first instance, the translator seeks to adhere as closely as possible to the language of the original, at the risk of making the target language seem unnatural and ungainly. In the second, the translator strives to create a translation that reads as if it were written in the target language. This kind of fluency essentially masks the fact that the text has been translated from another language.

While Schleiermacher first presents these as equally viable options, he clearly favors foreignizing translations. For Schleiermacher, the process of rendering a foreignizing translation is at once an extraordinary act of humiliation and the starting point for a transformative encounter with the foreign. This suggests that translation should orient the reader toward a foreign other rather than reinforce an already solidified image of the self. This form of translational orientation has clear moral underpinnings for Schleiermacher. In the course of the essay, he elevates a foreignizing—and implicitly German—approach toward translation above the domesticating style of translations in French classicism:

> [The foreignizing] method of translating cannot flourish equally well in all tongues, but rather only in those that are not confined within the narrow bounds of a classical style beyond which all else is deemed reprehensible. Let these bounded languages seek to expand their territories by inducing foreigners who require more than their native tongues to speak them . . . and let them appropriate foreign works by means of imitations . . . but this sort of translation they must leave to the freer languages in which deviations and innovations are more readily tolerated, such that these deviations may, in the end, combine to produce a new characteristic mode of expression.[84]

Several key assertions come to the fore in this passage. Schleiermacher's depiction of languages "bound by a classical style" as expansionist asserts that French classicism bears imperialist tendencies. Schleiermacher suggests in turn that Germans do *not* need more than their native tongue. In other words, Germans need not learn French as a means of gaining cultural capital. The French language is rather portrayed as inherently insular and the French method of translation as a violent means of appropriation. German, in contrast, is depicted as a "free" language, or a language that can not only tolerate foreignness but that also emerges renewed and rejuvenated from productive encounters with the foreign in translation.

Wilhelm von Humboldt advanced similar views in the 1816 preface to his translation of *Agamemnon*. Here, he depicts translations from Greek—and in particular those of Voss—as a unique success for the German language. Identifying hexameter as a defining feature of the Greek national character, Humboldt argues that only the Germans had been able to successfully render its rhythms into their language thus far.[85] In short, he describes

German as possessing a certain flexibility or openness to the foreign that other languages do not. This understanding of the German language as uniquely open to and receptive of the foreign was central to the surge in translation activity at the turn of the century, which brought about a subsequent regeneration of German language and culture.

Schleiermacher's and Humboldt's assertions hinge on the absence of both a German nation-state and German colonies in the early nineteenth century. Yet scholars such as Susanne Zantop have shown how Germany's lack of colonial possessions created an even stronger sense of entitlement for many Germans. In her examination of "colonial fantasies" during the late 1700s and early 1800s, she shows how authors forged an imaginary German colonial history. In the absence of actual colonies as a testing ground, these colonial fantasies provided more of a "mythological" than a clear-cut "intellectual authority" over the East. Yet, over time, German colonial fantasies established themselves so strongly that they eclipsed reality.[86] Through literature, Germans created a "colonial universe" that they inserted themselves into, with fictive colonial scenarios providing Germans the opportunity to imagine themselves in the role of colonizer.[87]

Scholarly Orientalism played a similarly important role in Germany's self-definition as European. In the absence of colonies, Orientalism provided a key opportunity for Germans to counter their sense of cultural and political subordination to other European powers, and to assert their position in a European civilization otherwise deeply marked by the colonial enterprise.[88] Building on Mary Louise Pratt's distinction between violent conquest and anticonquest, Todd Kontje shows how German scholarship dealing with the Orient was intimately linked to the triumphs of European civilization. German narratives of universal history in particular, which categorized peoples of the world along racial and temporal hierarchies, played an important role in establishing European hegemony,[89] all while asserting the "pure inwardness of the German nation" as the "proper ground for the liberation of the spirit."[90]

While Zantop and Kontje focus on the discursive power of German literature and philosophy, B. Venkat Mani uncovers the myriad material connections between German Orientalism and British colonialism in particular. Focusing on the institution of world literature and its origins in early nineteenth-century Germany, Mani highlights the influence of British translations from Sanskrit on early German Romantic authors, the manner in which German libraries acquired Oriental manuscripts through colonial trade routes, and the interconnections between Johann Wolfgang von

Goethe's statements on *Weltliteratur* (first published in 1836) and Thomas Babington Macaulay's "Minute on Indian Education" (1835).[91]

In his examination of the historical trajectory of global English, Aamir R. Mufti further elaborates on the relationship between British colonialism and German Orientalism. Tracing the origins of Orientalism to the British colonization of India, Mufti describes how an early generation of British Orientalists discovered "not one single culture of writing but rather a loose articulation of different, often overlapping but also mutually exclusive, systems based variously in Persian, Sanskrit, and a large number of the vernacular registers, often more than one in a single language, properly speaking."[92] Orientalists made sense of this diversity by restructuring it according to the historicist model of an evolutionary national history and retroactively applying European categories of literature. As such, the British colonial project of philologically based Indology was an important predecessor for German and, eventually, also a larger European discourse of world literature,[93] which set out to classify and evaluate diverse forms of textuality under the uniform title of "literature."[94] To put this more succinctly, Mufti traces the genealogy of world literature to the philologically based practice of modern Orientalism in the late eighteenth and early nineteenth centuries.[95] By producing a conception of the world as an assemblage of civilizational entities with specific textual traditions, he describes Orientalism "as an articulated and effective imperial *system of cultural mapping*"[96] and an organized classification strikingly similar to the contemporary discourse of (Anglophone) world literature.

UNHINGING WORLD LITERATURE

What does the historical nontranslation of *Carriage* tell us about the history of German–(Ottoman) Turkish translational contact? And how can the 2014 translation help us to read this history from a different angle? On one hand, *Carriage* confounds an Orientalist fixation with origins. As a novel that did not clearly conform to a nationalist paradigm, it was also not taken up into the philologically determined circuit of world literature. On the other hand, the 2014 translation appeared amid a surge in world literature scholarship in the twenty-first century. A transtemporal reading of *Leidenschaft* thus brings us from the rhetoric of untranslatability perpetuated by nineteenth-century Orientalism to postcolonial reconceptualizations of world literature in the present.

This time span is punctuated by no fewer than seventy-six "translations" of *Carriage* into modern Turkish. The need to constantly update the language of this novel is testament not only to the immense changes the Turkish language has undergone since the late nineteenth century but also to the enduring quality of *Carriage*'s narrative and style and the continued significance of its theme. Indeed, nearly thirty new versions of the novel have appeared in Turkey since 2015 alone.[97] On one hand, the multiple versions of *Carriage* attest to the novel's fundamental *translatability*, if we understand the shift from Ottoman Turkish to modern Turkish as a mode of intralingual translation.[98] On the other hand, the persistent move to render this novel into ever-more modern versions of Turkish also underscores the fundamental unreadability of the "original" for the general public. This gesture toward unreadability circles back to Orientalist worldviews that plagued Bihruz and his fellow Ottoman dandies.

I argue that it is through the shift to a linguistic register other than Turkish—and more specifically to a European language that is *not* thematized in the novel—that a translation such as *Leidenschaft* can open up new lines of interpretation for *Carriage* in the future. While a term for world literature had not yet entered into the Ottoman Turkish language in 1896, a novel such as *Carriage*—together with its contemporary translation—leads me to revisit the stakes of world literature across this time frame.

In one of the most influential definitions of the term, David Damrosch describes world literature as "all literary works that circulate beyond their culture of origin, either in translation or in their original language."[99] While this may encompass any work that somehow transcends its home culture, Damrosch qualifies that "a work only has an *effective* afterlife as world literature whenever, and wherever, it is actively present within a literary system beyond that of its original culture."[100] While we might read a novel such as *Carriage*—which actively negotiates the tropes of authenticity and originality—as understanding itself and its subject matter *in translation*, under a definition such as Damrosch's, it would only join the sphere of world literature with its translation in 2014.

In her focus on the widespread teaching of select—mainly Anglophone and Francophone—texts in English translation, Emily Apter has drawn attention to "singular modes of existing in the world's languages,"[101] which are elided in the idiom of global English. Revisiting the terms of comparative and world literature, Apter thus argues for a right to untranslatability that safeguards cultural and linguistic specificity.[102] A novel such as *Carriage* provokes us to fundamentally rethink this argument; it demonstrates how the rhetoric of untranslatability was part and parcel of an Orientalist grand narrative about the Ottoman literary past that plagued Turkish authors well into the founding of the modern Republic of Turkey.

In this context, writes Walter Andrews, "no one (including the Turkish Republic, its actual descendant) had an interest in claiming or seeking origins in Ottoman culture." It is thus no surprise, he concludes, "that Ottoman literature remains on the distant margins of 'world literature.'"[103] Central to the late nineteenth- and early twentieth-century devaluation of the Ottoman literary tradition, Orientalist grand narratives profoundly influenced Turkish authors' perceptions of their own literary production well into the republican era. Even in the 1940s, when Turkish reformers and intellectuals fully asserted themselves as European, Turkish literature was rarely understood as world literature (*dünya* or *cihan edebiyatı*). Coded as decidedly European, world literature was set in contrast to the *national* literature of the new republic.

By contrast, this book uncovers profound interconnections between German and (Ottoman) Turkish literary spheres that have otherwise been imagined as separate. In doing so, it asks what implications the German–(Ottoman) Turkish relationship might have for our understanding of world literature—for which German culture is often imagined as a crucial site of inception but from which Turkish literature has been historically excluded. At the same time, this book does not call for a reading of Turkish literature as world literature by means of simply widening the canon. Taking inspiration from Gayatri Chakravorty Spivak's call to "rethink comparativism [by approaching] translation as an active rather than a prosthetic practice,"[104] it argues rather that translations between German and Turkish—*in both directions*—negotiate the meaning of world literature as an event or a relationship to come.[105] Even as the German–(Ottoman) Turkish translational relationship emerged from within the discourse of Orientalism—which at its core seeks to relegate the Orient and Occident to separate positionalities—the translations analyzed in this book generate instability. This instability holds, in turn, a disorienting potential, which does not simply manifest itself as a category of cultural crisis but rather serves as a site of opening for new configurations of the German-Turkish relationship in the future.

What new role might late Ottoman translations—such as those that ultimately led to the adaptation of the genre of the novel and the kind of radically modern narrative employed in *Carriage*—play when we approach them as active rather than reactive forces? Responding to the work of Damrosch and others, Spivak has also called for a "loosening" of the terms that make up world literature. Rather than seek a clear-cut definition, she argues that world literature has not necessarily already happened in a manner that can be easily defined; world literature points rather to the power of texts—and texts in translation—to project a future that is still open to imagination and interpretation.

Spivak underscores here Goethe's own comments on world literature as an epoch, the approach of which, he states, "we must *strive* to hasten."[106] The open-endedness of this statement imagines the aporetic nature of world literature as an event that is yet to be fully realized. This conception of world literature allows us to revisit late Ottoman translation movements—and novels that register the profound effects of these translations—not simply as a sign of belatedness within a societal reorientation toward Europe but rather as productively inconclusive. As such, the German translation of *Carriage* does not catapult the Ottoman Turkish novel into the realm of world literature; it rather extends and reconfigures the modes of (dis)orientation in the novel, which defy the Orientalist philology at the heart of world literature as we know it, even as it portrays a late Ottoman internalization of philological conventions.

This understanding of world literature as productively inconclusive also sheds light on the first translations from Ottoman Turkish into German in the early nineteenth century. Undertaken exclusively by diplomats, these texts raise questions about the role of translation in Orientalist practice. While diplomats such as Heinrich Friedrich von Diez (1751–1817) and Joseph von Hammer-Purgstall (1774–1856) were in contact with and even strongly influenced the trajectory of German scholarly Orientalism, their positionality as nonprofessionals provides an opportunity to explore previously understudied aspects of the German–(Ottoman) Turkish cultural relationship in the nineteenth century. Marked by the dynamics of cultural exchange and diplomacy, their translations did not always line up with the basic tenets of Orientalism.

Notably, translation figures into Said's broader theory of Orientalism as a metaphor of cultural encounter based on a specific form of positionality. According to Said, the manner in which a Western author writes about the Orient serves as a form of strategic location: "Everyone who writes about the Orient must locate himself vis-à-vis the Orient; *translated* into his text, this location includes the kind of narrative voice he adopts, the type of structure he builds, the kind of images, themes, motifs that circulate in his text—all of which add up to deliberate ways of addressing the reader, containing the Orient, and finally, representing it or speaking on its behalf."[107] Such strategic self-positioning occurs via a process of translation-as-interpretation. As an exercise of control, to "translate" the Orient is to fixate it in both space and time through the process of textual representation. In the terms of orientation, translation involves a process of directing oneself toward a specific image of "*the* Orient," which in turn constitutes the position of its assumed counterpart, "*the* Occident." Translation-as-interpretation thus enables the production of geographic and temporal distance, thereby reaffirming the stability of the Orientalist/self.[108]

Translation nevertheless takes on new contours across the long arc of Said's argument. In his discussion of latent and manifest forms of Orientalism, translation becomes a means of rendering the Orient intelligible in a much more ambiguous manner: "The relation between Orient and Orientalist was essentially hermeneutical. Standing before a distant, barely intelligible civilization or cultural monument, the Orientalist scholar reduced the obscurity by translating, sympathetically portraying, inwardly grasping the hard-to-reach object."[109] Transformed here into a *sympathetic* gesture, the process of translation-as-interpretation entails a negotiation of the very terms of representation. As a trained expert, the Orientalist's main job was to interpret the Orient for his compatriots. Yet Said gestures here toward a paradoxical acknowledgment on the part of the Orientalist—which occurs through a hermeneutically inflected process of translation—that the Orient is on some level difficult to read and thus also difficult to describe and fully comprehend. Within Said's theory of Orientalism, translation thus emerges as a key form of containment—but also as the very process that renders such containment impossible. If, in other words, to translate the Orient is to produce an essentialized and localized image of it, the very *need* to translate also attests to the Orient's unknowability and thus its resistance to being fixed in space and time. Contrary to a form of orientation that begins with and reaffirms the self, such resistance can produce disorienting forms of contact by rendering the instability and interdependence of both self and other, Orient and Occident, visible in new ways.

The translations of diplomat Heinrich Friedrich von Diez are an excellent example of this. While his translations were received within an Orientalist framework, Diez dedicated the better portion of his life to collecting and translating Ottoman Turkish source texts, which he hoped would overturn stereotypes about the "despotic" Turk as an Oriental other. Diez's work was then taken up by Johann Wolfgang von Goethe, who adapted numerous translations from Ottoman Turkish in his monumental *West-East Divan* (*West-östlicher Divan*, 1819). Notably, neither Diez's translations nor Goethe's poetic adaptations result in a fixation of the Otto-man other. Unlike the systematizing force of Orientalism as a discursive form of knowledge production about the East, they destabilize Diez and Goethe's positions as Western authors.

It is no coincidence that such poetic destabilization occurs within a text that was central to Goethe's conceptualization of world literature. A reading of the *Divan* in this light—with close attention to the Ottoman Turkish–inspired elements throughout—uncovers an alternative paradigm of *Weltliteratur* that is open to diverse forms of translational disorienta-tion. Rather than serve as a strict form of cultural mapping, this early German–(Ottoman) Turkish encounter engenders a malleable and messy form of *Weltliteratur* marked by the transtemporal movements of translation.

Moving forward from this historical starting point, this book attends to the idiosyncrasies of German–(Ottoman) Turkish literary-cultural contact from approximately 1811–1946 through the lens of three key figures: Johann Wolfgang von Goethe (1749–1832), Friedrich Schrader (1865–1922), and Sabahattin Ali (1907–1948). Divided into six chapters, it moves between German and (Ottoman) Turkish contexts, examining each figure within a broad network of translation activity. Rendering visible an aspect of the German–(Ottoman) Turkish relationship that has remained largely neglected in scholarship to date, this book sheds light on translations that are not bound by the terms of economic imperialism, Orientalism, or modernization history. While the diverse case studies I take up are all in some way connected to Orientalism—and thus marked by modern Orientalism's investment in historicism—they also work against the basic premises of containment and originality that undergird its system of discur-sive knowledge production. By engaging multiple time frames, overlapping with authorial practice, and linking disparate literary traditions across retro-actively applied periodizations, the translations I examine do not merely orient themselves toward an original they are assumed to follow. As points of connection they instead produce new directionalities and thus also serve as sites of opening for new configurations of the German-Turkish relation-ship in the future.

SUMMARY OF CHAPTERS

If, as scholars Mani and Mufti argue, the paradigm of *Weltliteratur* emerged through Orientalist and colonial practices that asserted a binary coding of the world into developed and underdeveloped, center and periphery, major and minor, chapter 1 asks what role the Ottoman Empire and translations from Ottoman Turkish played within this framework. Due to both a strong French influence in the late Ottoman literary sphere and the incompatibility of Ottoman Turkish with the dominant paradigms of German and Austrian scholarly Orientalism, literary translations between Ottoman Turkish and German in the nineteenth century have been treated as either insignificant or exceptional. In response, I interrogate the category of exceptionality by asking what *was* translated, why, and how.

Chapter 1 addresses this question through a reading of Johann Wolfgang von Goethe's *West-East Divan*, which incorporates and adapts translations from Ottoman Turkish into its poetry. Contrary to Goethe's scattered comments on *Weltliteratur*, which articulate a form of literary-cultural exchange in the service of a self-affirming universal progress, I argue that the poetry of the *Divan* embraces a more productive form of disorienting cultural contact. Thematizing excess, spatial instability, and disorientation, the Ottoman Turkish–inspired elements of the *Divan*, in particular, envision a messier form of *Weltliteratur* as a radical questioning of the self.

Chapter 2 takes up the first translations from German into Ottoman Turkish, which were coincidentally of Goethe's *The Sorrows of Young Werther* (*Die Leiden des jungen Werther*, 1774). In my analysis of these translations within shifting conceptions of originality in the late nineteenth-century Ottoman Empire, I argue that they do not simply consecrate Goethe's role in a canon of world literature; they rather actively negotiate the terms of originality and cultural transformation. As such, they engender an open-ended conception of world literature as process: rather than a sign of belatedness within the historical reorientation of the late Ottoman literary realm toward Europe, they reveal *Werther*'s account of modern subjectivity to entail processes of mediation that undermine the authority of an assumedly original German or Western narrative voice. Thus, the *Werther* translations also speak back to Goethe's own use of poetic experimentation in the *Divan* some sixty years prior and the specific vision of *Weltliteratur* it engendered.

Chapter 3 examines the short story "My Nephew" ("Yeğenim," 1899) by Ahmet Hikmet Müftüoğlu (1870–1927). Published on the eve of the twentieth century—following decades of political agitation for modernizing reforms—"My Nephew" weighs the consequences of losing one's cultural bearings amid far-reaching processes of societal reorientation. A satire of the superficially Westernized Ottoman dandy, the Paris-educated "nephew"

of this story returns to Istanbul, only to undertake the "spread of civilization" (*neşr-i medeniyyet*) among household members. As a figure fraught
with the anxieties of Westernization and the fear of cultural disorientation,
the Ottoman dandy was an archetype of late Ottoman literature, which
generally took France as its site of reference in the "West." This chapter
asks what new implications "My Nephew" gains in German translation.

Orientalist and journalist Friedrich Schrader's 1908 translation of "My
Nephew" appeared in the *Ottoman Lloyd*, an official newspaper that upheld
Germany as a neutral role model for the Ottoman Empire in the era leading
up to the German-Ottoman military alliance in World War I. Yet Schrader's German title—"Der Kulturträger (Mein Neffe)" ("The Bearer of Culture
[My Nephew]")—brings the rhetoric of the white man's burden to the fore.
In the specific context of the *Ottoman Lloyd*, I argue that Schrader's translation practice calls attention to aspects of the civilizing mission operating
in Germany's economic and military interactions with the Ottoman Empire
in the late nineteenth and early twentieth centuries. As such, Schrader's
translation shows both that Germany was far from a neutral model for the
Ottoman Empire and that translation in this time period was anything but
a neutral enterprise. Taking Schrader's training as an Orientalist—but also
his diverse roles as journalist and cultural curator—into consideration,
this chapter asks how the German translation of "My Nephew" prompts
us to consider what kind of cultural labor might reach beyond the civilizing missions of colonialism and Orientalism toward a more meaningful
process of German-Turkish cultural exchange in the future.

Picking up where chapter 3 leaves off, chapter 4 considers Friedrich
Schrader's late-career embrace of Ottoman divan poetry (1920–22) in relation to his 1916 translation of Halide Edip Adıvar's *The New Turan* (*Yeni
Turan*, 1911). Schrader enthusiastically endorsed Turanism (pan-Turkism)—
and its valuation of a specifically Turkish race—in his translator's preface
to *Das neue Turan*, which was published at the height of the German-Ottoman military alliance. While his 1916 translation reflects a clear investment
in the forces of ethnic nationalism that led to World War I, I show how
his journal articles from the 1920s are more closely aligned with Edip's
very specific vision of a politically liberal and democratic form of Turanism. More specifically, I argue that Schrader's late-career investment in
the Persian-inflected genre of Ottoman divan poetry entails a rethinking of the rhetoric of authenticity and originality, which forms a basis for
ethnic nationalism, philology, and humanism alike. In conclusion, I show
how Schrader's late-career writing opens up a vision of humanism that is

dislodged from Europe as an imagined birthplace and that points toward new forms of cultural orientation for the Ottoman Empire in the future.

Chapter 5 turns to early republican Turkey and a reading of modernist author Sabahattin Ali's "The Comprehensive Germanistan Travelogue" ("Mufassal Cermenistân Seyâhatnâmesi," 1929) as a prescient alternative to conceptualizations of world literature that would emerge in Turkey in the following decade. Unlike the dominant depiction of world literature *in translation*—which underscored the act of transferring an intact European literature into the Turkish literary-cultural realm—Ali points to the elements of translation already at work in German culture as one so-called origin of world literary classics. Ali achieves this through a form of self-translative Ottoman Turkish, which I argue presents an early theorization of Turkish literature *as* world literature.

Whereas the 1920s and 1930s saw a series of modernizing reforms that took the "West" as a stable entity toward which Turkey could orient itself, Ali depicts the local city of Potsdam as an unstable and thus disorienting force. He does so by translating the sounds of this place name into those of Ottoman Turkish. The resulting word, *Put-sedd-ümm*, takes recourse to the outdated grammar, vocabulary, and script of Ottoman Turkish, which had been labeled as illegible and untranslatable in the 1928 script reform. On the eve of more radical language reforms, which sought to uncover a "pure" and more legible form of modern Turkish, Ali takes recourse to the complexities of an outdated Ottoman Turkish to showcase the depths of its expressive capacity. The result is a form of translation that does not orient itself toward an original that it comes after. The translation rather moves forward and backward across multiple times, places, and languages to imagine an inherently open future in which new and unexpected meanings may emerge.

In conclusion, chapter 6 takes up Erich Auerbach's concept of the *Ansatzpunkt*—or point of departure—in its reading of Sabahattin's Ali's final novel *The Madonna in the Fur Coat* (*Kürk Mantolu Madonna*, 1943) and his 1943 translation of Heinrich von Kleist's *The Engagement in Santo Domingo* (*Die Verlobung in St. Domingo*). As an organic part of the literary object, Auerbach describes the *Ansatzpunkt* as so eminently clear that it can "speak for itself." Only by this definition can it form a "handle" from which to approach the material and engender a "radiating power" that in turn provides a form for viewing, dealing with, and ordering world history. In my examination of narrative gaps as an *Ansatzpunkt* in *Madonna* and *Engagement*, I ask how a textual silence might "speak for itself" or radiate outward: What implications might this have for both Auerbach's under-standing of world literature in the postwar era and for diverse Turkish intellectuals' usage of the term nearly a decade prior?

The 1940s Translations from World Literature series—for which Ali produced his Kleist translation—upheld a Eurocentric understanding of world literature, which was based on a more general conceptualization of Western civilization as a synthesizable whole. In line with larger Turkish humanist reforms of the time, the World Literature in Translation series thus sought to transfer assumedly universal Western values into the Turk-ish language and culture, through an orderly and systematic translation movement on a grand scale. In sharp contrast, my focus on Sabahattin Ali allows for a vision of world literature to emerge that is premised on the messy interrelationship of his writing and his translation practice. Whereas world literature in translation was meant to serve as a coordinate of cultural orientation in 1940s Turkey, Ali's work suggests rather that world literature is about a form of (inter)relationality that places the stability of each side of the literary exchange into question. As such, it also upends Auerbach's under-standing of world literature in the postwar era. While the world historical synthesis Auerbach still longed for in 1952 necessarily depended on the existence of stable component parts, the interrelationship of *Engagement* and *Madonna* betrays the fundamentally hybrid character of Germanness and Turkishness alike. Converging on—and radiating outward from—narrative silences in each text, this interrelationship conveys the unstable positions of translator/translated and source/target, thereby upending the premise of cultural originality itself.

PART 1

Johann Wolfgang von Goethe

*"Exceptional" Translations Across
the Nineteenth Century*

CHAPTER 1

Orientalism and *Weltliteratur*

The Ottoman Disorient in Goethe's West-East Divan

Written over a period of thirteen years, Johann Wolfgang von Goethe's *West-East Divan* (*West-östlicher Divan*) is indebted to translation.[1] With the Persian word *diwan* indicating a collection of poetry by a single author, Goethe's choice of title already reveals his increasing contact with non-European literatures in translation around the turn of the century. His own *Divan* was most famously inspired by that of Shams al-Dīn Muḥammad Ḥāfeẓ Shīrāzī (hereafter refered to as Ḥāfeẓ), a fourteenth-century Persian poet whose work Goethe accessed via the German translations of Joseph von Hammer-Purgstall in 1813. Yet numerous other translations also influenced the writing of Goethe's monumental work. As overseer of the library of the Großherzogliches Haus Sachsen-Weimar[2] from 1797 until his death in 1832, Goethe had access to works of non-European literature in both translation and original manuscript form while working on the *Divan*. A quick survey of his borrowing record reveals the diverse books he read in German, English, and French translation from 1815 to 1816. Among these sources were German translations of Saʿdī's poetry;[3] Heinrich Friedrich von Diez's *Memoirs from Asia* (*Denkwürdigkeiten von Asien*, 1811–15) and *The Book of Kabus, or Lessons of the Persian King Kjekjawus for His Son Ghilan Schach* (*Buch des Kabus oder Lehren des persischen Königs Kjekjawus für seinen Sohn Ghilan Schach*, 1811), which contain German translations of Ottoman Turkish, Persian, and Arabic literature;[4] English and German translations of the pre-Islamic poems of the *Muʿallaqat*; a German translation of Rūmī's

Masnavī-yi maʿnavī (The Spiritual Couplets)";[5] and an encyclopedic work entitled *Scholarship of the Orient (Wissenschaften des Orients*, 1804).[6]

From among these diverse sources, Goethe indicated his conscious incorporation of translations from Ottoman Turkish into the *Divan*: "[I have taken] Oriental poetry and literature in general into consideration ... yes, the Turkish poets have not been disregarded."[7] Dated to 1815, this statement signals the centrality of Ottoman Turkish source texts to the *Divan* from its early stages of inception. In an era when Ottoman Turkish literature was rarely translated into German—or into any European language for that matter—what weight does a statement such as Goethe's carry?

In answer to this question, this chapter considers the significance of Goethe's *Divan* for his subsequent conceptualization of *Weltliteratur*. On one hand, I show how the *Divan*—and the translations that inspired it—was enabled by the interrelationship of British colonialism and German Orientalism. To this end, the *Divan* participates in a genealogy of world literature that can be traced back to the emergence of modern Orientalism in the late eighteenth and early nineteenth centuries. With its strong philological basis, modern Orientalism sought to classify and organize the world according to the historicist model of an evolutionary national history. Emerging in this historical moment, the discourse of *Weltliteratur* also sought to make sense of diverse cultures of writing by ordering them into retroactively applied European categories of literature.

On the other hand, I show how the *Divan*—and in particular poems inspired by translations from Ottoman Turkish—runs counter to such attempts to map the world and give order to its literary traditions. Engaging in themes of excess, spatial instability, and disorientation, the Ottoman Turkish–inspired poems of the *Divan* underscore omnidirectional practices of translation and adaptation, destabilizing the positions of source/target, Occident/Orient, and self/other in the process. While enabled by the trade routes and scholarship of Orientalism, the *Divan*'s poetic cycles thus do not exert an Orientalist logic of discursively locating—and thereby asserting power over—an inferior cultural other. On the contrary, they render the positionality of both Orient and Occident unstable. As such, I also argue that the poetry of the *Divan* provides an alternative conception of *Weltliteratur* from Goethe's otherwise scattered remarks on the concept, which articulate a Eurocentric form of literary-cultural exchange in the service of a self-affirming universal progress. Rather than a concept of literary exchange that leads to a heightened sense of self-orientation, I show how the Ottoman Turkish–inspired elements of the *Divan* envision a messier form of *Weltliteratur* as a radical questioning of one's own positionality.

This conception of *Weltliteratur* affords, in turn, an opportunity to reflect on the exceptionalities of the Ottoman Turkish language and its primary literary genre of divan poetry. Incorporating elements of Arabic and Persian, the Ottoman Turkish language was inherently multilingual, thus defying the Orientalist-philologist search for links between a specific *Volk*, geographic area, and national language. Deeply influenced by Persian, Ottoman divan poetry was deemed inferior to outside models and thus not "original" enough to stand as a national literature in its own right. As a literary tradition that defied philological conceptions of an evolutionist national history, it was furthermore labeled as difficult and illegible. As a result, very few works of Ottoman divan poetry were translated into German.

However, rather than disregard the few existing translations from Ottoman Turkish into German in the first half of the nineteenth century as exceptions, this chapter takes up the category of exceptionality to ask what *was* translated, why, and how. In conclusion, it shows how Goethe's engagement with existing translations evinces a more complex approach toward originality than that of Orientalist philology. Marked by processes of interpretation and adaptation—rather than some inherent uniqueness—Goethe's adaptation of Ottoman Turkish sources in his *Divan* embraces the multiple modes of translation prevalent in Ottoman divan poetry itself.

ORIENTALISM, COLONIALISM, AND *WELTLITERATUR*

Unlike France and England, where the colonial enterprise had helped to establish an academic practice of Orientalism, no similar historical impetus existed for German universities. On the contrary, German Orientalism had traditionally been driven by Bible criticism. With its strong theological basis, the field was centered on the study of religious languages such as Hebrew, classical Arabic, Chaldean, and Aramaic.[8] Even as the field underwent significant changes at the turn of the nineteenth century, this historical basis continued to inform German Orientalists' self-perception of their work as distinctly separate from that of British and French scholars. The result was a form of contradictory self-positioning. By participating in the intellectual project of Orientalism, Germans sought to overcome their

sense of cultural and political subordination to other European powers—
in particular France—suggesting that although they had neither nation
nor empire, they nevertheless belonged to European civilization.[9] At the
same time, they also sought to distinguish themselves from other European
powers by asserting the "neutral" character of their scholarship, which was
ostensibly free from colonial forms of political domination.

This second viewpoint is succinctly expressed by Georg Forster, whose
1791 translation of Kālidāsa's Śakuntalā into German was an important insti-
gator for impending shifts in the field of German Orientalism. Notably,
Forster did not translate directly from Sanskrit but rather worked with the
English version by Sir William Jones—Orientalist, linguist, and Supreme
Court judge for the British East India Company—who had translated the
text three years prior. Despite the fact that Forster's translation was clearly
enabled by the British colonial enterprise, he was careful to distinguish the
differences between German and British attitudes toward Indian literature
and culture in his preface. Due to their lack of colonial interest, political make-up, and geographic condition, Forster argues, Germans have a
unique intercultural receptivity in relation to other Europeans, in particular the English. Whereas the English had imported various cultural *artifacts*
from India, it was the task of German scholars to interpret and evaluate foreign *texts* in an altruistic manner: "Our geographic position [and]
political constitution have lent us an eclectic character, with which we can
altruistically research the beautiful, the good, and the perfect . . . for its own
sake, until the construction of human knowledge has been completed—
or we have played our role, and future generations can use the stones that
we have brought together to construct a new building."[10]

Inspired by Forster's translation, Johann Gottfried von Herder
composed the essay "On an Oriental Drama" ("Über ein morgenländisches
Drama") in 1792. In the effort to promote intercultural dialogue, Herder
instructs his readers to approach the play in an Indian rather than a European spirit, all while intimating the difficulty of this task. Both Forster and
Herder thus differentiate German scholarly Orientalism from the British practice of colonization without recognizing their indebtedness to the
colonialist enterprise. This same sense of denial applies more generally to
Herder's philosophical historicism, which was informed by the ideas of
cultural difference elaborated by scholars such as William Jones.[11]

The circulation of Śakuntalā, in particular, initiated a new tradition of
translations and comparative literary scholarship in Germany.[12] Indicative
of the early German Romantic fascination with India, it paved the way for

the establishment of scholarly Orientalism as a humanistic field. As a text that brought rigorous linguistic research together with the study of philosophy and history, Friedrich Schlegel's 1808 monograph "On the Language and Wisdom of the Indians" ("Über die Sprache und Weisheit der Indier") then laid the groundwork for a philological turn in the field of German Orientalism.[13] In *Recoding World Literature* (2016), B. Venkat Mani ties the translation of *Śakuntalā* to the life and work of August Wilhelm Schlegel, the first professor of Sanskrit at the University of Bonn and the founder of German Indology. A. W. Schlegel's later comparison of Sanskrit texts to classical Greek and Latin literatures drew connections between the translation of non-European texts and the development of comparative scientific knowledge for the first time. Among the fruits of Schlegel's labors was also the establishment in 1820 of the periodical *The Indian Library* (*Die indische Bibliothek*), which published German translations from Sanskrit and, in 1829, Schlegel's own Latin translation of the *Ramayana*. Schlegel's theoretical and comparative interest in Indology formed an important precursor to Goethe's theorizations of *Weltliteratur* as a mode of international literary exchange in the early nineteenth century. As such, the translation of *Śakuntalā*, as well as the work of the Schlegel brothers in forging the field of Indology, reveal the close relationship between *Weltliteratur*, British colonialism, and German scholarly Orientalism, laying bare the diverse systems of geopolitical inequality in which the first theoretical explorations of world literature were steeped.[14]

Whereas Mani focuses largely on the German fascination with India and its implications for *Weltliteratur*, I explore here a second turn within the field of German Orientalism toward the realm of the classical Orient. This turn was solidified by Joseph von Hammer-Purgstall, who in 1808 founded the first successful academic journal devoted to Orientalist studies, *Repository of the Orient* (*Fundgruben des Orients*).[15] In the introduction to volume 1, Hammer-Purgstall clearly states that theology—and in particular biblical exegesis—should play as minimal a role as possible within the space of this journal.[16] He solicited, rather, scholarship on topics as diverse as geography, rhetoric, poetry, physics, mathematics, medicine, history, philology, and translation, to name only a few. Hammer-Purgstall distinguished *Repository* from more established journals in the field through this unusually broad scope, which attested to the journal's "manifold connections to and direct contact with the Orient."[17] Such connections were forged not through academic contexts but rather through "friends" reporting from major metropoles in the Middle East and Asia. Despite the journal's initial intention to focus on the Orient in the broadest sense (from Turkey to China), Hammer-Purgstall had already introduced a second important shift in the introduction to volume 2. The *Repository* would limit itself to "the three languages"—Arabic, Persian, and Turkish—in effect aligning itself with the School of Oriental Languages in Paris where Antoine Isaac Silvestre de Sacy taught.[18]

Goethe's decision to compose a *Divan* in the Persian style took shape amid these paradigm shifts in the modern field of German Orientalism. As an avid reader of the *Repository*, he was well aware of Hammer-Purgstall's scholarship. Indeed, Hammer-Purgstall's translations of Ḥāfeẓ were arguably the single most important influence on Goethe's *Divan*. Yet many other translations and literary traditions also helped to shape the *Divan*, including those of Ottoman Turkish.

While the Ottoman Turkish–inspired elements of the *Divan* have remained largely underresearched in contemporary scholarship,[19] I argue for their significance based on a number of historical factors that speak to the interrelationship of *Weltliteratur*, Orientalism, and colonialism. The first is a longstanding history of Ottoman contact with German-speaking lands, outside the frame of academic Orientalism. As Ottomans gained control over sections of Hungary in the 1520s, for example, the Hapsburg and Ottoman empires came into direct geographic proximity. Diplomatic contact necessarily ensued: the first Ottoman interpreter was dispatched to the Viennese Court in 1541[20] and the first Hapsburg interpreter to the Sublime Porte in 1547.[21] While the Ottoman Turkish language was taught at the University of Vienna from 1674 on, Kaiserin Maria Theresia later deemed language instruction at the university inadequate for Austria's diplomatic needs. A stronger language program was established in 1754 at the Royal Academy of Oriental Languages with the express purpose of training court interpreters. Numerous prominent interpreters and diplomats studied at the Academy, including Joseph von Hammer-Purgstall, who later played a crucial role in the restructuring of German scholarly Orientalism in the early nineteenth century.[22] After a brief diplomatic career in Constantinople and Cairo (1799–1807), Hammer-Purgstall returned to Vienna, where he would meet scholars such as Friedrich Schlegel and go on to found the aforementioned journal *Repository of the Orient* in 1809.[23]

The Ottoman Empire and Prussia also had a long-standing history of diplomatic relations. Following the 1757 establishment of a Turkish embassy in Vienna, a second sizeable embassy opened in Berlin between 1764 and

1765. The opening of this embassy was preceded by the Ottoman ambassador Ahmed Resmî Efendi's (1700–1783) first visit to Berlin in November 1763; Resmî Efendi was ceremoniously received and remained in Berlin for five and a half months. Throughout the Russo-Turkish wars of 1768–74, the Ottoman Empire then came into the increasing focus of European foreign policy. German newspapers, such as Hegel's *Bamberger Zeitung* and Kleist's *Abendblättern*, published information on Constantinople, including courtly news, small translations, and reports on the Russian-Ottoman conflict.[24]

Despite these long-standing Ottoman-Hapsburg and Ottoman-Prussian relationships, secondary scholarship tends to either overlook translations from Ottoman Turkish into German or to characterize Turkish studies as less rigorous than other German and Austrian Orientalist scholarship of the eighteenth and nineteenth centuries. Such scholarship emphasizes the relatively minor role Ottoman Turkish played vis-à-vis the study of Arabic and Persian, noting that even Orientalists who were knowledgeable in Ottoman Turkish generally did not consider it a central component of their research.[25] Even Heinrich Leberecht Fleischer (1801–1888)—who had a lasting impact on the field of Turkology through the students that he trained—worked primarily as an Arabist in his position as chair for Oriental Philology at Leipzig University from 1836 to 1888.[26]

The reasons for this are complex. In contrast to Persian and Sanskrit, which lent themselves well to a historical-comparative approach to linguistics, the relative youth of the Ottoman Empire and its language did not comply with a German tendency to historicize the Orient through reference to ancient and mythic cultures.[27] On the contrary, the Ottoman Empire exhibited what Andrea Polaschegg terms "an excess of presentness."[28] From a linguistic standpoint, Ottoman Turkish also posed a challenge to the field of modern German scholarly Orientalism with its strong philological foundations. Written in the Perso-Arabic script, Ottoman Turkish utilized a combination of Turkic, Persian, and Arabic grammar and vocabulary, thereby defying German philological scholarship that sought to trace etymological lines between a language, a culture, and a specific *Volk*. Its heteroglossic qualities—with different registers utilized for everyday, courtly, scholarly, and poetic purposes—furthermore rendered Ottoman Turkish incompatible with nineteenth-century conceptions of an authentic *Volkssprache*. Together with the multiethnic makeup of the Ottoman Empire, the Ottoman Turkish language thoroughly frustrated an Orientalist-philologist investment in pure national languages, which sought to narrate a descent from origins.[29]

The Persian-inflected genre of Ottoman divan poetry was often deemed unoriginal according to these Orientalist standards. Such was the opinion, for example, of the Orientalist, translator, and poet Friedrich Rückert (1788–1866). While an important figure for Turkology, Rückert consistently downplayed the significance of the field. As professor of Oriental languages at the University of Erlangen, Rückert taught Persian, Arabic, and Ottoman Turkish and translated from all three languages. Yet his translations from Ottoman Turkish served mainly private purposes. In Rückert's estimation, these translations did not deserve publication; too dependent on Persian models, Ottoman divan poetry was not "original" enough in its own right.[30]

If, compared to Arabic and Persian, Ottoman Turkish did play a relatively minor role in the field of German scholarly Orientalism, this chapter calls for a shift in attention from the realm of the academy to that of Ottoman diplomatic relations with German-speaking lands. During the first half of the nineteenth century, *all* translations from Ottoman Turkish into German were undertaken by diplomats rather than academics. While these diplomat-translators were at the forefront of paradigm shifts occurring in the academy, they were also ostracized from the scholarly Orientalist community due to their lack of university training. In what follows, I choose not to participate in historical debates centered on questions of inferiority. I suggest, on the contrary, that a focus on diplomacy brings nuance to the otherwise negatively coded category of exceptionality, which has often been employed to describe translations from Ottoman Turkish into German. Rather, I ask, how can we embrace exceptionality to underscore the significance of translations that *were* undertaken?

Notably, the Ottoman Empire also plays an exceptional role in Edward Said's account of Orientalism: the empire was in close geographic proximity to Europe through its border with the Hapsburg Empire; the Islamic lands were on top of the biblical Holy Lands, and Islam was theologically much closer to Christianity than the religions of China, India, and Japan. Citing the British colonial enterprise in India, Portuguese presence in the East Indies, China, and Japan, and French colonialism in North Africa and the Levant, Said argues that "*Islam excepted*, the Orient was for Europe until the nineteenth century, a domain with a continuous history of Western dominance."[31]

The translations of diplomat Heinrich Friedrich von Diez—which Goethe read with great interest—reflect the idiosyncratic character of the

Ottoman Empire in both German scholarly Orientalism of the nineteenth century and Said's broader theory of Orientalism. A self-proclaimed "enthusiast,"[32] Diez did not formally train as an Orientalist. His knowledge of Ottoman Turkish was gained rather during the six years he lived and worked as a diplomat in Constantinople. Together with Joseph von Hammer-Purgstall, he was nevertheless central to shifts underfoot in German scholarly Orientalism around 1815 and its newfound emphasis on the languages of the "classical Orient" (Arabic, Persian, and Ottoman Turkish).[33]

Diez's knowledge of languages was largely self-taught. After obtaining a law degree from the University of Halle in 1769, he began a legal clerkship, during which he continued to study languages, philosophy, and linguistics in his spare time.[34] In 1784, Diez applied to be, and was ultimately appointed as, Prussian *chargé d'affaires* to the Sublime Porte, despite his lack of previous diplomatic experience and his mediocre French skills.[35] Considering this background, Diez was met with an extremely difficult diplomatic mission. His main job at the Porte was to advance Prussian interest in the Eastern Question without offering any material support to the Ottomans. Diez arrived in Constantinople just one year after the Ottoman territory of the Crimea had been annexed by the Russian Empire. In his first official report to Prussia he warned that the Ottoman Empire was on the verge of collapse and in danger of coming under complete Russian control within the next ten years.[36] Yet both Friedrich II and his successor Friedrich Wilhelm II remained reluctant to enter into an official alliance with the Porte. Following the outbreak of the Russo-Turkish War in 1787, after which Austria also declared war on the Ottoman Empire in 1788, Diez urged Prussia to intervene. While Prime Minister Ewald Friedrich von Hertzberg took Diez's warnings seriously,[37] he ultimately refused to offer any form of support beyond the symbolic. On January 31, 1790, Diez nevertheless signed an alliance with the Sublime Porte, stating that Prussia would enter the Russo-Turkish War on the side of the Ottoman Empire; he was subsequently dismissed from his position even before the treaty was ratified on the grounds that he had overstepped his authority.[38]

While Diez's treaty negotiation was informed by his own assessment of the European balance of powers, it is also indicative of his close relationship to the Turks, which he noted in detail to his friend Christian Dohm upon his dismissal: "For the past two days, my quarters have been full with Turks, who have come to me, crying, in order to bid farewell. The same thoughts pour forth from each man's mouth: 'We have never had an envoy like him before, and surely a second will not follow!' This was too much for my heart!"[39] While these comments certainly reflect some degree of self-promotion, they are an indication of the lifestyle Diez led in Constantinople. He maintained close contact with a diverse circle of Turks, dressed in traditional Ottoman clothing, and devoted a significant portion of his time to learning Ottoman Turkish, Persian, and Arabic. While Diez's language skills were largely conversational, he also utilized his political connections during the six years he lived in Constantinople to acquire more than four hundred manuscripts, which he shipped to his home near Potsdam upon his dismissal.[40]

With the financial security of a generous pension, Diez was then able to devote all of his time to reading and translating these manuscripts until his death in April 1817. During the first twenty years following his return, Diez translated primarily for his own sake, to keep up the linguistic knowledge he had gained abroad. He began to self-publish these translations in 1811 with volume 1 of *Memoirs from Asia*; a second volume followed in 1815. With approximately eight hundred pages of translations and an additional six hundred pages of commentary, the *Memoirs* cover diverse subject matter, ranging from a Turkish sea atlas to the epic stories of the Oghuz Turks and from Ottoman proverbs to a historical account of Sultan Selim I's life.

Diez brought forth his *Memoirs* at a time period when the field of German scholarly Orientalism was in the incipient stages of a paradigm shift. This publication—which contained predominantly Ottoman Turkish but also diverse Arabic and Persian translations with accompanying source texts—both contributed to changes that were already underway and helped to solidify a new scholarly focus on languages of the classical Orient. Yet Diez's introductory framing of his translations deviated significantly from standard paradigms of the field. In the introduction to volume 1, for example, Diez reverses the standard Orientalist trope that Western scholars are better equipped to preserve knowledge about the East than Orientals themselves. On the contrary, he describes scores of valuable texts that have been brought to the West only to collect dust in libraries. Rather than standard-bearers of civilization and a safeguard of cultural artifacts, Diez depicts European libraries as the "graves of Oriental manuscripts."[41] In clear contradistinction to the necropolis-like European library, Diez figures Ottoman archives as repositories of knowledge and valuable cultural information. Underscoring, in particular, the important role played by the Ottoman Empire in preserving great works of Arabic and Persian poetry, Diez sought to correct European Orientalist stereotypes of the "terrible Turk." On the contrary, he depicts the Ottoman Empire—and

Constantinople in particular—as an intermediary between Europe and the Orient and an important site of literary contact.[42]

Notably, Diez also understood *himself* to be a cultural intermediary who sought to capture the spirit (*Geist*) of the Orient in his translations and convey this to the West. In his writings, he emphasized the significance of his physical residence in Constantinople, which enabled him to establish direct contact with Ottoman Turks. In doing so, Diez further emphasized his knowledge of Ottoman Turkish as a *spoken* language, which he viewed as key to better understanding the Turkish character.

Diez's self-declared role as a "spokesman for Orientals"[43] is simultaneously problematic and productive. After returning to Germany, Diez continued to dress like a Turk, employed a Turkish servant, and imported Turkish furnishings for his home.[44] On one hand, this very ability to appropriate certain facets of Turkish culture already signals Diez's own position of power. His self-designation as "spokesman" further suggests that Diez understood himself not only in a position to speak about but also *for*—or rather in place of—the Oriental. At the same time, Diez's move to Orientalize himself points to the epistemological dimensions of Orientalism as one means of forging a "sympathetic identification" with an otherwise alien culture. Marginalized within the realm of German scholarly Orientalism and rendered suspect by the Prussian government for enacting policies too much in favor of the Ottomans, Diez's self-positioning also calls into question the very power relationships that structured German Orientalism as an academic field in the nineteenth century.[45]

Diez's emphasis on his own knowledge of the Orient as alive (*lebendig*) is key to understanding the challenges he presented to scholarly Orientalism at the time. For Diez, the Orient was not relegated to the past; similarly, his passion for collecting, studying, and translating manuscripts was not just about acquiring knowledge as a means of consolidating power. On the contrary, Diez described his dedication to the manuscripts he had collected in Constantinople as an act of love. He further understood this relationship to be fundamentally different from that of academically trained Orientalists to their subject matter. As Diez expressed in a letter to Goethe on November 28, 1815, he did not want to be like professional scholars, "who failed to see the spirit [of the Orient] before the words."[46] This aspect of Diez's legacy helped initiate a new theoretical approach to the study of Oriental languages outside the confines of the university.[47]

While guided by the desire to serve as a mediator between Eastern and Western cultural realms, Diez's approach to translation was also influenced by his own commitment to Pyrrhonian skepticism, or the belief that certain forms of absolute knowledge are impossible to attain. Unlike an open-minded inquirer, who maintains the ultimate discovery of truth as a future possibility, Pyrrhonists advocated for the assemblage of opposing arguments or viewpoints in order to suspend a final judgment.[48] Diez expressed a similar outlook in his 1774 letter to Jakob Mauvillon: "The doubter does not decide absolutely, because he does not know on which side the truth is. I, however, am not searching for any truths, and deny that they exist or could exist. I set aside the distinctions that one makes between truth, error, bias, falsehood, etc. and bring everything back to the word 'ideas' that everyone makes according to his nature."[49] As such, Diez positioned himself against the fundamental premise of the Enlightenment that certain truths can be uncovered through recourse to reason.

Diez's commitment to skepticism comes to bear on his translation practice in the preface to *Mirror of Princes* (*Qabus Nameh*, ca. 1080 CE), an ethical didactic work of Persian literature that he rendered into German: "Everyone can only visualize the world and humans as he sees them, and everyone sees them only according to the relationship of the place where he stands, according to the business that he conducts, and the proportion of the perception and experience he has accumulated."[50] Diez's comments are particularly noteworthy here in the preface to a work dedicated to the rules of social conduct. Above all, Diez places his own position as (Western) translator and interpreter of Persian social and cultural norms into question, suggesting that he can never fully know this text or the ideas expressed therein.

While Diez doubted the premise of absolute knowledge, he also strove for accuracy in his translations, based on his belief that primary sources constituted the most "secure medium" for teaching about other cultures.[51] Diez understood primary materials, even if mediated by translation, to constitute a direct source of information far superior to secondary scholarship. Consequently, Diez valued a literal (*wörtlich*) approach to translation, which aimed to reproduce the source text in unabridged (*unverkürzt*) form. Whenever possible, Diez also provided the original source text alongside his translation with the goal that his work could serve the purpose of language study.[52] While this approach appears, on the surface, to contradict his skepticism, it also evinces his refusal to adapt the source text to European tastes. Through an emphasis on fidelity, Diez emphatically set himself against the French tradition of Orientalist translations in particular, which was dominated by the tendency toward domestication. Central to Diez's self-positioning here was a larger critique of European superiority grounded in the Enlightenment. In seeking to understand other cultures through their own writings, Diez worked against a hierarchy of cultures that figured Europe at the apex of development. On the contrary, he understood translation as a means of learning from other cultures and thus reinvigorating a European cultural realm he believed to be suffering from moral decay.[53]

In the following sections of this chapter, I do not intend to pass judgment on Diez's translations but rather to investigate the manner in which Goethe appropriated and incorporated them into his *Divan*. On the surface, Goethe's poetic approach in the *Divan*—which is marked by experimentation and adaptation—stands in opposition to Diez's expressed commitment to fidelity in translation. A close reading of the Ottoman Turkish–inspired poems in the *Divan* does nevertheless reflect Diez's commitment to Pyrrhonian skepticism, in that they resist the Orientalist desire to discursively locate the Orient as a fundamentally knowable other. In doing so, they align themselves with literary techniques of the Ottoman divan tradition, which engaged in diverse forms of translation, including parallel and response poetry. As such, Goethe's *Divan* demonstrates attention to more complex Ottoman conceptions of originality that did not align with the philological traditions of German Orientalism. Like Diez, who asserted that he could never fully know the texts he translated and interpreted, Goethe does not employ translations of Ottoman divan poetry as representations of an Ottoman cultural realm with clear and identifiable origins. On the contrary, his engagement with and adaptation of Ottoman source texts play into the overall cyclical nature of the *Divan*'s poetry, which blurs the distinction between source and target, original and translation.

Indeed, the *Divan* as a whole challenges Said's depiction of translation as a process of self-localization. Orientalist writing, Said argues, involves locating oneself vis-à-vis the Orient via a process of hermeneutic translation. Through the implementation of specific images, themes, and motifs, the Orientalist strategically positions himself in relation to his text and subject matter.[54] By asserting knowledge about and authority over the Orient, he both contains it and renders it unchanging and stable. A distinction between the space of the Orient and the Occidental position of the Orientalist thereby crystallizes, enabling a form of self-localization.

In the space of the *Divan*, such a clear-cut distinction between Orient and Occident never crystallizes. By bringing together elements from diverse source texts, the *Divan* rather collapses times and spaces, rendering any attempt to locate a fixed perspective or site of narration impossible. While replete with oppositions—such as East/West, poetry/prose, love/hate, voice/script, past/present—the text's seeming dualities work together to create cycles of mirror relations that mediate one another. This use of oppositional pairs begins with the title itself. The use of a hyphen in the German title, *West-östlicher Divan* (*West-easterly Divan*), suggests a geographic and poetic fusion of East and West. Conversely, the Arabic subtitle, which translates to *The Eastern Divan by the Western Author* (الديوان الشرقي للمؤلف الغربي), reinforces a clear distinction between cultural spheres, in line with Goethe's initial conceptualization of the *Divan* as a collection of German poetry written in an Oriental style.[55]

Goethe's understanding of an "Oriental" quality or style of poetry nevertheless breaks down this distinction between East and West once again. In the chapter "General Observations" ("Allgemeines"), Goethe depicts Oriental poetry as having an awe-inspiring diversity (*Mannigfaltigkeit*)[56] capable of bringing the most unrelated of concepts together. Central to the introduction of free forms to modern literature and art, the concept of *Mannigfaltigkeit* represented an important break with uniformity of thought (*Einheitsdenken*) in the German Romantic tradition and was thus one critical indicator of cultural modernity during Goethe's lifetime.[57] His utilization of this term to describe Persian and pre-Islamic poetry poses a challenge to the logic of Orientalism as a project of post-Enlightenment Western modernity, which asserted Western civilization as an ideal that non-Western societies should aspire to. It suggests, on the contrary, an instance of "virtual contemporaneity"[58] between Goethe and the authors of the various Eastern traditions incorporated into his *Divan*.

This contemporaneity of Western and Eastern textual traditions is embodied by Goethe's metaphorical depiction of Oriental poetry as a market: "Not always are the most costly and cheapest wares widely separated in space. They mix before our eyes, and often we behold also the barrels, boxes, and sacks in which they have been transported."[59] Goethe draws a clear connection between the market and his own *Divan* by referring to himself as both a traveler and a merchant in the opening section of the "Notes and Essays" ("Noten und Abhandlungen").[60] While the market metaphor signifies the inherently modern situation of an intensified, inevitable interaction between diverse literary traditions, the concept of Goethe as traveling merchant also implies a power relationship in the market structure. Goethe is free to pick and choose the poetic goods of his choice and present them to his European readership accordingly.

In the following sections, I ask more specifically how Goethe figures his own positionality as a Western author in relation to more complex instances of East-West contemporaneity that arise in poems inspired by Ottoman Turkish source texts. Central to my analysis are Goethe's own remarks on *Weltliteratur* and their bearing on his relationship to both Diez and the Ottoman Empire.

GOETHE READING DIEZ

From late 1814 through spring 1815, Goethe engaged in an extended letter exchange with Diez, whose translations and commentaries he had read with great interest. The two then shared select correspondence until Diez's death in 1817. While Diez clearly influenced the composition of the *Divan* in some manner, Goethe's relationship to Diez's work and the Ottoman Empire is contested in secondary scholarship. Ian Almond argues that while Goethe was familiar with and valued Diez's work, he nevertheless chose to ignore the information at hand with overly simplistic depictions of Turks. Almond notes a stark disparity between Goethe's keen interest in both Islam and Ottoman literary culture and his selective, negative portrayals of Turks in works such as *Philipp Hackert* (1811) and *New Greek Piraean Sagas* (*Neugriechisch-epirotische Heldenlieder*, 1822). Almond reads this as a contradiction of aesthetic and political interests: as a potential threat to Europe, the Ottoman Empire in general posed a challenge to Goethe's view of Islam as a civilizing and inspirational force.[61]

Katharina Mommsen argues, on the contrary, that many of Goethe's statements on Turks and the Ottoman Empire demonstrate a marked independence in thought, despite persistent negative indoctrination from a young age. Rather than as the archenemy of Christianity, she notes that Goethe often depicted Turks in a neutral, if not overtly positive, light: *The Pastor's Letter* (*Brief des Pastors*, 1773) portrays a Protestant pastor who shows brotherly love toward both Jews and Turks, looted Turks in *Faust* (1808; 1832) offer an important counterpoint to the image of Turks as barbaric plunderers of Christian lands, and *Götz von Berlichingen* (1773), which offers a historical portrayal of the Turks as the archenemy, nevertheless expresses the humanity of Turkish prisons in comparison to the treacherous conditions in Germany.[62]

The *Divan* in particular offers remarkably positive portrayals of Ottoman *muftis*, Muslim jurist-interpreters of religious law with the authority to deliver a *fatwā*. The poems "Fatwā" and "The German Offers Thanks" ("Der Deutsche dankt") in the "Book of Hafez" ("Hafis Nameh—Buch Hafis") express gratitude to the Grand Mufti Ebussuud Efendi for upholding the poetic value of Ḥāfeẓ's divan against Orthodox theologians wishing to ban it due to erotic content,[63] thus ensuring the survival of this work for future generations. Goethe's declaration of Ebussuud's sainthood in relation to this matter is particularly noteworthy; it underscores the value of Turkish appreciation for art and liberal thought in the face of religious dogma.[64]

In contrast to these examples, Goethe's adaptations of Ottoman Turkish source texts in the *Divan* rarely make explicit reference to Turks or the Ottoman Empire. Tracing an "Ottoman Turkish" element in the poetry section of the *Divan* requires rather a close comparison of Diez's translations to Goethe's own poetic output.[65] While at times significantly altered, Goethe's adaptations of Ottoman Turkish source texts are thus firmly embedded within the poetic structure of the *Divan* as a whole, which is itself marked through and through by processes of translation.

Within the "Notes and Essays" that addend the *Divan*, Goethe describes translation as a medium through which Germans move toward the Orient.[66] This formulation bears a striking resemblance to the virtual movement he seeks to enact throughout the *Divan* as a whole. The opening stanza of the "Notes and Essays" reiterates this idea: "Poetry if you would know, / To its country you must go; / If the poet you would know, / To the poet's country go."[67] This layered conception of travel replicates a strictly Orientalist logic in which it is Goethe's role to articulate and represent the Orient for a Western readership: Goethe travels to the "land" of poetry—or rather the diverse Oriental texts that inspired his *Divan*—while the reader travels to the poet's land—or the pages of Goethe's text.

A parallel poem from the opening sections of the *Divan* nevertheless questions what it means to both travel and to stay at home: "Let me get my saddle, don't need rest! / Stay in hut and tent, for you they're best! / I'll be riding footloose, free, and far; / And above my cap, many a star."[68] The Bedouin lifestyle evoked by "huts" and "tents" in line two suggests that by engaging with the *Divan*, Goethe's assumedly German or Western European readers have already placed themselves in an Eastern setting, which in turn questions where the "poet's land" actually is. Reading Goethe's essay alongside these stanzas suggests the need to reconsider what it means to engage with the foreign through translation and posits the *Divan* as a translational space in which this occurs.

According to Goethe, all acts of translation occur within the temporally and spatially determined relationship of text to nation. He outlines three progressive stages of translation in which the third and final stage is described as a *Zeitraum*—an epoch but, rendered literally, "time-space"—in which the translator follows the original so closely as to give up the originality of his own nation in the process.[69] Such a relationship is fostered through translation as identical to the original as possible. In its approximation of the original, it initiates a movement between the foreign and the local, known and unknown.[70] This movement both completes the cycle of translational stages and points to the fundamental incompleteness of any act of translation, as all three stages repeat themselves endlessly. This cyclical theory of translation suggests neither a dissolution nor the complete synthesis of source and target languages/nations. It demands rather a constant, intensified engagement with different translational formats in flux, which in turn places the concept of originality itself into question.

Goethe attributes the third stage of translation to Johann Heinrich Voss's breakthrough renditions of the *Odyssey* (1781) and the *Iliad* (1793) into German. Voss's close attention to the syntax, word order, and forms of Greek, together with his approximation of Greek hexameter in German, paved the way for a new tradition of foreignizing translations with an increasingly nonidiomatic use of German. Despite Friedrich Gottfried Klopstock's initial criticism that Voss had "done violence to the idiom of the Germans,"[71] Voss's translations had come to be regarded as classics by the turn of the century. Highly influenced by Voss's attention to meter, Wilhelm von Humboldt expressed the significance of Voss's work for the development of a German national literature in the introduction to his own translation of Aeschylus's *Agamemnon* (1816).[72]

Arguing that translators are as crucial as poets to the "expansion of the significance and expressive capacity of one's own language,"[73] Humboldt cites Voss's innovative translations as an example of the German language's flexibility and openness to the foreign. His emphasis on the unique expressive capacity of German is nevertheless built into a larger theory of untranslatability. Drawing an essential relationship between language and culture, Humboldt's theory of untranslatability is based not simply on the original nature of the work being translated but also on the nature of language itself. Arguing that no two words form absolute equivalents across languages, he describes words not as individual signs for a concept but rather as a network of ideas or a process of thinking: "The indeterminate activity of the power of thinking condenses into a word, just as light clouds originate in a blue sky."[74] The word is thus both an individual and a collective being. Within the text, it is the manifestation of a particular artist's imagination. Yet as a word that developed within specific cultural circumstances, it is also essentially national in character. Rather than understanding this as an obstacle, Humboldt sees this essential uniqueness of the original as a characteristic that demands translation, despite the seeming impossibility of this task. He develops a theory of fidelity that aims at precise imitation, even though the text can never be perfectly imitated in another language.

While the unique national character of language necessitates translation for Humboldt, it also leads to the ultimate limitations of his theory. In order for the expressive capacity of German to be realized in translation, Humboldt describes an important threshold that must not be crossed: the translation should render the foreign (*das Fremde*) aspects of the original, but not its strangeness (*die Fremdheit*), into the target language. The strangeness of the source language, he writes, holds the potential to completely overcome the target language. This could lead to an undoing of the uniqueness of the original, which Humboldt depicts as a translational betrayal.[75] Goethe's cyclical model of translation forges an opening out of the national parameters of Humboldt's theory. The impossibility of fully completing the translational process is ultimately a liberating factor for Goethe. It leads into a series of translations and retranslations that not only serve different purposes but also undermine the essential discreteness of national target and source languages through their mediation of one another.

Considering Goethe's discussion of translation in the closing sections of his *Divan*, it seems no coincidence that he also figured the entire book as unfinished. In its first 1819 publication, the *Divan* contained a chapter titled "Future Divan" ("Künftiger Divan") in which Goethe described the current state of his work as incomplete or imperfect (*unvollkommen*)[76] and expressed the desire to eventually publish a complete second edition. Notably, a second, 1827 publication of the *Divan*—which was expanded with forty-three new poems—did not correspond to his own projections for revision eight years prior. On the contrary, it contained an exact replication of the original chapter "Future Divan," suggesting a fundamental openness of the text. Together with the cyclical nature of its structure—in which widely separated poems reflect on one another thematically—this suggests that the *Divan* is itself exemplary of the translational time-space of Goethe's theory.

GOETHE'S *WERKSTATTSPLITTER* AND THE OTTOMAN DISORIENT

Goethe's figuration of the *Divan* as fundamentally incomplete or imperfect raises further questions regarding the approximately three hundred documents—ranging from notes, sketches, excerpts, charts, and poem drafts—in his personal archive categorized under this work. While many of these documents were not incorporated into the published version of the *Divan*, they provide insight into the genesis of individual poems and the texts Goethe engaged with while conceptualizing the work as a whole.[77]

One document of note is the May 1815 draft of a second (unpublished) dedication panel for the *Wiesbadener Divan*. Goethe's ability, within this brief draft, to draw diverse connections between pre-Islamic Arabic poetry, thirteenth-century Persian poetry, and a collection of pre-Ottoman Turkic proverbs exemplifies the way Ottoman Turkish elements are drawn into the composite of places and authors that make up the *Divan*. Meant to balance out a December 1814 title page that directly refers to the Persian poet Ḥāfeẓ, this dedication closes with the following lines: "The ethical constellations / Kabus and Oghuz / locked in sight."[78]

"Kabus" and "Oghuz" refer here to Diez's translation of *The Book of Kabus* and to the twelfth section from volume 1 of his *Memoirs*, "Book of Oghuz" ("Buch des Oghuz"), both of which Goethe read earlier in 1814. Goethe's use of the adjective "ethical" (*sittlich*) echoes lines 3–7 of the dedication, which reference the ethically didactic *Book of Advice* (*Pandname*) by the twelfth-century Persian Sufi poet Farid-al-Din Attar.[79] The word "constellations" (*Sternbilder*) refers in turn to the title of Anton Theodor Hartmann's 1802 translation of the *Mu'allaqat*, an eighth-century collection of seven pre-Islamic Arabic poems mentioned in lines 13–17 of the dedication.[80] Hartmann's title, *The Luminous Pleiades in the Arabic Poetic Sky, or the Seven Arabic Poems Hanging on the Temple in Mecca* (*Die hellstrahlenden Plejaden am arabischen poetischen Himmel, oder die sieben am Tempel zu Mekka aufgehangenen arabischen Gedichte*), connects the meaning of the word *Mu'allaqat*—the suspended odes or hanging poems—to the beautiful and luminous constellation of stars known as the Pleiades, which is visible to the naked eye due to its proximity to Earth. Hartmann's title further connects these blue-hued stars to the common Arabic description of the *Mu'allaqat* poems as precious gems that hang in the mind and are watched in silence. Goethe's use of the single word "constellations" condenses this reference to the *Mu'allaqat* as stars or gems of Arabic literature and draws a connection between these pre-Islamic poems and Diez's translations, suggesting their unique value to him as an author. With the final phrase "locked in sight," Diez's translations then become a navigational guide or site of ethical orientation.[81]

A collection of approximately two hundred proverbs that can be traced back to the Oghuz Turks, Diez's "Book of Oghuz" emphasizes the significance of proverbs as phrases that maintain a unique national character, despite their tendency to migrate across cultures.[82] In the collection *Proverbial* (*Sprichwörtlich*), Goethe reformulates Diez's depiction of proverbs as "national testimonies"—or signs of national mentality, customs, and traditions—as "proverbs denote nations."[83] Despite Goethe's keen interest in proverbs as phrases that somehow reflect on their national origin, many of the *Divan* poems inspired by Diez's translations emphasize acts of transgression, suggesting that these proverbs gain value by exceeding the level of the national. Consider, for example, the following couplet from "Book of Proverbs" ("Hikmet Nahmeh—Buch der Sprüche"): "Das Meer flutet immer, / Das Land behält es nimmer."[84] ("The sea is flowing ever, / The land contains it never.")[85] Inspired by proverb 140 in *Memoirs*, Goethe's succinct couplet significantly shortens Diez's translation, which reads as follows: "Tritt nicht über wie das Meer und umfasse keine Sache, welche du nicht ausrichten kannst"[86] (Don't overflow like the ocean and don't embrace anything you cannot justify). Through its expression of the inevitable, Goethe's couplet takes away the didactic character of this Oghuz saying. By bringing the opposition between land and water in direct visual focus, it renders the proverb more explicit. At the same time, Goethe creates ambiguity in the second line regarding the pronoun "it." As the potential object or poetic subject of the line, "it" refers both to the water's inability to cover the land and to the land's inability to contain the water.

The following parallel poem from the *Book of Proverbs* suggests the significance of this overwhelming force of flooding for the realm of poetry: "The flood of passion storms in vain / The never conquered solid land. – / Poetic pearls thrown on the sand! / And that, for living, is a gain."[87] While these two poems are often read in conjunction as a reflection on the raw and uncontrollable forces of nature, the shore's inability to contain the poetic flood of passion is clearly figured in this second quatrain as positive. It suggests the circulation of poetic ideas in which the individual components—shore and land—cover and exceed one another but do not simply merge. They engage rather in a constant ebb and flow that undermines simplistic one-way movement between self and other.

Rather than act as a navigational guide, such moments of excess are emblematic of a larger problem of orientation staged in the *Divan* and the impossibility of identifying purely Eastern or Western spaces. While Goethe often constructs spaces that appear to be Eastern, the integrity of these spaces is often broken down and destabilized shortly thereafter.[88] This tendency is already apparent in the first two stanzas of the opening poem "Hegire":

> North and West and South—they shake!
> Thrones are cracking, empires quake,
> To the purer East, then, fly
> Patriarchal air to try:
> Loving, drinking, songs among,
> Khizer's rill will make you young.
>
> There, in what is pure and right,
> Generations I, with might,
> Urge to depth of origin
> Where they from the Lord would win
> Earthly-worded Heaven-lore;
> They will rack their brains no more.[89]

Here Goethe figures his own poetic journey as both a political flight from a fractured Europe, as well as a personal journey of rejuvenation. While this stanza clearly reiterates the Orientalist trope of the East as a site of originary purity, the conception of civilization in the second stanza is multifaceted. The reference to "Heaven-lore" could refer to Moses's receiving of the Ten Commandments on Mount Sinai, Muhammad's divine revelations in the Arabian Desert, or Zoroaster's receiving of the Zend-Avesta in ancient Persia.[90] Only in the following stanza is the poem clearly locatable in the Arabian Desert, through reference to the divine revelations Muhammad received as spoken word.

The "East" of Goethe's *Divan* is often a composite of several different places. At times this includes ancient Greece, as, for example, in "Book of Zuleika" ("Suleika Nameh—Buch Suleika") or the section "Summer Night" ("Sommernacht") in "Book of the Cupbearer" ("Saki Nameh—Das Schenkenbuch"). Such mixing of Eastern and Western references raises the question as to where the *Divan*'s textual journey leads its reader and points to a problematic of worldly self-positioning that developed throughout the eighteenth century. In a time of great European expeditions and increased colonial expansion, the need for reliable world maps grew immensely. The impossibility of rendering three-dimensional space accurately on a two-dimensional map, together with the absence of an identifiable east-west meridian, nevertheless rendered the very concept of orientation problematic. Whether isogonic or homolographic, maps are truly to scale only at the point the imaginary globe touches its projected space on paper. And unlike the north-south axis on which one's relative position can be determined through reference to the sun and stars, there are no earthly signs that reveal one's easterly or westerly location.[91] In the absence of reliable signs, the concept of geographic and cartographic orientation developed into a more specific problematic of self-orientation (*sich orientieren*), as is exemplified by the following definition from Grimm's dictionary: "from the Italian *orientare*, French *orienter*, trans. and reflexive. (in absence of the compass needle) to try to find the excess—namely, the East—of one's familiar worldly location, and generally, to orient oneself in an area, a space, a situation or a relationship."[92]

That the task of orienting oneself is measured upon the ability to locate the East as opposed to the West is due to the etymology of the word "Orient." Derived from the Latin *oriens*, it can be translated as *sich erhebend*, soaring or uplifting, and designates the space of the Orient as the land that lies in the direction of the rising sun (*sol oriens*). Accordingly, the verb *orientieren* (to orient) originally meant to turn toward the East.[93] Grimm's quote—which identifies the East as the unknown or excess (*die übrigen*) of an implied West—suggests the development of a problematic form of *Weltorientierung*, or worldly self-positioning, that is nevertheless impossible to achieve with accuracy. It points to the inherent meaning of the word "Orient" as a nonlocatable space that changes according to one's own position. Any attempt to locate the East thus reveals one's own position to be unstable.

Goethe's depiction of Diez's translations as "constellations" is emblematic of such spatial instability: within the context of the *Divan*, these translations become navigational signs that nevertheless reveal the impossibility of a clear-cut system of East-West orientation. Consider, for example, the cosmic imagery in *Book of Zuleika*, which forms the core of the *Divan*'s poetic section. The following motto for this book is adapted from a *distichon* of Sultan Selim I, which is quoted in translation in Diez's *Memoirs*. Goethe gives this quote a proverbial character by breaking it into four short lines: "I was thinking, in the night, / That in sleep I saw the moon; / But when

I awakened, / Unawaitedly the sun arose."[94] While originally intended for the *Book of Proverbs*, Goethe later positioned this poem more prominently as the motto for the *Book of Zuleika*. This decision is significant considering Goethe's first "encounter" with the Ottoman Empire in 1758. At the age of eight, he was given the task of translating the following from German into Latin: "Selimus [Sultan Selim I] has become Kaiser in the Turkish Empire, after murdering his father Bayezid and chasing away his brother Zizimus."[95] Such model sentences were commonly used to emphasize the barbaric character of Ottoman rulers during the period of *Türkenfurcht* in the eighteenth century. Considering this background, what might it mean for Goethe to incorporate a quote from a feared Ottoman ruler into the love story at the center of his *Divan*? In contrast to the kind of educational indoctrination Goethe experienced as a child, it underscores Diez's desire to depict Sultan Selim I not simply as a political ruler but also as a poet, a thinker, and a person.

This motto becomes the core of a "dream-day and sun-moon symbolism"[96] that develops throughout the poetic dialogues of the *Book of Zuleika*. The series of oppositions this section encapsulates—sun/moon, waking/sleeping, day/night—repeats in different forms throughout cycles of union, separation, and reunion with the beloved. Within the book, the opposition of sun and moon becomes a symbol of cosmic-erotic conjunction: "The rising sun, a splendor shining! / The sickle-moon enclasped it round. / To solve the riddle, your divining / In time the answer will have found!"[97] This reference to the crescent or sickle moon—an important symbol for the Ottoman Empire—is significant in relation to Goethe's later figuration of the sun as Helios, personification and god of the sun in Greek mythology, within the same book.[98] It suggests a specifically Ottoman role in the East-West love affair of Hatem and Zuleika.

That the Ottoman element in this relationship contributes to a complex portrayal of the "East" in the *Divan* is underscored by a later stanza also taken from Diez's *Memoirs*: "When from your love you're riven, rent, / As Orient from Occident, / The heart is through the desert sent—/ Our guide no matter what we are. / Baghdad—for lovers—can't be far!"[99] This poem is inspired by a scene from Diez's translation of *The Mirror of Countries* (*Spiegel der Länder*), the travelogues of the Ottoman diplomat Seydi Ali Reis, also known as Katib-i Rūmī. When an interlocutor attempts to dissuade Seydi Ali Reis from traveling to Baghdad, he responds by reciting the following line from the divan of the Ottoman Turkish poet Necati: "If the distance between you and your lover should be so far as from Orient to Occident: /

then simply run, oh heart! for lovers Baghdad is not far."[100] By contrasting the desert to the urban setting of Baghdad, Goethe's transformation of this quote puts forth a seemingly insurmountable geographic barrier, only to then break it down through a collapsing of otherwise oppositional spaces and the suggested ability of love to overcome even unthinkable distances. As such, it reveals the difficulty in discursively locating the diverse "Oriental" textual geographies of the *Divan*, among which the Ottoman Empire and Ottoman Turkish literary texts comprise one important part.

The "distance" from Orient to Occident expressed in the original quote is complicated by Goethe's position as an "Occidental" author with access to Orientalist scholarship and texts in translation. Within the context of the *Book of Zuleika* and the *Divan* as a whole, it suggests the need to reflect on the role translations played within Orientalist discourse in the construction of an assumed distance between West and East. This is a question central to any reading of the *Divan*, which drew its inspiration overwhelmingly from texts in translation. Yet, as the poetic interpretation of a translation of a quote by an Ottoman statesman who was himself *quoting* Necati, this stanza in particular suggests the need to consider the *Divan* as a fundamentally mediated text that reflects critically on its own methods of representation.

CONCLUSIONS

Goethe's method of adapting Ottoman Turkish source texts throughout the *Divan* is fundamentally open-ended. As such, it does not align with the Orientalist-philological treatment of textual meaning as something finished and complete in and of itself. Dateable and locatable to a specific time and place, philology approaches primary materials as historically traceable sources that can be analyzed to glean information about their origins.[101] On the contrary, Goethe's engagement with Ottoman Turkish sources in translation more closely aligns with the flexibilities of the Ottoman lyric tradition itself. In the words of Walter Andrews, for example, Ottoman lyric poetry did not prize a concept of originality "that demands a poem unique in all its features with a discernible origin in a particular author. This is a more recent concept. The situation of Ottoman poetry more closely resembles that of improvised jazz, rock, or hip-hop, where masters of the art render common themes in unique and original ways and the less accomplished only mix and match familiar riffs."[102] In conclusion, I consider what bearing such a conception of originality might have on our understanding of *Weltliteratur*. Curiously, Goethe's *Divan* has been largely overlooked in recent theoretical discussions of the term. John Pizer and Angus Nicholls have analyzed sections of the lengthy "Notes and Essays" that accompany the *Divan's* poetry cycle in order to address their significance for the concept of comparison and the relative Eurocentricity of *Weltliteratur*.[103] I argue further that, as a text that owes its existence to non-European literatures in translation, the poetry of the *Divan* provides a richer perspective on *Weltliteratur* than Goethe's essays or even his direct reflections on the term.

In his various comments on *Weltliteratur*, Goethe often comments on the act of reading his own work in translation. Yet rather than a consecration of the work's fundamental Germanness, Goethe describes translation as a transformative process. In a letter to Thomas Carlyle from January 1, 1828, for example, Goethe inquires about the Englishness of his own *Torquato Tasso* (1790) in translation: "It is just this connection between original and the translation," he writes, "that expresses most clearly the relationship of nation to nation and that one must above all know if one wishes to encourage a common world literature transcending national limits."[104] Alternately, Goethe also viewed translation as a means of reinvigorating a national literature, which would exhaust itself without the contributions of foreign texts.[105] In an 1831 letter to Sulpiz Boisserée, for example, Goethe argues that certain aspects of his botanical studies were more understandable in French than in his original German.[106]

To what extent and in what manner did Goethe refer to non-European texts in translation as part of this invigorating process? Goethe informed Johann Peter Eckermann on January 31, 1827, that he was reading a Chinese novel in French translation. Rather than remark on the cultural particularities of this text, however, Goethe notes that its characters think, act, and feel just like Europeans.[107] As shortly thereafter he declares poetry to be the "universal possession of mankind,"[108] this succession of comments begs the question of what Goethe means by "universal." The system of literary exchange he envisioned—while playing out between national literary elites—was dedicated to the advancement of universal human progress.[109] Goethe's specific understanding of universalism entailed not the dissolution of differences but rather the integration of any number of particulars into the universal via a process of negotiation.[110] But to what extent did this process remain open to the world? Goethe upheld ancient Greece as the model of perfection[111] and figured Europe as the site of the universal on at least two occasions. In one instance, he titled an unpublished schematic list regarding mutual intra-European literary influences as "Weltlitera-tur, that is to say European literature," thus equating the two.[112] In another instance, he qualified his reference to "European" literature as universal: "In venturing to announce a European, in fact a universal, world litera-ture, we did not mean merely to say that the different nations should get to know each other and each other's productions; for in this sense it has long since been in existence, is propagating itself, and is constantly being added to. No, indeed! The matter is rather this—that the living, striving men of letters should learn to know each other, and through their own incli-nation and similarity of tastes, find the motive for corporate action."[113] In the spirit of this passage, Antoine Berman understands *Weltliteratur* as a historical concept addressing modern relations between different national and regional literatures. In asking what it means to speak of an "age" of world literature, he argues that literatures do not simply interact but rather conceive of their existence within the framework of this interaction.[114]

Numerous scholars have weighed in on the relative scope of such inter-actions by investigating the Eurocentric character of *Weltliteratur* and the conditions of its initial theorization. Already in 1946, Fritz Strich argued that intra-European literary exchange was the first and thus preparatory stage for the future inauguration of a *Weltliteratur* that might truly encompass the world. Yet even as Strich argued against accusations of Eurocentrism, he figured European literature as the "seed" from which the living and growing organism of *Weltliteratur* would emerge.[115] More recently, John Pizer has argued that Goethe was limited by the existing communication networks of the time, during which "prolific translation activities were still restricted to [the European] continent."[116] And yet, as mentioned above, one of Goethe's most famous ruminations on *Weltliteratur* involves commen-tary on a Chinese novel he read in French translation. Beyond this oft-cited passage, B. Venkat Mani has shown how the very concept of *Weltliteratur* emerged amid colonial and orientalist practices that divided the world into the uneven categories of East/West, center/periphery, and modern/premodern.[117]

The *Divan* in particular owes its existence to the histories of Oriental-ism and colonialism. While Germany had not yet emerged as a colonial power—or even as a nation—in the 1820s, the ability of libraries such as the one of Haus Sachsen-Weimar to acquire non-European manuscripts was necessarily dependent on the colonialist activities of countries such as England and France undertaken in Asia and Africa.[118] And yet, as my readings have shown, the *Divan* itself does not replicate the hierarchies of power or the investment in origins so central to colonialism and Oriental-ism. Academic Orientalist philology in particular was deeply invested in producing universal world histories through the categorization and hier-archization of individual cultures and literary traditions. While Goethe's assertion of a "European, in fact a universal world literature" does buy into the grand narrative of Orientalism, his *Divan*, arguably, does not. Rather, the poetry of the *Divan* collapses times and geographic locations, thereby exhibiting shifting relationships between different languages and literary traditions. This is not a form of literary exchange that might lead to a more refined understanding of the self in the name of universal progress. The cyclical nature of the *Divan*'s poetry exhibits, instead, a deep questioning of originality, thus aligning it more closely with the Ottoman lyric tradi-tion than the criticism of Orientalist philology. Within the pages of the *Divan* we thus glimpse the potential for an alternative conception of *Welt-literatur* that does not serve a strictly Eurocentric ordering of the world; rather it forges meaningful alliances with literary traditions, such as those of Ottoman Turkish, that lay outside the scope of academic Orientalism.

CHAPTER 2

Translations with No Original
Reading Werther *in Ottoman Turkish*

Across a nearly five-hundred-year time frame, Ottoman Turkish authors engaged with Arabic and Persian literature through diverse writing practices, such as rewriting, parallel poetry, call and response, commentary, and literary evaluation (*tezkire*). Within these diverse forms of cultural and textual interaction, numerous concepts existed to describe translation in all of its guises: in addition to *terceme* (translation), terms such as *taklid* (imitation), *iktibas* (borrowing), *imtisal* (modeling), *tanzir* (emulation), *ahz* (taking), and *idhal* (importing) differentiated between aspects of a translation process that was not predicated on the strict separation of source and target texts. Unencumbered by the norms of fidelity, the shifting and mediated forms of translation that existed in Ottoman lyric poetry demonstrated a more flexible approach toward the relationship of texts across languages and toward the concept of originality itself. Only in the mid-nineteenth century, with the first literary translations from French, did a stricter understanding of originality as something completely new and unique enter into the Ottoman Turkish literary-cultural realm. This reconceptualization inaugurated in turn a stricter understanding of translation in binary opposition to an "original" source text.

In this chapter, I examine the mid- to late nineteenth century as a period of profound semiotic reorientation for late-era Ottoman Turkish authors in their turn toward Western European sources of inspiration. In particular, I show how this period of reorientation also produced the conditions under which Ottoman Turkish authors began to understand their own translation practice and literary production as belated. Amid shifting conceptions of originality, the West and its literary traditions took on the status of an original that Ottoman Turkish authors could only attempt to translate into their cultural realm. Translation, in turn, began to be understood in terms of temporal succession rather than as a powerfully mediating force. In short, authors began to view translations as texts that must orient themselves toward a given original. Only in this process of orientation did translation come to be understood as a text that *follows* an external point of reference in both space and time.

In my examination of the first translations from German into Ottoman Turkish, I argue that even so, the semiotic shifts underway in the late nineteenth century proved literary translation to be an extremely generative realm of experimentation that did not adhere to such unidirectional movement. Translated by five authors, different sections of Johann Wolfgang von Goethe's *The Sorrows of Young Werther* (*Die Leiden des jungen Werther*, 1774) appeared in leading literary journals between 1886 and 1894. Attesting to intense debate in the late Ottoman Turkish literary-cultural realm regarding questions of cultural reform and the role Western European literature should play therein, these translations mediate and respond to one another more than to a single authoritative source text. At the same time, competing translational decisions on the part of Ottoman Turkish authors reveal *Werther*'s account of modern subjectivity itself to entail processes of mediation that undermine the authority of an assumedly original German or Western narrative voice.

Given the status of *Werther* as a text that catapulted Goethe into the international spotlight—affording him a new role in the realm of *Weltliteratur*—this chapter also asks what it means to read the Ottoman Turkish translations of *Werther* as *Weltliteratur*. As such, they do not simply consecrate Goethe's role in a canon of world literature but actively negotiate the terms of originality and cultural transformation that also inform his work. This reading entails taking seriously the omnidirectional nature of the *Werther* translations as texts that do not simply respond to and follow an "original" in time but rather serve as an active and creative force in and of themselves.

To contextualize, I read the *Werther* translations against the Classics Debate of 1897—which reflected extensively on the role translations from Western European literatures should play in the Ottoman cultural realm. The Classics Debate, I argue, aligns closely with speculations over

Weltliteratur made by late nineteenth-century German authors who sought to anthologize the literatures of the world. In doing so, they understood *Weltliteratur* as a retrospective category that could be applied to representative works of literature. In contrast, the *Werther* translations engender an active vision of *Weltliteratur* more closely aligned with the kind of poetic experimentation Goethe undertook in his *Divan* some eighty years prior. Pointing toward an open-ended conception of *Weltliteratur* as a process rather than a canon, the *Werther* translations are productively inconclusive. Rather than signs of inferiority or belatedness, the tensions that emerge between divergent translations, in terms of style, word choice, and emphasis, hold the power to enact debate in the public sphere regarding not only processes of modernization in the late Ottoman Empire but also the concept of *Weltliteratur* itself.

CONTRA THE DISCOURSE OF BELATEDNESS

On September 5, 1897, Ahmet Mithat (1844–1912) initiated the Classics Debate with his detailed definition of a "classic" as a European work of literature, approximately 100 to 150 years in age, the value of which does not decrease over time. As examples, he cites authors such as Goethe, Corneille, Shakespeare, Molière, and Racine. In contrast to the literatures these authors represent, Mithat states that Ottoman authors have not yet entered their own classical period.[1] In the myriad response articles that followed, Mithat's ideas were met with intense debate regarding the meaning of the term "classic" in relation to contemporary and ancient texts and the application of the term to non-European literatures. This gave way to a questioning of the existence of Ottoman literary "classics," which itself engendered an examination of the state of the Ottoman language, its perceived im/maturity, and its in/ability to produce a classical period (*klâsik dönem*) via classical works of literature. Very specific debates regarding the definition of the term "classic," its etymology, and to whom or what it should be applied ensued: Should the term "classic" refer to authors or individual works? Can—and should—the word "classic" be applied to art forms other than literature, including the plastic arts? Must the word be traced back to its Latin etymology, or can the meanings of "classic" be illuminated by reference to Arabic grammar?

While Goethe stands high on the list of classic authors in Mithat's account, Goethe had himself debated the concept of the classic in relation to

German literature one century prior. And while the term *Weltliteratur* had not yet entered his vocabulary, Goethe's 1795 essay "Literary Sansculottism" ("Literarischer Sansculottismus") arguably foregrounds the contradictory position German authors would occupy in his later conceptualization of this term. Goethe states here that the conditions necessary for a classical—or national—author to come into being had not yet been achieved in Germany. These conditions all revolve around the existence of a specific *National-geist*, which is produced through the highest level of culture, marked by social and political unity at the national level, and capable of inspiring a writer's inherent genius to sympathize with the nation's past and present.[2] Some seventy-six years prior to the establishment of a German nation-state, Goethe laments the absence of a political center that could serve as a gathering place for Germany's greatest authors and help to counter the overt influence of French classicism, which "prohibited the Germans from developing as Germans earlier on."[3]

While Goethe's 1828 proclamation of a common world literature was predicated on the transcendence of national boundaries, the conditions he had described in 1795 still held sway in German-speaking lands. About fifty years prior to its national unification in 1871, Germany existed as a *Kultur-nation*, a shared cultural realm bound together by language and tradition rather than political rights provided by the state. If Germans thus enjoyed a certain clarity of aesthetic perspective that was not limited to a national political identity, they also stood on shaky ground: "Please note that the world literature I have called for is deluging and threatening to drown me like the sorcerer's apprentice," Goethe wrote to Carl Zelter in May of the same year.[4] Unable, in the absence of a political cultural center, to develop into classical authors, Germans were in danger of losing themselves in the expansiveness of world literature.[5] Read together, Goethe's 1795 essay on "Literary Sansculottism" and his late-career remarks on *Weltliteratur* reveal certain tensions: On the one hand, Goethe's conceptualization of *Weltliter-atur* as a poetic aesthetic ideal stands in contrast to the concept of a literary canon constituted by the works of representative "classic" authors. On the other hand, if Goethe highlighted a process of transnational intellectual exchange in the service of universal humanity through the concept of *Welt-literatur*, this very concept of exchange also presupposed individual ethnic or national actors coming together for a higher purpose.[6]

These ethnic underpinnings of *Weltliteratur* came to the fore in the aftermath of Goethe's death, as the term became more closely aligned with the "classic." Published in 1848, Johannes Scherr's *Gallery of Weltliteratur*

(*Bildersaal der Weltliteratur*) is indicative of this shift. In the introduction to this seven-volume anthology, Scherr describes his work as the first attempt to realize what Goethe had only expressed as a thought. In short, this realization entails drawing a "total picture (*Gesamtbild*) of the poetic works of all civilized peoples from ancient to modern times, who truly possessed or possess a literature."[7] As this quotation suggests, Scherr imagines his work to be all-encompassing with regard to questions of form and genre, as well as in terms of the languages and regions it covers. These include (1) literature of the Orient (China, India, "Hebrew Land" [*Hebräerland*], Arabia, Persia, and Turkey);[8] (2) ancient Greece and Rome; (3) the "Roman lands" (France, Italy, Spain, and Portugal); (4) the Germanic lands (Germany, the Netherlands, England, Scotland, Ireland, Scandinavia, and North America); and (5) the Slavic lands (Czechoslovakia, Poland, Russia, Hungary, and Greece). Suffice it to say, this is clearly not a comprehensive anthology of the world's literatures—if such an anthology is even possible—but rather a selective grouping of translations from literatures deemed to be of signal importance.

Even more telling than Scherr's selection criteria are the specific qualities he attributes to the Germans. The very ability to undertake such a project, he writes, is attributable to the poetic art of translation (*poetische Übersetzungskunst*) that only the Germans possess. In conclusion, Scherr declares Germans to be the true owners (*Besitzer*) of a *Weltliteratur* that the great author Goethe had himself announced some twenty years prior. Scherr's rhetoric of ownership and appropriation marks a strong departure from Goethe's remarks on *Weltliteratur*. While Goethe referred to *Weltliteratur* as a common good (*Gemeingut*), he also pointed to a process of intellectual exchange across national boundaries and a mode of circulation that was not bound by an understanding of the world in a specifically geographic sense. By contrast, Scherr's anthology clearly divides the world's literatures into recognizable categories, which are then mediated through the German language. At the same time, *Gallery of Weltliteratur* echoes diverse eighteenth- and nineteenth-century authors' celebration of German as a language uniquely suited to translate even the most difficult of texts. From Georg Forster's celebration of German's cultural receptivity to Wilhelm von Humboldt's emphasis on the unique capacity of German to successfully imitate Greek hexameter, Johannes Scherr's comments partake in a long tradition of authors upholding a specific proclivity of the German language toward translation as a sign of openness to the world.

In contrast to the history of translation in Germany, nineteenth-century Ottoman Turkish authors tended to internalize the basic premises of

Orientalism, which "placed Europe at the center and pinnacle of development, and . . . ordered the globe spatially and temporally in accordance with
the criteria of European development. Non-European societies were characterized in this reordering of the world not by what they had but by what
they lacked—in other words, the lack of one or more of those characteristics
that accounted for European development." As a result, "they were perceived
predominantly to be located at some rung or other of the ladder of development that Europe already had left behind."[9] In the literary realm, Ottoman
Turkish authors registered their own "lack" in what they saw as the need to
translate from European literatures in order to gain cultural capital. This
self-perceived belatedness emerged in the wake of Tanzimat era reforms,
which sought to adopt certain innovations from Europe in the realms of
technology, the military, and bureaucracy. Increasingly familiar with European modes of government, Ottoman Turkish intellectuals of this era also
began to turn to European literature as a source of inspiration. Accordingly,
the Tanzimat era saw the first translations from Western European source
texts into Ottoman Turkish: İbrahim Şinasi's translation of collected classical French poetry, *Translations of Verse (Tercüme-i Manzume)*, in 1859
set the stage for the dominant role French literature would play in the late
nineteenth-century Ottoman Turkish literary-cultural realm. Following a
nearly five-hundred-year history of translations from Arabic and Persian,
translations from French and other European languages introduced new
genres, such as the novel, the short story, and literary criticism, as well as
new idea(l)s to late Ottoman readerships, sparking heated debates on issues
as diverse as language reform and political governance.

Within this period of semiotic reorientation, literary translation was
broadly conceived as a method of social reform, as a means for achieving
literary and cultural progress (*terakki*) and for "catching up" with the more
"developed" literatures of Europe. In the introduction to his summary-
translation of Pierre Corneille's *Le Cid*, for example, Ahmet Mithat argues
that awareness of the classics of European literature is the first step toward
achieving (European) progress. In short, Mithat viewed Europe as a source
for importing new literary models into the late Ottoman intercultural realm.
The development of Ottoman literature was in turn premised on its successful emulation of European literary models.[10]

The rhetoric of Mithat's argument here has been replicated and
reworked in a variety of scholarship through to the present moment. Ahmet
Hamdi Tanpınar's monumental study *A History of Nineteenth-Century
Turkish Literature*, for example, attributes a perceived lack of innovation

in pre-nineteenth-century Ottoman Turkish literature to a lack of literary models; such models, he argues, were first provided through translations from French in the Tanzimat era.[11] This accusation tends to be at the core of scholarship examining the centrality of translation to late Ottoman and modern Turkish participation in a form of Western modernity. Recurring terms such as "civilizational transfer,"[12] "translating the West,"[13] and "importation"[14] emphasize the problematics of this encounter, highlighting a lack in the Ottoman Turkish literary realm and an imagined one-way transfer of modernity from West to East.

This imagined one-way movement of modernity rests on a linear conception of time and processes of modernization, through which one group's present (the West) is defined as another group's future (the rest). Johannes Fabian describes this dynamic in terms of chronopolitics, or the manner in which time "accommodate[s] the schemes of a one-way history: progress, development, modernity."[15] In his critique of the field of anthropology and the conditions under which it emerged, Fabian argues that the relationship between anthropology and its objects of study was configured not only in terms of difference but also in terms of *distance* in both space and time. While the process of fieldwork necessarily occurs in coeval time, through the interaction of anthropologists with their human subjects, the manner in which nineteenth-century anthropologists wrote about said interactions entailed a denial of that very coevalness, by portraying other cultures as existing in a separate and static time. The resulting assertion of different historical epochs of time served to promote the linear discourse of progress so central to the justification of European imperialist expansion. In short, the denial of coevalness reveals a hidden agenda of anthropology: the universalization of Western progress in order to justify its colonial domination of the world.[16]

While the Ottoman Empire was never colonized, late Ottoman Turkish authors did often perceive themselves and their work as derivative of a Western model, amid the empire's sweeping cultural-political reorientation toward Western Europe in the second half of the nineteenth century. Within the cultural realm generally, and in the field of literary translation in particular, this self-perception was informed by the self-presentation of Western modernity as perennially "new," and thereby also unique and singular. In the words of Timothy Mitchell, modernity, as such, appears to "form a distinctive time-space, appearing in the homogenous shape of the West and characterized by an immediacy of presence that we recognize as the 'now' of history."[17] This necessarily creates a situation in which the "non-West" has been fated to unsuccessfully mimic a history already performed by the West.[18]

In the following sections, I argue that literary translations from Western European source texts provide a particularly fruitful realm from which to challenge assertions of the West's originality and uniqueness. The *Werther* translations in particular negotiate a more flexible concept of originality at a historical moment when "original" and "translation" had not yet solidified into oppositional terms in the late Ottoman realm. Thus, even as diverse Ottoman Turkish authors began to *discuss* translation in these terms, the actual practice of translation did not necessarily uphold such a rigid binary distinction.

TRANSLATING MODERN SUBJECTIVITY

Sâkine Eruz's work on Ottoman translation movements marks an important departure from the rhetoric of translation as a mode of one-way cultural transfer, through her focus on Istanbul/Constantinople as a historically multilingual and multicultural city. She situates translation not as a strictly modernizing or Westernizing process but as a natural outcome of the interactions among diverse Turkish, Greek, Armenian, and Ladino-speaking Jewish communities in the Ottoman Empire.[19] Similarly, Johann Strauss has documented extensive translation and transliteration movements *within* the empire—particularly among the Greek and Armenian communities—that occurred well before the first Ottoman Turkish translations from French. While Yusuf Kâmil Paşa's 1859 translation of *The Adventures of Telemachus* marks the beginning of literary translations from French into Ottoman Turkish, this work had enjoyed popularity among diverse communities of the Levant long before this date. The first Greek translation dates to the eighteenth century, and an Armenian version was published in the same year as the Turkish.[20] There is also evidence that Ottoman Turkish translation decisions were to some extent influenced by translation activity into the other languages of the empire. Ahmet Mithat Efendi, for example, undertook a translation of Émile Richebourg's *The Cursed Girl* (*La Fille Maudite*, 1876) in 1883 after observing its success as a serialized novel in Greek and Armenian newspapers. Furthermore, popular Turkish literature, such as the novels of Mithat, was transliterated into the Armenian and Greek scripts for Turkish readers in those communities.[21] More recently, Etienne Charrière has examined the Tanzimat era as a landscape of "transcommunal translational communities." In his survey of translations from contemporary French literature into Greek, Armenian, Ladino, and Greek-scripted Ottoman Turkish (*karamanlidika*), Charrière argues that trends within this corpus of texts "cut across linguistic and communal boundaries within the empire."[22]

My interest in nineteenth-century German–(Ottoman) Turkish literary relations is informed by these various calls for a more holistic and differentiated approach to translation activity in the Ottoman Empire. While my focus remains on translations into Perso-Arabic scripted Ottoman Turkish (and not into or among other minor languages of the empire), I argue that many smaller acts of translation, particularly from languages other than French, remain understudied. Housed largely in rare book sections of major research libraries, smaller-scale translations, such as poetry, short stories, and excerpts from novels, comprise an important element of a larger movement. Many such translations appeared in literary journals, which were subject to less rigorous censorship than printed books and served as important forums for political, social, and cultural debates.[23]

Uncovering diverse late Ottoman translations that remain unanthologized and untransliterated can help create a more complex picture of nineteenth-century translation initiatives. Such diversity runs counter to early republican accusations in particular, which charged Ottoman Turkish translations from Western European literatures with being inaccurate, rudimentary, and incomplete. In the following case study, I show how the first translations from German into Ottoman Turkish reveal, on the contrary, intense debate regarding the value, use, and method of translation. At the same time that translators expressed anxiety regarding the (in)expressive power of Ottoman Turkish, their translations bring forth a myriad of views on the subject that testify to both their own and the language's expressive capacity.

Between 1886 and 1894, the first thirteen letters of Goethe's epistolary novel *The Sorrows of Young Werther* were rendered into Ottoman Turkish by a total of five translators (Ahmet Rasim (1864–1932), Hüseyin Daniş (1870–1943), Halil Edip (1863–1911), Mustafa Fazıl, and one anonymous author) and published in leading literary journals of the time period. This series of translated letters prefigured a complete translation of the novel by Ali Kâmi Akyüz (1873–1945) in 1911. The first letter from *Werther* was translated anonymously and published by *Sebat Dergisi* in 1886. A translation by Ahmet Rasim of the fourth letter followed shortly thereafter in *Gülşen Dergisi*, together with an article by Rasim on Goethe. *Say Dergisi* then published a series of four translated letters by Halil Edip in 1888. Finally, throughout the year 1894, *Malumat Dergisi* published four letters translated by Hüseyin Daniş, two letters translated by Mustafa Fazıl, and one anonymously translated letter. While it is impossible to know if these translators were in direct contact, it is likely that they were at least aware of one another's work; the translations are not redundant and were translated fairly systematically, starting from the beginning of the book and moving forward chronologically.

In contrast to early republican Turkish rhetoric that criticized late Ottoman translations for their haphazardness, erroneousness, or superficial adaptation of Western values, this case study demonstrates the need to read translations in relation to one another rather than simply against a single, presumably original source text. Indeed, reading the *Werther* translations in dialogue reveals the intense level of debate generated by questions of what and how to translate in the late Ottoman context. As opposed to passive models of importation and imitation, they reveal translation to be an *active* process that expresses individual translators' relative positions as literary agents.

As such, the role of the translator largely resembles Ahmet Mithat's depiction of the literary critic. In the first extended work of literary criticism in Ottoman Turkish, *A General Look at Literary Works* (*Ahbar-ı Asara Tamim-i Enzar*, 1890), Mithat depicts the literary critic (*müntekid*) at a level of development above that of the master. A figure normally treated as secondary in the realm of literary production, the critic is elevated here to the level of a torch in the darkness, leading the author down the right path.[24] This amounts to a depiction of the writer as his own harshest—and therefore best—critic. Mithat argues, nevertheless, that there are no true Ottoman Turkish critics, as there is no Ottoman Turkish novel to speak of, and the latter cannot come into being without the former. This is a remarkable statement from an author of almost fifty novels. More than an expression of self-insufficiency vis-à-vis an assumedly superior Western model, however, Mithat outlines a model of unachievable perfection in his emphasis on the extreme rarity of what he understands to be the ideal critic. Literary criticism is thus not simply an imitable object located in the West; rather, it is a positive and constructive process that allows for a negotiation of the self through its interaction with a foreign form (the novel).

Reading Ottoman Turkish translations in this vein, as an emergent form of literary criticism, suggests the need to situate them not simply in relation to a static ideal set by the source text but rather through an active negotiation of source and target languages that occurs, in part, through the translations' interactions with one another. This approach is closely in line with the Ottoman tradition of *terceme*, a term for translation that also incorporated practices such as parallel and response poetry.[25] Adopted from Arabic before the thirteenth century, this term eventually dropped out of Turkish discourse in the 1960s. Its modern variant *tercüme* is quite similar to the meaning of *çeviri*, which no longer connotes a broad range of translational practices. Saliha Paker has shown how a republican Turkish ideological emphasis on Westernization has deproblematized the Ottoman concept of *terceme* through a modern nation-building process aimed at both a cultural and political break with the past: "[As] linguistic and poetic inventiveness or originality in Turkish became important elements for literary studies to seek, locate and foreground," she argues, "translations identified as *terceme* by their authors or by tradition were superficially evaluated in terms of the modern concept of fidelity."[26]

While this shift toward a fidelity-based understanding of translation was solidified in the republican era, the concept of originality (*özgünlük*) it was based upon had already entered into Ottoman Turkish discourse as a literary term by the second half of the nineteenth century. Namık Kemal in particular—who was also central to the introduction of European literature and thought into the late Ottoman cultural realm—expressed the idea that in order to serve as a literary model, a text needed to have a quality original to itself or characteristics unlike those of any other text. Without using the specific word "original," Kemal utilized a variety of other terms to describe it in his writings, such as *has* (peculiar or special to), *mahsus* (on purpose, intentionally), *numune* (specimen, archetype), and *benzemezlik* (dissimilarity).[27]

These terms all bear on the concept of originality in literature, as was first elaborated by the British poet Edward Young (1681–1765). Young's *Conjectures on Original Composition* (1759) contrasts the concept of literary originality to that of imitation or emulation, arguing that only the genius can achieve a work of original stature.[28] Kemal, for example, viewed the writing of Victor Hugo in this manner, as both the product of a genius and as a metaphor for a (Western) model of literature that could be emulated in the Ottoman Turkish literary sphere.[29] As such, the work of Kemal and others indicates important shifts in the Ottoman Turkish conception of originality that occurred vis-à-vis a Western literary-cultural counterpart, which Ottoman Turkish authors sought to emulate. In contrast to the more flexible concept of *terceme*, this new focus on originality produced a self-perceived spatial and temporal gap between Ottoman Turkish and Western European literary production. It further upheld a conception of translation as a text or process that can only ever come into being retrospectively, vis-à-vis an original it is assumed to follow in time. Learned from the West, this reconfiguration of the terms of originality served to corroborate Ottoman Turkish authors' internalization of modernity as unique to the West, against which their own literary and translational production appeared as inherently belated.

Reading the *Werther* translations within the *terceme* tradition suggests that they orient themselves toward one another rather than toward an authoritative "original" text that they temporally follow. They thus partake in a more flexible understanding of originality that also reflects on the structure of Goethe's novel itself. A text that notably garnered fame for Goethe and the German literary realm by way of its translation into French, *Werther's* narrative of modern subjectivity could also be read as a discourse on translation and the impossibility of a single, unmediated, or original narrative voice. The insertion of an editor toward the close of the novel stages a break of its epistolary form. Pointing to a lack of original documents, the editor describes his efforts to reconstruct the final days of Werther's life leading up to his suicide. While not uncommon for the epistolary form, the insertion of an editorial voice in *Werther* is notable, in that it signals the introduction of a multiplicity of voices and mixed narrative forms into an otherwise univocal text.[30] The closing sections of *Werther* take extratextual references and citations to an extreme—perhaps most notably through Goethe's own translations from James Macpherson's collected edition "The Poems of Ossian" (1765). A collection of allegedly ancient Gaelic folk songs incorporating multiple voices, this poetry was "discovered" and "translated" into contemporary English by Macpherson in the 1760s. Extremely popular among German intellectuals of the Sturm und Drang movement to which *Werther* belongs, Macpherson's translations inspired, in particular, an influential essay by Johann Gottfried Herder, "On Ossian and the Songs of Ancient Peoples" ("Über Ossian und die Lieder alter Völker"). Written in 1773, just one year before the publication of *Werther*, Herder's essay praises the sensual immediacy of oral folk poetry as the direct, collective expression of a *Volk's* natural characteristics. While recognizing the necessity of preservation, Herder laments the transformation of the embodied folk song into the disembodied "dead letters" of a written record. His own writing style—full of exclamation marks, dashes, and ellipses—could be described as an attempt to simulate the immediacy of the folk poetry it describes at the same time that it recognizes the impossibility of fulfilling this task.

Lotte's request that Werther read his *Ossian* translations aloud expresses a similar desire to recuperate the oral character of these "original" songs. The extended *written* quote in the novel—which spans a full eight pages— nevertheless attests to the fact that Werther can only ever achieve a form of mediated immediacy. Rather than a strictly Herderian investment in the originary, untranslatable quality of the Ossian songs, I read this scene within the staged multivocality in the final sections of the novel as a commentary on the impossibility of an unmediated originality. This argument gains new meaning today with the knowledge that Macpherson's translations were actually a hoax reproduction; as such, *Werther* presents its contemporary readers with a translation of a translation with no original.

The reality of this translation stands in stark contrast to Werther's own desires for originality and individuality in the face of convention. These two poles pulling at Werther—alternately represented by his own fits of intense inner emotion and his admiration for an image of pastoralized domesticity in the maternal figure of Lotte—are central to the experi- ence of modern subjectivity. In particular, modern inwardness and the affirmation of everyday life are core elements in the making of a modern identity, for which the competing claims of the original and the ordinary are central to the pursuit of self-expression.[31] Within the structure of the novel, I suggest that Werther's impossible pursuit of originality is tied to a translational experience of modern subjectivity. This idea is informed, first, by an understanding of modernity as experience—as opposed to an epoch or set of institutions—that places the creative potential of the indi- vidual at its center.[32] Yet beyond a tension between individual autonomy and the constraints of social norms, I argue that acts of literary translation and textual mediation are central to Werther's emergence as an inherently modern subject. In this respect, the Ottoman translations of the novel add another key level of cultural mediation to Werther's character. As a multi- vocal collection of texts, they reflect on Werther's impossible quest for originality, through their negotiation of the state of the Ottoman Turkish language and the significance of translating Goethe's "classic" of European literature into the late nineteenth-century Ottoman context.

THE *WERTHER* TRANSLATIONS AND THE CLASSICS DEBATE

Several of the *Werther* translators also participated in the Classics Debate. Ahmet Rasim, for example, penned a largely metaphorical article—"Literary

Observations Inspired by the Classics Affair (Past)" ("Klâsikler Meselesinin Verdiği Bir Fikr-i Edebî [Mâzî]")—which described classics as works from the past that help us learn from our mistakes. In contrast to authors such as Sâid Bey (1848–1921), who supported the translation of more recent European classics on the basis of their chronological proximity and perceived historical relevance to current European political and literary thought, Rasim criticized what he saw as a desire to progress forward by way of rejecting the past. He advocated, instead, for the translation of ancient Greek and Latin literature due to its foundational role for European civilization. According to Rasim, translating only from contemporary literature would be like groping in the darkness, after having been born into the nothingness of an unknown desert through which one must find one's own way. In contrast to such exhausting circumstances, Rasim argues that Ottoman intellectuals should enter the future with weapons of knowledge (*silâh-ı irfân*) and critical guides (*müdekkik rehberler*).[33]

Considering the content of his article, it seems surprising that Rasim chose to translate from *Werther* at all. His decision to translate the fourth letter before the second or third (the first had already been translated) is nevertheless notable, as this letter contains the first of several references to Homer. Rasim's emphasis in his article on figures from the past as guides (*renümâlar/rehberler*) resonates strongly with his depiction of Homer's words as soothing songs (*nağmeler*) capable of containing his emotions, which are in turn depicted as his worldly guide (*mehd-i cihan*). A comparison of Rasim's and Akyüz's translations of the same passage—with important differences marked in bold—reveals the specific emphasis Rasim places on Homer as an emotional guide. Rasim's translation reads as follows:

Ah! **Benim kalbim bir seylâbdır ki kemâl-i sür'atle cereyân eder**. Bana, daha henüz reside-i mehd-i cihân olmuş olan kalbimi mahsûr edecek nağmeler lâzımdır. Bereket versin **benim (Omer)im** bu nağmeleri bana tedârik etmiştir. Galeyân ve heyecân-ı hûnumu teskîn etmek için **o kitaba kaç defa mürâca't ettim**![34]

Oh! **My heart is a flood, flowing at a perfect pace.** I am in need of a song to surround my heart, which has recently arrived at its worldly guidance. Thank heavens **my Homer** has provided me with these songs. How many times have **I appealed to this book** to soothe my agitated and excited blood!

In Rasim's version of the passage, it is specifically by returning to Homer's book that Werther is able to soothe his volatile character. This places an added emphasis on Homer as a healing force, whereas the need to calm oneself (*teskîn etmek*) is an act grammatically separated from the reading of Homer both in Akyüz's version and in the German:

> **Zira bu kalb kendi kendine derece-i kâfiyyede tahammür etmek-tedir.** Hatta benim—ondan ziyade—ninni gibi hâb-aver bir süruda ihtiyacım var. Bunu ise **(homer)de** ma-ziyadeten bulurum. Kaç defalar galeyâna gelen dem-i şebâbımı teskîn etmek ihtiyacında bulundum![35]

> **Because this heart ferments at a sufficient degree on its own.** I need—rather—a soporific song like a lullaby for the time being. This I find in abundance **in Homer**. How many times have I needed to soothe the agitated blood of my youth!

In contrast to the later translations of Mustafa Fazıl and Ali Kâmi Akyüz, Ahmet Rasim also chooses to directly translate Werther's reference to "*my* Homer." While an arguably minor linguistic issue, this personal pronoun is significant as one of the subtle ways in which Goethe expresses Werther's fatal egocentricity.[36] Rasim's decision to maintain "my" where other trans-lators choose to eliminate it sustains an emphasis on Werther's inherently romantic character. This is underscored by Rasim's insertion of the word "flood" (*seylâb*) to describe the state of Werther's heart. By drawing a connection between Werther's uncontrollable intellectual fervor and the destructive natural force of raging waters, Rasim foreshadows a real flood that occurs toward the close of the novel and the final flood of emotions that ultimately lead Werther to commit suicide.[37]

Notably, Mustafa Fazıl eliminates *all* references to flood vocabulary from his translations. At times, this entails the removal of entire passages, including key references to the awesome but destructive character of artistic creativity and romantic genius.[38] Read together, Rasim's and Fazıl's trans-lations reflect on larger problems of artistic self-expression and modern subjectivity. In either highlighting or downplaying the sentimental roman-tic tendencies of Werther's search for self, they bring out key tensions in the source text regarding his impossible desire for originality and singu-larity in the face of social convention.

Similar issues surface in Hüseyin Daniş's translations, with a more specific focus on the very possibility of self-representation in language or the translation of subjective experience into words. Notably, all of the letters Daniş translated are predominantly concerned with the faculty of imagination, the relationship of life to art, and the ability to express one's feelings accurately. Consider, for example, the following excerpt from the close of Werther's May 10 letter:

> Ach könntest du das wieder ausdrücken, könntest du dem Papiere das einhauchen, was so voll, so warm in dir lebt, dass es würde der Spiegel deiner Seele, wie deine Seele ist der Spiegel des unendlichen Gottes![39]

> Ah! I would that I could express it, would that I could breathe onto paper that which lives so warm and full within me, so that it might become the mirror of my soul as my soul is the mirror of the eternal God!

Whereas Daniş's translations are generally inclined toward embellishment, his translation of this passage is particularly striking, in that he shortens the source text:

> Şâir! Seni müstağrak-ı lücce-i hayret eden şu menâzır-ı âliyyeyi niçin teşhirgâh-ı beyâna çıkaramıyorsun? Acaba, hissiyât-ı âliyye-i derûnunu musavvir olabilecek bir eseri meydâna koyamaz mısın?[40]

> Poet! Why can't you publicly declare this sublime view that has immersed you in deep wonder? Or is it that you cannot make public a work of art capable of depicting feelings of deep sublimity?

On the surface, this translation upholds Daniş's contribution to the Classics Debate, where he argues that no language's form and style could be accurately represented in another but that a certain level of information (*bilgi*) could be transferred through translation.[41] The May 10 letter offers a form of meta-reflection on this very idea. In it, Werther laments the impossibility of transferring the sublime joy he derives from nature to canvas, suggesting that the utter singularity of his experience is untranslatable. This very lament is nevertheless expressed through a detailed depiction of his feelings in epistolary form. The words of this letter thus form an *impossible* translation or a potentially imperfect mirroring of Werther's soul.

Daniş's translation does not exactly "mirror" the syntax and meaning of the May 10 letter. As such, it serves both as an interpretation and a continuation of the German passage it translates, as well as an expression of Daniş's views on the state of the Ottoman Turkish language. In his contribution to the Classics Debate, Daniş argues that a classic could only be produced once a language has embodied the ideals of its nation.[42] Through a negative inversion of this argument, he then claims that if classics did exist in Ottoman Turkish, the language would have already reached its highest level of maturity.[43] Daniş's own heavy usage of Persian vocabulary and his tendency toward embellishment are in line with a longer history of Divan poetry that he implicitly criticizes for not being reflective of Ottoman values. It thus expresses the relative stagnation of the Ottoman Turkish language and suggests that no other translation was possible due to a lack of appropriate syntax and structures.

Daniş's emphasis on the importance of making one's feelings *public* relate back to and counter his own criticism of the Ottoman Turkish language. As a character who attempts to escape the confines of bourgeois society by moving to the countryside, Werther is marked by his search for a solitary lifestyle. In his retreat from the confines of social life, it is a desire for the impossible—ranging from his impossible love for Lotte to an impossibly perfect unity with nature or expression of his feelings in another medium—that offers a (temporary) confirmation of the singular and original nature of the self. Goethe's staged polyphony in the final sections of the novel nevertheless suggests the impossibility of an unmediated narrative of the self. Daniş's transformation of Werther's conversation with himself into a rhetorical question posed by the writer/translator to the literary character is thus in line with the novel's ending. Daniş hereby opens the posed question to a broader context, which in turn speaks to the role of translation in opening a source text to an entirely new public. As such, the information Daniş reveals through this translation is precisely a statement on the impossibility of an exact transmission of meaning, even as his translation continues the meaning of the original, albeit in a new context.

To reiterate my argument in simpler terms: Daniş's translation from *Werther* in 1894 exceeds his later remarks on translation in the Classics Debate of 1897. If the Ottoman concept of *terceme* was thoroughly deproblematized following the establishment of the Turkish nation-state in 1923, Daniş's comments show that the shift toward a fidelity-based model of translation (*tercüme* or *çeviri*) was already underway at the turn to the twentieth century. His emphasis on accuracy and the impossibility of a perfect translation in the Classics Debate is constitutive of this shift, while at the same time, his *Werther* translations render his own argument moot.[44]

PRACTICING WORLD LITERATURE

Through its emphasis on the conditions necessary to engender an Ottoman classic—which were largely deemed to be lacking—the Classics Debate underscored the idea of a classic as the representation of a national-cultural identity. While this definition of a classic clearly harkens back to Goethe's early thoughts on the term, it also closely aligns with the German conception of *Weltliteratur* in the second half of the nineteenth century. Understood as the compilation of representative classical works, *Weltliteratur* in this time period presupposed a division of the world into clear-cut literary-cultural categories.[45] Among other factors, this investment in categorization and separateness fueled Ottoman Turkish authors' perception of their own literary output as belated vis-à-vis the "West." On the contrary, the Ottoman Turkish translations of *Werther* embrace a more dynamic conception of *Weltliteratur*. They constitute—to use a term of Goethe's—a kind of translational mirroring that draws out and revitalizes certain aspects of the "original" text. In doing so, they attest to both the role of translation as a valid mode of interpretation and the expressive capacity of the Ottoman Turkish language.

Scholars such as Franco Moretti and Pascale Casanova have rightly emphasized profound inequalities in the circulation of texts between literary cultures imagined to be at the "core" and "periphery" of a world literary system.[46] Yet a closer examination of Ottoman Turkish translation activity in the nineteenth century suggests the need to challenge this discursive division of the world. Contrary to the assumption that target literatures on the periphery are interfered with by source literatures that completely ignore them,[47] the Ottoman Turkish renditions of *Werther* reveal the agency of its Turkish translators within the Europeanization process. As a group of texts, the *Werther* translations stage a salient debate regarding methods of translation and the value of European literature for the development of a modern Turkish literary canon. By extending the core tenets of Goethe's novel into a new historical context, they underscore the inherently translational nature of modern subjectivity and the impossibility of an unmediated

narrative voice. In contrast to theories of translational influence or importation, which fuel perceptions of Turkey's belatedness vis-à-vis the "West,"
they thus reveal the power of omnidirectional translation practices to effectively place the authenticity of a source text into question.

The omnidirectional and multivocal character of the *Werther* translations also speaks to the role this novel plays in the larger context of Goethe's
career. Preceding Goethe's essay on sansculottism by more than twenty
years, *Werther* demonstrates a strong Romantic influence. Yet in contrast to
the conservative Romantic discovery of a national and Christian past, the
multivocal quality of the *Werther* translations points instead to Romanticism's conception of its own era as both fractured and incomplete. Rather
than simply understanding its own modern condition as a repudiation of
the past, the Romantic tradition set itself more specifically against classicism or the very possibility of a classic, timeless work.[48] On the contrary, the
modern came to be understood as a state of unfinished reflection, open to
future emendation through the critic, the translator, and the philosopher.

Although Goethe became a leading author of what is now known as
Weimar Classicism, there is significant overlap between his later conception of *Weltliteratur* and the Romantic conception of modernity. The system
of circulation and exchange inherent to *Weltliteratur* necessitates an active
coexistence of contemporary literatures, as well as a fundamental recon-
sideration of the relationship of the (national) self to the other. Goethe
not only argues that any national literature would exhaust itself without
the counter-perspective of translation, he also sees translation as an act of
giving up the "originality" of the translator's nation in the process of identifying with the source language.[49]

The late eighteenth and early nineteenth centuries in which Goethe
composed his major literary works coincidentally witnessed an unprecedented amount of translation in the German context, whether from ancient,
contemporary European, or "Oriental" literatures. Regardless of the power
structures undergirding these translations—many of which were clearly
tied to Orientalist and colonialist practices—Goethe's historical conception
of *Weltliteratur* gestures toward the translational experience of modernity itself. Arguing that the first Ottoman Turkish translations of *Werther*
put this conception of world literature into practice is to say that they
participate in an experience of modernity that renders the self subject to
processes of translation: their emphasis on the difficulty of self-expression
reveals a translational experience of modern subjectivity, and their structure as a group of texts mediating one another undermines the presumably

"originary" authority of their source text. By opening up new spaces of negotiation regarding translational practices and the expressive capacity of the Ottoman Turkish language, they show that late Ottoman Turkish literature was not merely "interfered with" by source literatures and that authors did not simply import works of European literature into the Ottoman realm. On the contrary, translation provided an important realm for debate and an alternative form of literary criticism.

PART 2

Friedrich Schrader

Translating Toward the Future

CHAPTER 3

Translating Beyond the Civilizing Mission

Ahmet Hikmet Müftüoğlu and the Ottoman Dandy

Ahmet Hikmet Müftüoğlu's short story "My Nephew" ("Yeğenim," 1899) weighs the consequences of losing one's cultural bearings amid the far-reaching processes of societal reorientation in the late Ottoman Empire. Published on the eve of the twentieth century—following decades of agitation on the part of Ottoman intellectuals in pursuit of modernizing reforms—"My Nephew" warns against the dangers of over-Westernization but also stops short of advocating for the "return" to an imagined form of pure Turkishness. Told from the perspective of an uncle who has financed his nephew's university education in Paris, "My Nephew" recounts a process of cultural estrangement. Upon returning to Istanbul, the nephew kisses his uncle on the mouth instead of the hand, forces the maids to listen to Western music, and recounts the stories of Boccaccio to his mother-in-law. Aghast at the seeming absurdity of these actions, the uncle declares his nephew's "duty" to be nothing less than "the 'spread of civilization'" (*neşr-i medeniyyet*).[1]

This offhand, tongue-in-cheek declaration reveals how a longstanding, powerful empire never historically colonized by France nonetheless internalized the rhetoric of the civilizing mission as it undertook modernizing reforms. It further expresses Müftüoğlu's critical approach toward Westernization, while also implicating himself in the "civilizing"/Westernizing process. As the stem of *neşretmek*, *neşr* means to spread or diffuse but also, more specifically, to publish or broadcast, gesturing both toward the actions of the nephew and the role of Müftüoğlu as author. Coincidentally, while

Müftüoğlu was central to the development of a *milli edebiyat*, or national Turkish literature, "My Nephew" is written in the European genre of the short story and is a reflection of Müftüoğlu's diverse experiences living and working in Europe. This contrast of form and content is but one way in which "My Nephew" reveals the process of forging a "national" Turkish literature to paradoxically involve the orientation of Turkish society toward Europe, as opposed to a strictly inward orientation of Turkish culture toward itself.

Whereas Müftüoğlu takes France—with Paris at its imagined center— as a site of reference for the Westernization of Turkish culture, this chapter asks what new implications "My Nephew" gains in German translation. Orientalist-turned-journalist Friedrich Schrader's 1908 translation of "My Nephew" appeared in the *Ottoman Lloyd*, an official newspaper that upheld Germany as a neutral role model for the Ottoman Empire in the era leading up to German-Ottoman military alliance in World War I. Yet Schrader's German title—"Der Kulturträger (Mein Neffe)" ("The Bearer of Culture [My Nephew]")—brings the rhetoric of the white man's burden to the fore. In the specific context of the *Ottoman Lloyd*, I argue, Schrader's translation practice calls attention to aspects of the civilizing mission at work in Germany's economic and military interactions with the Ottoman Empire in the late nineteenth and early twentieth centuries. As such, Schrader's translation shows both that Germany was far from a neutral model for the Ottoman Empire and that translation in this time period was anything but a "neutral" enterprise.

Indeed, that questions of political power come to the fore in the realm of translation is no coincidence. Although few in number, translations from Ottoman Turkish into German at the turn of the century were generally undertaken within the parameters of *Orientalistik*. These translations were furthermore central to the establishment of Turkology and a broader *European* assertion of a national Turkish character that was distinct from the other ethnicities of the Ottoman Empire. In the literary realm in particular, this European Orientalist investment in Turkishness proved central to Ottoman Turkish authors' denouncement of their own literary heritage in favor of a modern, national literature. In line, again, with the basic premise of the civilizing mission, this late Ottoman process of self-devaluation represents an internalization of the superiority of Western models.

In my examination of Friedrich Schrader's translation work in particular—including "My Nephew" and other stories by Müftüoğlu that appeared in the extensive Turkish Library (Türkische Bibliothek, 1904–29) publication series—I show that Schrader was clearly implicated within the power dynamics of Orientalism. He completed his doctoral studies in philology at an important epicenter for scholarly Orientalism and remained in close contact with other German Orientalists for his contributions to the Turkish Library in particular. At the same time, I ask how his early translations—together with his more prolific work as a journalist—prompt us to ask what kind of *Kulturarbeit*, or cultural labor, might reach beyond the civilizing missions of colonialism and Orientalism, toward a more meaningful process of German-Turkish cultural exchange in the future.

THE "TERROR OF DISORIENTATION" AND THE OTTOMAN DANDY

Fearful of the potentially negative consequences of living and studying in Europe, Ahmet Hikmet Müftüoğlu advocated for an education at home that placed emphasis on Turkish language and history. Only once students were well versed in these subjects did Müftüoğlu believe they should travel to Europe to "complete" their education.[2] Sending an uninformed Turkish student to Europe, Müftüoğlu warned, could only produce negative results, including "languagelessness," "homelessness," and the state of being neither a European in Europe nor a Turk in Turkey.[3]

Müftüoğlu renders such consequences concrete in his short story "My Nephew." Following the nephew's university studies in Paris—during which he flits from one field of study to another—he returns to Istanbul as the caricature of the *züppe*, or Westernized Ottoman dandy. Rather than gaining any lasting knowledge during his studies abroad, he has undergone a superficial process of Westernization. His new fixation on French cultural habits leads him to extravagance, pretentiousness, and superficiality: obsessed with external appearances, the nephew maintains carefully manicured nails, applies cold cream to his face at night, and engages in absurd measures in the name of French fashion, such as elevating his feet in order to drain them of blood and more easily squeeze them into a pair of stylish shoes. Yet even more appalling to his uncle is the manner in which the nephew seeks to regulate the appearances of other household members: he makes the maids unbutton the tops of their blouses to expose their *décolleté* and encourages the servants to shave their mustaches and don white gloves.

Müftüoğlu's short story is clearly a light-hearted work of satire; yet the implications of this nephew character, who seems doomed to mindlessly imitate Western culture, run deep. By 1899, when "My Nephew" first appeared, the dandy was already an iconic figure in late Ottoman

Turkish novels. Based on real-life Turkish Francophiles educated in Western languages and practices, the Ottoman dandy was most often the subject of satire. This move to poke fun at the Ottoman dandy expressed both criticism of the figure's over-Westernization but also a more deep-seated anxiety regarding larger processes of Westernization underway in the empire.

The Ottoman government began to undertake certain aspects of modernization in the second half of the eighteenth century, following significant military losses to Europe. During the early phases of this process, Ottomans sought to achieve superiority over Western Europe by learning from and adopting its technological advancements but without affecting change in the Ottoman cultural realm. In an effort to acquire scientific and technological knowledge, for example, the Ottoman government sent students to study in Paris. Fearful of the undue influences of French culture, the government housed students in mansions outside of the city and instructed them to speak only Turkish and Arabic among themselves. But such attempts to circumscribe students' encounters with Western European culture proved impossible, and the generation of students educated in Paris soon affected significant transformations in late Ottoman intellectual spheres.[4]

At the same time, secular reforms such as the 1839 Edict of Gülhane—which ushered in the Tanzimat era (1839–76) by granting certain civil liberties to all citizens of the empire regardless of religion or ethnicity—also brought about new modes of epistemological reorientation. During the late nineteenth century, the Ottoman Empire was still based on the traditional *millet* system, which divided communities along clearly demarcated religious lines. The secularizing reforms of the Tanzimat era nevertheless began to challenge the finality of such epistemological certainties. In the words of Korhan Mühürcüoğlu, Tanzimat reforms "made it possible to survey the changes in political and social matters through the perspective of progress; a perspective that necessitates a certain relation to the present perceived of as a boundary between the past and the future."[5]

At this juncture of cultural-political reorientation, Ottoman intellectuals began to conceive of their present as deficient, which drove them toward a simultaneous "will to change" and "terror of disorientation."[6] How could the Ottoman Empire Westernize without simply imitating the West? And how could Ottoman society modernize and transform without losing its religious and cultural particularities? At the forefront of Tanzimat and post-Tanzimat era novels, such questions crystallized around the figure of the dandy as a deep-seated expression of anxiety over processes of Westernization already taking place.

While the dandy represented a fundamental "fear of the cultural unknown," Şerif Mardin also examines the move to ridicule the dandy as a "subtle form of social control."[7] Early novelists such as Ahmet Mithat, for example, built on the *meddah* tradition of oral storytelling by inserting their own voices into the narrative.[8] Openly lauding certain characters while denouncing others, they confirmed correct and incorrect ways to modernize. Yet such techniques were most prominent in the earliest representations of the Ottoman dandy, suggesting that, in its full evolution, not all aspects of this archetype are so easily explained as a simple measure of social correction. In her analysis of *The Carriage Affair* by Recaizade Mahmut Ekrem, for example, Nurdan Gürbilek argues that its dandy figure, Bihruz Bey, addresses the problem of originality itself:

> The mainstream critical opinion is that Tanzimat novelists filled their novels with clichés stolen from Western writers, with puppets complete strangers to us since they lacked introspection. . . . [But w]hat if that *is* what they saw there? When they were looking inside themselves, what if someone else—a deformed and a distorted figure but someone else indeed—looked back at them? What if the place called inside consists of an outside? What if the inner world is made up of accidents and traumas rather than being a "natural treasure" that is always already there? What if it is "the ideas spreading like malaria" or the "unwanted guests" themselves that make up the place we call the interior?[9]

To rephrase Gürbilek's argument here in the terms of translation: The Ottoman dandy is often considered as nothing more than a bad translation. Doomed to imitate a Western "original," the dandy can never be original in and of himself but will always remain secondary to a primary model for emulation. Caught in this double bind, the snobbishness and performative excessiveness of the dandy serve as a screen to hide his fears of inadequacy, peripherality, and belatedness—in short, his unoriginal qualities.

As a genre born out of translations from Western European source texts, the Ottoman Turkish novel was plagued by these same fears. Yet as Gürbilek so cogently argues, the novel genre itself upends the very premise of originality. By taking its subject matter from the realm of interiority and individual experience—rather than previous literary models or the realms of mythology, legend, or history—the novel makes a claim of locality, individuality, and originality. And yet, born in the "epoch of contagious ideas and contaminative desires," the very idea of a strictly "local" or "individual" experience is afflicted by the problem of belatedness from its outset. Rather than provide direct access to some inner world free of cliché or affectation, "the history of the novel involves the claim to originality as much as the experience of losing that originality."[10]

While the brevity of a story like "My Nephew" does not provide space for interiority of character, it hits precisely on this problem of an impossible originality. Exasperated with his nephew's behavior, the uncle seeks to reimmerse his nephew in Turkish culture by sending him to the Black Sea city of Zonguldak, where, lo and behold, he undergoes a form of local rehabilitation: "Exactly five years later, my nephew, who was like champagne that could not be contained to its cup, returned from Zonguldak. Dazed, he was as quiet and calm as ayran."[11] While underscoring the uncle's success, the ambivalence of this ending is also quietly unsettling. Champagne is pretentious but active and alive, and if the salted yogurt drink of ayran represents here a rejection of Western culture, it is also lifeless and dull in Müftüoğlu's estimation, mirroring the nephew's dazed state of mind. Thus, while "My Nephew" criticizes the superficial adoption of European cultural norms in the late Ottoman context via the figure of the dandy, it does not express straightforward anti-Europeanism or endorse the return to some imagined form of pure Turkishness.[12] Rather, its ending begs the question as to whether an originary Turkishness exists, one to which one might "return" without sustaining a loss of vitality.

In order to highlight the stakes of this premise, the following section examines the significance of philologically structured Orientalist scholarship to the assertion of an originary form of Turkishness in the first place. From the realms of historiography to literary translation, Orientalist scholarship engaged in a positivist grand narrative, which attempted to describe Turkish literature and culture by means of an evolutionary arc from its pre-Ottoman origins to the present.[13] With British and French sources at the forefront, Orientalist scholarship from numerous European countries affected the investment in a shared cultural heritage and a nascent form of nationalism among Ottoman Turks.

ORIENTALISM AND THE RISE OF TURKOLOGY

By calling attention to the historic ancestors of the Turks, European historians and Orientalists provided impetus for the establishment of Turkology, or the study of specifically Turkic—in contradistinction to other ethnicities of the Ottoman Empire—history, language, ethnography, and anthropology. Linguistic and historiographical research focusing on the Mongols and the Huns in particular provided evidence for ancient Turkic civilizations in Asia that predated the Ottoman Empire (1299) and Islam (610–32 CE), respectively.[14]

Such European scholarship deeply informed the "discovery" of a specific linguistic and cultural Turkish heritage on the part of Ottoman Turkish intellectuals. Political activist Ali Suavi (1839–78), for example, published numerous articles in 1869 highlighting the cultural achievements of the Turks throughout history; one of his primary sources was the historical introduction to Arthur Lumley Davids's *A Grammar of the Turkish Language* (1832). Ottoman military commander Süleyman Hüsnü Paşa (1838–92) utilized Joseph de Guignes's *General History of the Huns, Turks, Mongols and Other Western Tatars* (*Histoire generale des Huns, des Turcs, des Mongols et des autres Tartares occidentaux*, 1756–58) as a main source for the universal history textbook he prepared for military secondary schools in 1876. In it, he expounded on the political and military history of the pre-Islamic Turks. Historian and Turkologist Necib Asım Yazıksız (1861–1935) also undertook an adaptation of Léon Cahun's *Introduction to the History of Asia: Turks and Mongols, from the Origins to 1405* (*Introduction à l'Histoire de l'Asie: Turcs et Mongols, des Origines à 1405*, 1896) into Turkish in 1897–98.[15] Cahun's work, which describes ancient Turks as nomadic conquerors who degenerated once they accepted Islam as their official religion in the seventh century, was regarded by Ziya Gökalp (1876–1924) as a treatise to "incite the ideal of Panturkism"[16] in the early twentieth century and served as one catalyst for the developing nationalist sentiment among Turkish intellectuals.[17]

This time period also saw the emergence of important linguistic studies and dictionaries of the Turkish language. Calling for a simpler and more accessible prose style free of Persian and Arabic vocabulary, such studies emphasized that spoken Turkish was fundamentally separate from the high or courtly language of Ottoman Turkish. Scholarship by Şemseddin Sami (1850–1904) and Veled Çelebi İzbudak (1868–1950) in particular placed newfound emphasis on a shared language and common history, thus contributing to a burgeoning sense of literary and cultural nationalism within the political framework of the empire.[18]

This devaluation of Persian and Arabic was again learned from Orientalist philology. It encapsulated a widespread assertion that Persian and

Arabic influence on Ottoman Turkish and its literary genres led to a degeneration of the language and its expressive capacity over the centuries. Ironically, this idea was perhaps most forcefully expressed by the British Orientalist E. J. W. Gibb, who produced the six-volume *A History of Ottoman Poetry* (1905). While Gibb dedicated the better portion of his life to studying and translating Ottoman poetry, his scholarship details the history of its "decadence and its decay."[19] The final volume of *History*—which was pieced together from notes by Gibb's student Edward G. Browne—then points to the "dawn of a new era" and the "recreation" of the Turkish language and its literary ideals via a turn away from Persian and a critical reorientation toward French models in the mid-nineteenth century.[20]

As Walter Andrews notes, Gibb did undertake important work in his readings, interpretations, and translations of Ottoman poetry. Yet the narrative he constructs of the Ottoman literary past ultimately fixes it in an unnatural manner, rendering the complex and multifaceted tradition of Ottoman divan poetry one-dimensional and static.[21] His translations—which ironically seek to make Ottoman poetry accessible to a new European readership—corroborate this narrative. Annotated with excessive biographical, historical, and philological details, the translations uphold excessive prior knowledge as a prerequisite for reading Ottoman poetry. Central to a European coding of Ottoman Turkish and its literary genres as difficult, this style of translation signaled the failure of an elite, high-culture Ottoman literature and the success of a more streamlined and nationally oriented "Turkish" literature.[22]

While Friedrich Schrader does not utilize "difficulty" as a specific term, his early-career articles certainly uphold this evaluation. To this end, they reflect his various connections to German scholarly Orientalism: Schrader completed his doctoral studies in philology, Indology, and art history at the University of Halle, which was an important nineteenth-century epicenter for the study of Orientalism.[23] It was furthermore through the connections of his advisor Richard Pischel, who served as director and librarian of the German Oriental Society, that Schrader first received a position teaching German at Robert College in Constantinople in 1891.[24] While Schrader slowly gravitated toward the profession of journalism in Constantinople, his philological training is starkly apparent in his early articles.

In 1900, for example, in one of his first articles as a foreign correspondent in Constantinople, Schrader assesses the language of Ottoman divan poetry as "fossilized" (*versteinert*). Accordingly, he describes Ottoman literature as "lacking in original creative energy."[25] Suffocating under the bombastic influence of Persian models, he writes, divan poets had made little progress over the past four hundred years. Only with the recent interventions of innovative, reform-minded authors like İbrahim Şinasi and Namık Kemal had a modern Turkish voice finally come into its own. This voice was marked by both the creation of a sleeker and clearer prose style "free" of cumbersome Persian elements and the agitation for democratic reform under an absolutist regime.

In his assessment of both of these characteristics of modern Turkish prose, Schrader is quite clear: to modernize is to simultaneously nationalize and Europeanize. Despite his dismal depiction of the Ottoman literary past, Schrader expresses hope for this Europeanizing impulse. Under the right circumstances, he argues, Turkey could become a "viable member of the European family of nations."[26] And yet the emphasis here lies in Schrader's use of the subjunctive. Under the brutal censorship of Sultan Abdülhamid II's regime, he writes, Turkish authors striving to become full-fledged members of the European cultural realm were left "glowing under the ashes"[27] of their own intellectual spark.

In this article, Schrader clearly identifies Europe as a site of progress. By drawing on a discourse of freedom, he links the perceived need to "free" the Turkish language of foreign elements to the introduction of democratic principles such as freedom of speech. Alternately, he describes Turkish authors as in need of "the freedom to move" (*Bewegungsfreiheit*) within intellectual, political, and material spheres, with the nation as the cultural-ideological ground upon which such mobility is both founded and brought to fruition. Schrader takes recourse here to the legacy of the French Revolution and to a civic understanding of the nation as granting its citizens rights and freedoms.

Yet this "freedom" of expression that Schrader articulates is also reminiscent of ethnic nationalism, which links a specific people to the delineated geography of a given nation and seeks to demarcate the "origins" of that people via a historical trajectory leading to the present. Such investment in origin stories is also clearly upheld by the work of Orientalist philology. With regard to the study of Turkish, European philologists sought to understand modern Turkish literature via recourse to an "origins" story that predated the legacy of the multiethnic and multilingual Ottoman Empire (1299–1923). In the realm of language, this meant looking backward to a time before the development of a hybrid Ottoman Turkish language—which incorporated elements of Turkish, Persian, and Arabic—in the attempt to identify a "purer" form of Turkish.

Although Schrader notes a lack of original creative energy in Ottoman divan poetry, he identifies a paradoxical freedom to express an authentic—or *original*—Turkish voice as the key to Europeanization. Unsurprisingly, he then identifies language as the core realm of possibility for such an achievement. Recognizing İbrahim Şinasi as a pioneer in the movement to Europeanize the Turkish literary realm, Schrader views Namık Kemal as bringing the work that Şinasi had begun to fruition: "Şinasi . . . wed old Asian wisdom with the virgin thought of Europe. Namık Kemal was the first who was able to bestow a brilliant new style and shine to this combination. . . . The tools had been created: out of an unstructured paper jargon, which a native Turk would require a dictionary to read, Turkish had transformed into a modern language capable of expression. . . . Scientific works could now be translated into Turkish from European languages; the vehicle to introduce [European] culture to Turkey was now available."[28]

This brief citation is steeped in the assumptions of German scholarly Orientalism. By describing Ottoman Turkish as an "unstructured paper jargon," Schrader points to a perceived rift between a courtly language (and its classic literary genre of divan poetry) and the spoken language of the people. He furthermore depicts Ottoman Turkish as existing only on paper and as being inaccessible to the people due to its "unstructured" qualities. Schrader echoes here a common assumption on the part of Orientalists that the hybridities of Ottoman Turkish posed a fundamental hindrance to its comprehension. Similar to the translations of Gibb, Schrader's depiction of Ottoman Turkish as a language in need of deciphering—for example, with the aid of a dictionary—stands in clear contradistinction to the category of "nativeness" that he introduces. The bottom line of these remarks is clear: in its previously hybrid form(s), Ottoman Turkish could never stand the test as a "native" language or an authentic expression of Turkishness.

And yet equally clear in Schrader's remarks is that the process of forging a "native" Turkish language is paradoxically tied to the translation of European scholarship into modern Turkish. More specifically, it is tied to the *ability* of a modern Turkish, understood as "native," to express European ideas and values. Complicating this argument is Schrader's role as a European writing about Turkish literature. If, in Schrader's estimation, Namık Kemal's language constituted the vehicle to introduce European thought to Turkey, Schrader's language then also constituted the vehicle to represent this very process *to* Europe. While journalism was one prominent realm in which Schrader sought to do so, literary translation also played a central role in this process, both for Schrader and for other German Orientalists of the time. Before returning to Schrader's translation of "My Nephew" in the conclusion, the following section thus examines his earliest translations from Ottoman Turkish for the publication series the Turkish Library: three short stories from Müftüoğlu's collection *Thorns and Roses* (*Haristan ve Gülistan*, 1901). Schrader's translations, which appeared as volume seven of this series, both corroborated other Orientalist scholarship of the time and complicated the role of Orientalist translators who sought to represent a clear-cut vision of "Turkish" literature to Europe.

THE TURKISH LIBRARY

Writing in 1902, Orientalist Paul Horn asserted in no uncertain terms that "modern Turkish literature is no longer aligned with Asia but rather only with Europe."[29] And yet his monograph *A History of Turkish Literary Modernity* (*Geschichte der türkischen Moderne*, 1902)[30] appeared in the publication series *Monographs on Literatures of the East* (*Die Litteraturen des Ostens in Einzeldarstellungen*, 1901–22),[31] and Horn identified the inaccessibility of modern Turkish literature *in* Europe as the main obstacle to his scholarship: whether in original or translated form, European libraries offered at best haphazard collections, and scholarly journals published only the occasional article in this burgeoning field.[32] Only the German Oriental Society, he argues, had undertaken a systematic method of acquisition.[33] Horn's comments point here to two important issues I highlight in this section: first, the manner in which Orientalists like Horn, who expressed the *Europeanness* of modern Turkish literature, continued to relegate it to a non-European "East," and, second, the power of libraries, in both physical and other forms, to contribute to these kinds of systematic categorizations.

As B. Venkat Mani shows in *Recoding World Literature*, libraries are far from neutral spaces. Whereas individual books preserve and proliferate cultural memory, libraries serve as social and political agents through the acts of collection and dissemination.[34] Such processes are not limited to the physical space of a library that houses books but pertain equally to publication series and catalogues of titles. Libraries, in all of these forms, hold the power to render books in/accessible and un/interpretable, by either providing or withholding access to the public. Systems of classification furthermore play an important role in the wider reception of individual books and the cultures they are often deemed to represent. To this end, libraries not only contribute to the "worlding" of texts but "also play a very important role in nationalizing and even racializing literatures."[35]

If physical libraries codify texts through processes of ordering and organization, publication series do so through means of selection, advertising, and distribution. Individual titles further frame, and thereby codify, texts through prefaces and introductions. Questions of framing prove especially pertinent to the Turkish Library, a twenty-six-volume translation series from Ottoman Turkish into German that ran from 1904 to 1929. Published with the Mayer and Müller Verlag in Berlin and Leipzig, the Turkish Library was overseen by Georg Jacob—who is widely recognized as the founder of modern Turkology in Germany—together with Orientalists Theodor Menzel and Rudolf Tschudi. In terms of selection, this series boasted a rather diverse set of translations. Source texts included late nineteenth-century authors Ahmet Mithat, Mehmet Tevfik, and Ahmet Hikmet Müftüoğlu; folk literature and the oral stories of Turkish *meddahs*; scholarly texts on Ottoman history and Islamic mysticism; and the official report of Ottoman ambassador Azmi Efendi's diplomatic journey (*sefâretnâme*) to Berlin in 1790.[36] Yet in contrast to this diversity of texts—which traversed multiple registers and genres—the prefaces to the literary works in particular express a repeated desire to render some form of unspoiled Turkishness, as yet untouched by the effects of Europeanization, into German in translation.

Perhaps unsurprisingly—as a publication series overseen by a group of academic Orientalists—the Turkish Library adopted an approach to translation very much in line with that of Gibb. Riddled with footnotes and parenthetical explanations, the Turkish Library more closely resembles a set of academic treatises than literary translations. If this style of translation had previously been central to the *de*valuation of Ottoman divan poetry as a genre deemed difficult and thus illegible, to what end was it applied and what effects did it have on both the modern and folk literature represented in the Turkish Library?

The Turkish Library does not so much uphold the linguistic difficulty of the modern literary texts it rendered into German as gesture toward a pervasive sense of cultural otherness that requires extensive explanation. Thus, even as the translators and editors repeatedly express the Europeanizing tendencies of modern Turkish literature in their prefaces, the translation series as a whole clearly differentiates Turkish literature from European literature. This process of differentiation is perpetuated by the series' self-professed goals of accuracy and philological fidelity,[37] which lead the literary volumes of the Turkish Library to take what Lawrence Venuti has termed an instrumentalist approach toward translation. By treating source texts as contained, unmediated entities, instrumentalism suggests they can be successfully transferred intact and wholesale into a new target language. Fostering the illusion that immediate access to a given source text is possible, instrumentalist translation thus denies its own status as *one* possible interpretation among many and treats translation rather as a simplistic form of reproduction.[38]

To this end, the Turkish Library's investment in accuracy and fidelity boasts an ability to provide an unmediated window into Turkish culture for the receiving audience. In the introduction to volume seven, for example, editor Georg Jacob explicitly states the goal of "objectively allow[ing] Turkish texts to speak for themselves."[39] Translators and editors alike corroborated the series' ability to do so, by upholding a romanticized image of a static traditional Turkish culture in their introductions, prefaces, and reviews. Yet this investment in fidelity paradoxically upholds the need to explain—or in other words, interpret—Turkish literary texts through recourse to excessive footnotes, parenthetical information, and diverse prefatory materials. These various forms of explanation ultimately belie the fact that, regardless of genre, no text can be transferred unchanged into a new language, as translation always involves a hermeneutically inflected process of interpretation.

Consider, for example, Theodor Menzel's framing of *A Year in Istanbul* (*Istanbul'da Bir Sene*) by Mehmet Tevfik. First published in 1883, this book depicts everyday life in the city, together with its diverse traditions and customs.[40] In his translator's preface, Menzel attributes sociological significance to *A Year in Istanbul*, as a work that preserves the idiosyncrasies of a bygone era for a new generation: "The old traditions and entertainments [described therein] have vanished, together with any distinct memory of them."[41] In declaring Tevfik's work unintelligible to a younger generation of Ottoman Turks, Menzel implicitly lauds his own translation practice as the preservation of a dying art. In short, he invests himself, as a German Orientalist scholar, with the power to render essentially "Turkish" customs legible to a German audience.

Menzel's assumption of power is in line with an instrumentalist approach toward translation, in that it entails the fixation of Turkish culture in the past as a contained and unchanging entity. And yet—within the space of his own preface—Menzel clearly contradicts his own superior position as a Western Orientalist and the essentialized image of Turkish culture he otherwise seeks to uphold through the act of translation. Noting the complexities of Mehmet Tevfik's writing—which incorporates informal speech, as well as the poetic and courtly registers of Ottoman Turkish— Theodor Menzel admits to receiving advice from a range of contemporary authors, including Ahmet Mithat Efendi, Rıza Tevfik Bölükbaşı, Recaizade Mahmut Ekrem, R. M. Fuad Bey, and Mehmed Ibrahim.[42] In doing so, Menzel highlights the dynamic qualities of Mehmet Tevfik's writing and the stratified layers of cultural influence it is embedded within. More pointedly, however, Menzel's admission to working with numerous Turkish authors points to translation as a complex process of meaning-making that requires reading and interpretation. His implicit admission that he *required* advice from Turkish contemporaries in order to first understand and then translate the work of Mehmet Tevfik stands in contrast to the basic premise of Orientalism as a textual representation of the Orient, which fixates it in both space and time.

Within the discursive contours of Orientalism, to fixate the Orient through one's scholarship is, of course, also to show that one knows it better than Orientals themselves. In Saidian terms, Orientalism thus depends on and perpetuates the imagined "positional superiority" of the Westerner vis-à-vis the Orient.[43] While translations *have* historically served the purpose of fixating the relative positionality of the Occidentalist scholar vis-à-vis his Oriental materials, in Menzel's preface, he admits that this is fundamentally not the case. Menzel gestures here toward a paradoxical acknowledgment that the Turkish Orient is on some level difficult to read and thus also to describe and fully understand. He furthermore admits the need to engage in a more collaborative process of interpretation, which ultimately undermines his singular power as expert.

Complicating the Turkish Library's instrumentalist-Orientalist approach toward translation is the manner in which editors, translators, and reviewers addressed Europeanization as a fundamental problem. In 1909, for example, Schrader wrote the following review of the Turkish Library's first eight volumes, in which he addressed the German translations of traditional folk stories by Nasreddin Hoca from the thirteenth century: "In these tales, the innate character of a Turk from the *Volk* that has not yet been corrupted by European *Bildung* is most beautifully revealed. In these tales his dry humor and dramatic and lively art of storytelling appear most clearly. Evidently the editor's primary aim was to portray the Turk from the *Volk*—who is influenced by the traditional customs and opinions of his forefathers and is as distanced as possible from European

CHAPTER 4

Political Orientations

On (Re)translating Halide Edip Adıvar's The New Turan

Despite lifelong support for Ottoman Turkish literature's simultaneous Europeanization and nationalization, Friedrich Schrader expressed an astonishing turn of thought in the wake of Germany and the Ottoman Empire's defeat in World War I: just months before the 1920 Treaty of Sèvres—which initiated the dismemberment of the Ottoman Empire at the hands of the triumphant Allied powers—Schrader called for the Ottoman Empire to (re)orient itself toward the Perso-Arab world after decades of Westernization. Central to this vision was a reinvestment in the Persian-inflected genre of Ottoman divan poetry, which he characterized as fundamentally Hellenistic in nature.

With the potential establishment of a Turkish nation-state based on the Western European model already on the horizon, Schrader's move to situate the Ottoman Empire within a Middle Eastern cultural realm appears out of sync with the times, and at a moment when the novel had gained increasing importance as the primary genre of Turkish literary expression, his turn to the outdated genre of divan poetry appears oddly nostalgic. In this chapter, I argue, nevertheless, that Schrader does not simply endorse the empire's "return" to a previous state of being or cultural affiliation. Rather, he looks forward to new cultural alliances for the Ottoman Empire that do not endorse the rhetoric of authenticity and originality so central to the forces of ethnic nationalism that led to World War I.

In order to draw out the complexities of Schrader's vision, I situate this late-career turn of thought against his 1916 translation of Halide Edip Adıvar's (hereafter referred to as Halide Edip) *The New Turan* (*Yeni Turan*, 1912). Schrader enthusiastically endorsed Turanism (Pan-Turkism)—and its valuation of a specifically Turkish race—in his translator's preface to *Das neue Turan*. Published at the height of the German-Ottoman military alliance, Schrader's 1916 translation thus reflects a clear investment in the rhetoric of ethnic nationalism. Yet his journal articles from the 1920s are more closely aligned with Halide Edip's very specific vision of a politically liberal and democratic form of Turanism. "The Young Turk Lausanne Program" ("Das Jungtürkische Lausanner Programm," 1920) and "The Turkish Culture" ("Die türkische Kultur," 1920) in particular endorse the complex synthesis of cultural nationalism and Western-inspired humanism that *The New Turan* articulates. Schrader's demand for a *Rechtsstaat*, for example, echoes an important political speech in the novel, which delineates a future Turanist state based on the premise of justice and equality for all constituents of the empire. His call for the Ottoman Empire to rekindle its previous cultural ideals is furthermore in line with the lifelong project of Halide Edip, who strove to create a synthesis between Western and Eastern influences in her writing. More specifically, I argue that Schrader's vision for the *future* of an empire that was clearly on the brink of demise picks up on the futuristic aspects of Halide Edip's novel, which he had failed to capture in his German translation four years prior. In her novel, which is set twenty years in the future, Halide Edip envisions a forthcoming utopia in which women have gained the right to vote and work in public and in which all minorities of the empire enjoy equal protection under the law.

Writing in 1920, Schrader's vision for the future is informed by his own disillusionment with the Armenian Genocide of 1915–17 and the failure of the Young Turks to establish a full-fledged constitutional democracy in the wake of World War I. Forced to escape Turkey after the occupation of Constantinople by British forces in 1918, Schrader furthermore writes from a war-ravaged Germany, where he struggled to find a place for himself after nearly three decades in Constantinople. It is at this impasse that Schrader turns to divan poetry, a genre he had starkly criticized as "unoriginal" in his earliest articles from 1900.

In contradistinction to the rhetoric of ethnic nationalism—with its emphasis on origins and authenticity—I read Schrader's late-career turn to divan poetry as a reinvestment in the forces of hybridity and multilinguality that define it. Moreover, I argue that by describing divan poetry as

of the empire with equal importance to the Turks.[11] Yahya Kemal Beyatlı—
who otherwise praised both Halide Edip and her novel—similarly asked
to what extent the future society Halide Edip imagined was actually Turanist in nature: "From top to bottom," he writes, "*The New Turan* represents
nothing more than a restoration of the outcome of the Tanzimat."[12]

Such insightful criticisms were nevertheless in the minority. *The New
Turan* was first published by *Tanin* in serialized format (1912) and then in
book format by Türk Yurdu Press (1913), the publication outlet of the Turkish Homeland (Türk Yurdu) organization.[13] Halide Edip was herself later
deemed "Mother of the Turks" by members of this nationalist organization,
an appellation that she accepted with humble pride.[14] In her memoirs, she
nevertheless recalls that *The New Turan* in particular was grossly misunder-
stood to represent a formulated doctrine of nationalism.[15] On the contrary,
Halide Edip describes the novel as looking forward to a future utopia in
which women have gained the right to vote and work in public, in which the
ideals of austerity and simplicity have overtaken the opulence of a degen-
erate Ottoman civilization, and in which a democratic and liberal form of
nationalism has developed in the absence of a chauvinistic administrative
system.[16]

While Schrader does stress the idealist and progressive quality of Halide
Edip's Turanism, his introduction to her work also places heavy emphasis
on the Turanist investment in a specifically Turkish race. In his own brief
historical justification for the movement, Schrader cites the independence
of Muslim-majority Albania (1912) as salt in the wounds of an Ottoman
Empire still reeling from a series of Christian revolts. Together, he argues,
these diverse nationalist movements led Turks to become more aware of
their own common heritage. As a means for Turks to develop their innate
(*ureigen*) national character, Schrader views Turanism, in turn, as a panacea
for the failing empire. While emphatically refuting the reactionary quality
of the movement, Schrader's defense of Turanism is couched in extremely
conservative terms. Weakened and deformed by centuries of foreign influence, he asserts, Turkish culture must strengthen itself by returning to its
original purity;[17] he then alternately describes this process as an "awakening
of [Turkish] racial consciousness."[18] Schrader partakes here in widespread
debates regarding the need to "free" the Ottoman Turkish language from
elements of Arabic and Persian. He furthermore takes a clear stance against
Pan-Islamist movements—which sought to salvage the Ottoman Empire
by uniting its diverse Muslim constituents—in favor of the shared Tura-
nist-nationalist investment in the cultural heritage of all Turkic peoples,

regardless of religion. Throughout this introduction, Schrader thus asserts, in no uncertain terms, that the Turanist movement is central to the realization of a Turkish national consciousness based on the concept of a specific Turkish race. This, he argues further, is an ideology learned from Europe: "[Turanism] seeks to enable the Turks, in the manner of European peoples, to execute progress on the basis of their own essence."[19]

As in his early career, Schrader still identifies nationalization with both Europeanization and progress in 1916, although his specific understanding of nationalism becomes both more complex and contested with the onset of World War I. In the early 1900s, Schrader supported the investment in a national-cultural Turkish identity within the framework of Ottomanism. He thus did not place emphasis on the concept of a Turkish race or advocate for the establishment of a Turkish nation-state. Schrader's 1916 endorsement of Turanism indicates a more specific but also paradoxical understanding of nationalism. His identification of Turanism as the bearer of social progress is closely tied to the figure of Halide Edip and her support for women's emancipation. In subtitling *Das neue Turan* as *Ein türkisches Frauenschicksal* (*A Turkish Woman's Fate*), he draws specific attention to this aspect of the novel. Indicative of the leading role women play in Halide Edip's utopian vision, Kaya represents an educated, well-spoken, politically active, and yet humble working woman. While Kaya ultimately sacrifices her public presence for Oğuz, she embodies an almost mythical representation of Turanism and its ideals. Described as a natural teacher, her name is omnipresent among her supporters and the opposition alike. Indeed, the figure of Kaya serves not only to uphold a vision for women's emancipation but also to showcase societal resistance to the empowerment of women in the public sphere: the active presence of women in the Turanist party is what most horrifies members of the Ottomanist opposition, including the main characters of the novel, Hamdi and his nephew Asım.

Schrader's support for women's rights is closely aligned with the concept of civic nationalism, which would guarantee the basic civic and political rights of all citizens and uphold values such as freedom, tolerance, equality, and respect for the individual. In principle, civic nationalism is thus inclusive of all constituents who choose to participate in a common political structure.[20] This aspect of Schrader's introduction echoes his own calls to reinstate the 1876 Ottoman Constitution and his later insistence on the establishment of a Turkish constitutional democracy in 1920. Throughout his career, Schrader associates civic rights and democratic forms of government with Europe, and his introduction to *Das neue Turan* is no exception.

Here, he clearly attributes Halide Edip's own endorsement of women's rights to her education at the American Girls College rather than to Turanism as a movement. Via a negative turn of phrase, he then blames the conservatism of other Turkish women on their relative lack of a similar education. In short, he identifies a program of social progress that clearly originates in, and must be learned from, Europe. His depiction of Halide Edip's own drive for social reform as the fruit of a "civilizing instinct"[21] underscores this idea through its striking resemblance to the rhetoric of the civilizing mission.

While Schrader's investment in women's rights points to a civic understanding of nationalism, his enthusiasm for the Turanist movement as a specific form of racial awakening takes clear recourse to the elements of ethnic nationalism, all of which Turanism indeed provided. These include the valuation of the word Turk, which had previously been associated with uneducated Anatolian commoners, a common myth of descent and a shared history that stretched back to the Hun Dynasty and the Seljuk Turks, a distinct shared culture based on these origins, and an association with the specific territory identified as Turan.[22]

Admittedly, Halide Edip does employ the rhetoric of a specific Turkish race in *The New Turan*. Early in the novel, the young and charismatic leader Oğuz delivers a political speech in which he lays out the tenets of the New Turanist program. In this speech, Oğuz describes several stages of "Turkish" history, which he dates back to the existence of an original and homogenous (*yekpare*) Seljuk Turkish race. The racial purity of the Seljuks was so strong, he argues, that it served as the civilizational cornerstone for the Ottoman Empire. Via the incorporation of Serbians, Macedonians, and Albanians, the borders of the Ottoman Empire later began to stretch toward Europe, during which time period the Turks slowly mixed with neighboring races. Oğuz then describes the rise and fall of the Ottoman Empire over subsequent periods of invasion and expansion, with the bold military campaigns of Fatih Sultan Mehmed II and Sultan Süleyman the Magnificent at the apex of its success. In the periods following, he argues, Ottoman expansion was ultimately undertaken to the detriment of the Turkish race. In short, the Turks fought to build an empire that served multiple minority constituencies and were then unable to attend to the betterment of their own race because of their constant engagement in bloody conquest. Oğuz then likens the current political condition to an unwieldy Tower of Babel, which a centralized Ottoman government struggles to control. Asserting that the Turkish race will cease to exist if the current political course is allowed to continue, Oğuz calls for a decentralized system in which the diverse peoples of the empire would be gathered into a federation built around a strong, central Turkish government. Within this system, minority constituents would enjoy freedom of religion and relative political autonomy, both of which would be constitutionally guaranteed.

In short, *The New Turan* does uphold the ideal of an original, unadulterated Turkish race that predates the foundation of the Ottoman Empire; yet the novel does not suggest that a return to this original state would be desirable or even possible. On the contrary, Halide Edip looks forward to a utopian future, stressing the need to find common ground with the empire's Arab and Persian neighbors. Only in this manner, the novel concludes, can the Ottoman Empire protect itself "from the greedy eyes of Europe."[23] One irony of this vision is the fact that Halide Edip composed *The New Turan* in England. Halide Edip's vision of Turanism was furthermore influenced in numerous ways by European political, religious, and social movements. Oğuz's call for the constitutional protection of minorities, in particular, harkens back to the *Declaration of the Rights of Man and of the Citizen*, set forth by France's National Constituent Assembly in 1789.

In her memoirs, Halide Edip further recalls her first trip to England, in the immediate aftermath of the Counter-Revolution of 1909, during which her British friend Isabel Frye introduced her to important political and literary circles. Several events during this trip influenced *The New Turan*, which Halide Edip penned during a second trip to England in June of 1911.[24] In particular, a speech by John Dillon (1851–1927)—who was a strong supporter of home rule in Ireland—moved Halide Edip to tears. Recalling his sincerity and poise, Halide Edip openly admits that this speech was an important emotional catalyst for the development of her own national sentiment.[25] At the same time, Halide Edip identifies the British Parliament as both an inspiration for and a symbol of "Turkey's bloody struggle toward a representative government."[26] Finally, the simple, unadorned, and practical clothing worn by women in the Bristol Quaker community finds an echo in the white robes and sandals worn by New Turanist women. The relative independence of women in the Quaker movement also served as an important model for the character of Kaya.[27] As these diverse influences indicate, while Halide Edip was keenly aware of European economic and colonial interests in the Ottoman Empire, Europe writ large also served as an inspiration and a model of democracy for her writing.

TRANSLATING *THE NEW TURAN*

Schrader's translation of *The New Turan* appeared in the German Oriental Library (Deutsche Orientbücherei) publication series, which produced a record number of twenty volumes in just a two-year time span (1915–16). Edited by Ernst Jäckh, this series exhibited a strong inclination toward the political, with ten volumes dedicated explicitly to the Ottoman Empire.[28] Indicative of Jäckh's heavy investment in the German-Ottoman military alliance, the series covered the history of Prussian-Ottoman military relations under Frederick the Great[29] and significant material dealing with World War I, including: the fight for control over the Dardanelles Strait, the role played by the Caucasus, and the memoirs of Hilde Mordtmann, who served as a nurse for wounded soldiers in Constantinople.[30] It furthermore published three volumes related to Turanism, including Schrader's translation.[31] Volume 2 in particular advocated for Turanism as an important counterpart to Pan-Germanism; together, author Munis Tekinalp argued, these movements could form a significant bulwark against the common enemy of Russia.[32] Yet Tekinalp's understanding of Turanism was not explicitly irredentist in nature. For Tekinalp, the survival of the Turks as a race was predicated on the simultaneous processes of Turkification and nationalization. In short, Tekinalp declared that "[Turks] must become themselves again."[33] In his version of Turanism, Turan represented the originary and almost mythic homeland of the Turkish race rather than a site to be reintegrated into a Pan-Turkic territory.

Where exactly did Schrader's translation stand within the German Oriental Library? As the only work of fiction among twenty volumes, *Das neue Turan* provided a certain literary-cultural counterpart to the largely sociopolitical content of this series. Schrader's introduction in particular draws attention to Halide Edip's unique narrative style. He deems Halide Edip's fast-paced and witty dialogues, marked by a form of "pure movement" and "pure enthusiasm," to have achieved the status of "perfect music."[34] Yet his German rendition is anything but musical. Scarcely attentive to the aesthetic quality of Halide Edip's Turkish, it reads rather like an extended summary. Where characters speak with conviction in Halide Edip's Ottoman Turkish, Schrader's translation remains on the surface. Significantly shorter than the original, it paraphrases dialogues and glosses over lengthy inner monologues. The result is a text that appears more straightforward and factual but that robs characters of their individuality.

To this end, Schrader takes a clearly instrumentalist approach toward translation by treating his source text as an inherently contained, unmediated entity, the message of which can be successfully transferred into a new language at face value.[35] In short, translation is understood as a simplistic mode of reproduction rather than a hermeneutically inflected mode of interpretation. Within this instrumentalist approach, Schrader appears to deem form inessential to a reading of the novel's political message. And yet his translation style clearly serves as one potential interpretation of *The New Turan*. Together with the publication outlet of the German Oriental Library, Schrader's translation functions as a mode of political orientation, which is invested in the origins and expression of a specific Turkish race and is thus fundamentally backward-looking in nature.

That Schrader employs translation as a mode of political orientation is no surprise given the historical context. He translated *The New Turan* at the height of the German-Ottoman political relationship, which culminated in a military alliance during World War I and coincided with the rise of a general German enthusiasm for Turanism. Such enthusiasm is clearly evidenced in Otto Hachtmann's *Turkish Literature of the 20th Century* (*Die türkische Literatur des 20. Jahrhunderts*, 1916), which focuses exclusively on the Turanist movement and highlights Halide Edip as one of its leading authors. Whereas Orientalist Paul Horn had dismissed the German-Ottoman Turkish relationship as insignificant in 1902, Otto Hachtmann declares the very word "Turk" to be near and dear to Germans, for whom everything regarding "Turkey" awakened a deep and genuine interest.[36] Like Horn, Hachtmann identifies something fundamentally modern in contemporary Ottoman Turkish literature. Yet where Horn clearly understood modern to also mean European in a vague sense, Hachtmann draws sustained attention to the realm of the national:

> The immense political and emotional shock of the Balkan War and the World War have . . . led to a rejuvenation in the field of literature. It is a true joy to witness this spiritual rebirth! Turkish literature has shrugged off its anemia through its daily dose of iron in the war. Bright-eyed and conscious of its strength like a young, slim boy scout, it peers into the dawn of a glorious future. An entirely new and enthusiastic creative urge is swelling in both men and women: self-discipline, purity, and power have become the general ideals. . . . It is the expectant atmosphere before the sunrise: a bright dawn is on Turkey's horizon, which has contented

itself for so long with a dismal dusk. Soon the new sun of Turkishness will rise. Let us hope that its warm rays will promote new
life to blossom and maturity![37]

Without naming the Persian-influenced genre of divan poetry—
which dominated Ottoman Turkish literature from the fifteenth through
the mid-nineteenth centuries—Hachtmann portrays the Turkish literary
past as anemic, dismal, and dark. The "spiritual rebirth" he lauds is spurred
on by the shock of war and driven by a new nationalist sentiment that led
to significant territorial losses in the Ottoman Empire but also to a new,
self-determined expression of Turkishness. In contrast to "half-Turks,"
or authors who wrote "Turkish" content in "French" form,[38] Hachtmann
particularly directs his praise at a new type of Turk: the "New Turanist," an
appellation he derives from the title of Halide Edip's novel. Marveling at
their self-determined, pure, and genuine assertions of Turkishness, Hachtmann contends that for the New Turanists, "the alternatives are not: French
or German? But rather: European or Turkish?"[39]

Halide Edip's novel both performs and undermines the exaggerated
either/or of Hachtmann's statement: Cut off from her political activism and
her ties to the New Turanist party, the main character Kaya's mental health
wanes throughout her marriage to Hamdi. In an effort to revive his wife's
well-being, Hamdi brings Kaya on vacation to Europe. While he succeeds
for a time in distracting her from political events at home, Kaya remains
indignant to her husband's attempts to Europeanize her. Refusing to buy
and wear European-style clothing, she instead expresses her desire to travel
to Anatolia and support Anatolian artisans. And yet during the course of
their trip, Kaya reveals that she speaks both impeccable French and rudimentary German. Desperate for news, she requests newspapers in French
to keep abreast of political developments at home.

On the most basic level, this act of mediated reading points to the
fact that Turkish nationalism did not develop in a vacuum but was largely
learned from Europe. In fact, turning away from Europe via Turanism
thus entailed the process of becoming more European via the investment
in a national cultural identity. Hachtmann's dismissal of the ideological
underpinnings of Turanism as historically inaccurate fails to reflect on this
reality. Schrader, on the other hand, clearly traces the underpinnings of
Turanism back to Europe in his introduction to *Das neue Turan*. According to Schrader, the movement shows an energetic and ambitious form of
self-awareness on par with the nations of Europe.[40]

As a novel, *The New Turan*'s very form also points to the impossibility of forging a "pure" literary expression of Turkishness. Speaking in 1943 at Istanbul University, Halide Edip addressed this very idea through a focus on translation. Starting with authors of the Tanzimat and subsequent New Literature movements, Halide Edip shows how translation served to forge new local forms with innovative force. Halit Ziya Uşaklıgil (1866–1945) and Hüseyin Rahmi Gürpınar (1864–1944), she argues, were two vanguards of the New Literature movement heavily influenced by French realism who nevertheless utilized the European form of the novel to bring local characters to life.[41] More interestingly, Halide Edip argues that even the "national school" (*millî mektep*) of Turkish literature, which emerged around the turn of the century and reached its height during World War I, was spurred on by translations from French, German, Russian, and English. The result, again, was varying degrees of hybridity in content and form. As one example, she cites the work of Refik Halit Karay (1888–1965), who composed local stories (*memleket hikâyeleri*) in the style of French and Russian realism.[42]

In the early republican era and well into the late twentieth century, such hybridity was seen as a sign of inferiority, attributed to the writing of a novice.[43] And yet already in 1943, Halide Edip viewed this hybridity as a productive negotiation of self and other that allowed for a rediscovery of the self. If Hachtmann rejects Germany as a model for modern Turkish literature on the grounds that it would lead Turkey into a third "literary imprisonment," following its slavish imitation of first Persian and then French models,[44] Halide Edip proves this to be a moot point. Nationalist or not, all modern Turkish literature proves to be a negotiation of European forms and local content and thus cannot express something "essentially" Turkish. *The New Turan* is no exception. Rather than uphold the investment in a specifically Turkish race or an original Turkish identity, *The New Turan* displays a synthesis of diverse influences, from Western European forms of democracy and the Christian Quaker movement to Tatar cultural models and the system of decentralization supported by Ottoman sociologist Prince Sabahaddin. While Halide Edip's novel was upheld as a banner for Turkish nationalism both within Turkey and among German Orientalist scholars, the novel was clearly much more complex than this. It exhibits hybridity not only in the tension between "European" form and "local" content but also at the level of content itself, as well as in terms of character development.

Schrader's inattention to form thus not only streamlines its narrative but also strips the novel of its formal hybridities. By downplaying the aesthetic qualities of the novel through the techniques of summary and paraphrase, he transforms it from a work of literature to a political manifesto.[45] In doing so, he does not misrepresent Halide Edip's vision for a decentralized United Ottoman States on the level of information; his summary of Oğuz's speech accurately conveys the Turanist platform as a system of governance that makes space for the minorities of the empire. Nevertheless, his translation significantly alters the *form* in which this information is conveyed. In particular, by paraphrasing dialogues through the use of reported speech, Schrader detracts from the immediacy of the novel's language. Through the use of paraphrase, Schrader also alters the dialogic character of *The New Turan*, which represents the differences between the New Ottomanists and the New Turanists largely via the speeches delivered by and interactions between characters belonging to these opposing parties. That these alternating viewpoints are central to the novel's composition is made eminently clear by Halide Edip's decision to narrate *The New Turan* from the perspective of Asım, a dedicated member of the New Ottomanist party.

More importantly, as a general translation strategy, Schrader's inattention to form bypasses the fact that *The New Turan* is indeed a novel concerned with issues of form on more than one level: The decentralized system of governance Oğuz delineates is an imagined political form of the future, which stands in clear opposition to the backward-looking stance of a Turanist movement in search of a mythic homeland or origin story. This system of governance, which would guarantee relative autonomy to diverse minorities of the empire, is central to the democratic form of nationalism Halide Edip envisions. Thus, even as Schrader accurately conveys the content of Halide Edip's novel, his inattention to form detracts from the complexity of her utopian vision.

A CHANGE OF OPINION

Whereas Schrader had praised Halide Edip's Turanist aspirations in his 1916 translation, in 1920 he described Turanist poetry as gruff splutter that harbored unfounded hostility toward other national cultures.[46] What exactly led to this profound sea change in Schrader's approach to the movement? In order to answer this question, a brief timeline of the political situation is necessary: Halide Edip composed *The New Turan* in 1911, right before the Balkan Wars of 1912 and 1913, during which the Ottoman Empire lost nearly all of its European territories. It was published first in serial format in the newspaper *Tanin* in 1912 and then in book format in 1913. Thus, even in the two to three years before *The New Turan* appeared in publication, the expressions of ethnic nationalism sweeping through the European territories of the Ottoman Empire had rendered Halide Edip's utopian vision of Turanism at best a form of wishful thinking. In his introduction to the translation, Schrader nevertheless describes the novel in explicitly positive and realizable terms. He depicts Halide Edip's vision of a new Turan as a dream or vision (*Traumbild*) that has not yet come to full fruition but that serves as a guiding star (*Leitstern*) for Turkey's future development. Yet even as Schrader utilizes the language of futurity in these statements, he fails to realize that the novel is itself oriented toward the future. *The New Turan* is not invested in a clear-cut, retrospective confirmation of mythic origin stories but is more concerned with forging a viable future for Turkic peoples in peaceful coexistence with other ethnicities of the empire. On the contrary, Schrader identifies, in his introduction, the investment in a specifically Turkish racial *past* as the foremost "realizable" aspect of Turanism.

Schrader's 1916 translation of *The New Turan* appeared at the height of World War I and the German-Ottoman military alliance. His heavy emphasis on race in the introduction suggests his own complicity in the diverse expressions of ethnic nationalism that led in part to the outbreak of war. This idea is compounded by the fact that Schrader makes no reference in his introduction to the novel's focus on ensuring the rights of minorities in the empire. The ironies of Schrader's shortsightedness run deep: his translation appeared shortly after the mass extermination of Armenians in the Ottoman Empire in 1915. The extent to which Schrader was aware of the Armenian Genocide as it was unfolding is unclear. Schrader's close friend and colleague Paul Weitz, who served as Constantinople correspondent for the *Frankfurter Zeitung*, traveled to eastern Turkey in 1918, where he produced detailed internal reports on the extent of violence committed against Armenians; yet these reports were never published due to military censorship.[47] Whether he learned of the genocide from Weitz or other sources, Schrader's reflections in the diary he kept while escaping Constantinople via Ukraine at the close of World War I are clearly critical: "And we must not—as we have done abroad before—continue to support the party that undertook the rape of important minority constituents in favor of their own national hegemony. Such actions will avenge themselves, as they have avenged themselves in Turkey. We should not have been more Turkish than the Turks."[48] As this passage makes eminently clear, by 1918

Schrader was not only aware of—and horrified by—violence committed against the minorities of the Ottoman Empire, he also understood Germany to be complicit in this violence by way of its support for the Party of Union and Progress. His decision to publish these comments in 1919 suggests a significant change of thought with regard to his understanding of nationalism in the wake of World War I.

Schrader's recognition of the dangers of ethnic nationalism, I argue, manifests in his own statement of an alternative vision for the empire's future in 1920. Against the backward-looking rhetoric of ethnic nationalism—which was inextricably linked to processes of Europeanization underway in the Ottoman Empire from the mid-nineteenth century onward—Schrader articulates in 1920 a different mode of cultural orientation for the Ottoman Empire toward the Middle East. Rather than a return to previous cultural ideals, I argue that Schrader picks up on the future-oriented aspects of *The New Turan* that he had failed to capture in his own framing and translation of the novel in 1916. This entails highlighting the humanistic underpinnings of Ottoman divan poetry and thereby dislodging humanism from Europe as its supposed birthplace.

TOWARD A SHARED MEDITERRANEAN HUMANIST HERITAGE

In late November of 1917, Dr. Werner Richter, guest professor of German language and literature at Istanbul University, published a small article in the feuilleton section of the *Ottoman Lloyd* entitled "German Literature in the Turkish Language" ("Deutsche Dichtungen in türkischer Sprache"). Addressing the desire to forge new intellectual connections between Germany and Turkey by way of literature, Richter turns to the subject of translation. Yet in delineating a series of guidelines, Richter articulates not what to translate and how but rather the impossibility of rendering the great works of German literature into Ottoman Turkish. In closing, he emphasizes the incompatibility of Renaissance and humanist values with Ottoman Turkish language and culture and advises against the translation of any literary work that demands the aesthetic taste of a connoisseur, including but not limited to those by Lessing, Goethe, and Schiller.[49] Richter's emphatic suggestions elicited so many reader responses that the newspaper felt an obligation to report on them. One reader in particular questioned the deep divide between the "Turkish Oriental culture" and the spirit of humanism that Richter's article underscored: "Is not French literature, which has had such a deep influence on the Turkish intellectual classes, also a product of the Renaissance?"[50]

While Richter and his respondent put forth diametrically opposed arguments, each takes Europe as the basis of comparison and the yardstick of possibility. In Richter's estimation, Ottoman Turkish literature is deemed non-European and thus incapable of expressing the values of humanism. While the anonymous respondent stresses the humanist nature of contemporary Ottoman Turkish literature, he ultimately attributes this quality to the influence of French models. Each author thus upholds a tacit understanding of humanism as a fundamentally European practice.

The origins of humanism as a practice are generally traced to the rediscovery, interpretation, and assimilation of ideas represented in ancient Greek and Roman texts by European scholars from at least the ninth century onward.[51] Nevertheless, a scholarly term for humanism did not emerge in Germany until as late as 1809, and it indicated "a devotion to the literature of ancient Greece and Rome, and the humane values that may be derived from them."[52] This substantive refers to the *studia humanitatis*—centered on the subjects of grammar, rhetoric, history, poetry, and moral philosophy—through which Italian Renaissance humanists of the fourteenth and fifteenth centuries in particular sought to create an educated citizenry capable of fully participating in civic life.[53]

Schrader's 1920 article "Turkish Culture" is significant, in that it offers an alternative perspective to this accepted history and to the debate on humanism in the *Ottoman Lloyd*. Well before the first translations from French into Ottoman Turkish, Schrader suggests, the Persian-inflected genre of Ottoman divan poetry was already on par with the works of ancient Greek authors. Schrader sets up his discussion of Ottoman divan poetry via reference to Goethe's own fascination with the Persian poet Ḥāfeẓ (1315–90). Ḥāfeẓ strongly influenced Goethe's monumental *West-East Divan* (*West-östlicher Divan*), from which Schrader cites the following lines: "Herrlich ist der Orient / Übers Mittelmeer gedrungen / Nur wer Hafis liebt und kennt, / Weiß, was Calderon gesungen,"[54] ("Splendidly the Orient / Spread beyond the Middle Sea: / One who Háfiz love had lent / Calderón hears perfectly.")[55] This quatrain not only suggests that we must first read Ḥāfeẓ in order to comprehend the work of Pedro Calderón de la Barca (1600–1681), it also upholds the movement of ideas from the Orient to Europe rather than vice versa.

To put this argument differently: Dr. Werner Richter had argued for the impossibility of translating authors such as Goethe and Schiller into the Turkish language of 1917 precisely because their work was so influenced by what he calls "ancient forms and norms."[56] Richter points here to the important role both Goethe and Schiller played within Weimar Classicism, which viewed itself as the successor to Greek antiquity. In doing so, Richter emphasizes a fundamentally European-centered understanding of humanism, in which he argues that "Turkey" cannot partake, due to its "Oriental nature." In contrast, Schrader writes against the doctrine that in order to express humanist values, Ottoman Turkish literature must first become European. He suggests rather that humanism has a shared Mediterranean heritage stretching from ancient Greece to Persia, which Ottoman divan poetry not only participated in but also helped to shape.

Schrader's turn to Persian literature at this late stage in his career is particularly significant because of the historical antagonism between Greece and Persia, which was solidified in ancient Greek texts that later provided a foundation for Renaissance humanism. The word "barbarian," which was first utilized by Homer to denote speakers of a language other than Greek, later came to signify the entire non-Greek world.[57] While "barbarian" was first used in a descriptive manner, it took on new, derogatory meanings during the Persian Wars of the fifth century. Aeschylus was one of the first authors to use the term in a clearly pejorative manner in his play *The Persians* (472 BCE). According to Nancy Bisaha, referencing barbarian customs in order to demonstrate the superiority of the Greeks was a common trope in Athenian tragedies of the fifth century. References to Persians, or more generally Asians, as barbarians can also be found throughout the foundational works of Greek antiquity, including those of Aristotle and Hippocrates. And while the historian Herodotus displayed a certain receptivity and openness to other cultures, he maintained a depiction of the Persian Wars as a conflict between Greece and Asia, with Asia relegated to the East.[58]

The trope of the barbarian/foreigner, mapped onto the constructed dichotomy of Greece versus Asia, both resurfaced and gained new connotations during the Renaissance via the study of ancient texts. While ancient Greek authors had referred to a barbaric East, they did not provide a clear definition of the West. Rather, the concept of an implicitly Western Europe—understood in opposition to Asia—emerged in the fifteenth century, with Ottoman military advances on the Byzantine Empire. Greek humanist George of Trebizond (1395–1486) first invoked a clear dichotomy between Europe and Asia in order to summon Latin military support for Constantinople, which was under threat of occupation by the Ottoman

Turks. In his exhortation to Pope Nicholas V in 1452, he represents Greece as the "bulwark of Europe against the barbarians of Asia."[59] Pope Pius II (1405–64) gave further definition to the emergent concepts of West and East by coining the adjective "European," which he aligned with Christianity.[60] Through his writings, Pius II nevertheless gestured more toward seeing a common enemy in the "barbaric Turks" of Asia than any kind of clear cultural unity among "Europeans" in the West.[61]

With the fall of Constantinople to the Ottomans and the subsequent collapse of the Byzantine Empire in 1453, another significant transformation began to take place. Whereas Greeks had technically belonged to the Eastern Roman Empire (330–1453), they were often seen as both foreign and heretical by Western Europeans because of the schism between the Latin and Orthodox churches.[62] Yet the fall of Constantinople—which had been an important buffer between the Ottomans and Western Europe— was understood as a major loss to both Christendom and Europe at large. After the mass exodus of Greeks to Italy following the siege of their capital city, they eventually became an integral part of Italian society. As previous antagonisms began to fade in the wake of 1453, the perception of Greeks also shifted from "Byzantines" to "Hellenes."[63] In other words, contemporary Greeks of the Byzantine Empire were linked to the culture and texts of Greek antiquity, at the very moment in which a definition of Europe was beginning to take shape against an image of the "barbarian Turk."

Notably, Schrader's numerous reflective essays on Constantinople do not partake in the rhetoric of barbarism that figured the Ottoman Empire as a fundamental threat to Christian Europe. In his single essay that addresses the fall of Constantinople, Schrader narrates the event from the Ottoman Turkish perspective, which lends his depiction a celebratory rather than horrific tone: "The large outdoor camp in front of the city walls was swimming in well-warranted exhilaration and joy. The booty of gold and silver vessels, jewelry, and other valuables, was tremendous."[64] Written between 1911 and 1916, his Constantinople essays detail rather a selective yet multifaceted history of the city from Byzantine times to the contemporary moment. Published in book format in 1917 as *Constantinople: Past and Present* (*Konstantinopel: Vergangenheit und Gegenwart*), they address subject matter as diverse as Byzantine architecture, Venetian Carnival celebrations, the Genovese quarters, Armenian tradesmanship, a Koran school for girls, a dervish lodge, and much more. The specific reference to Ottomans as plunderers is softened by Schrader's further acknowledgment that Christians also pillaged one another in the siege. Both here and throughout his essay collection, Schrader clearly challenges historical portrayals of Ottoman Turks as barbarians and of 1453 as a fundamental civilizational break.

On the contrary, Schrader's essays as a whole write a palimpsestic history of the city by uncovering traces of the past in the present. An essay on the sea walls of the Golden Horn, for example, asserts that the markets of Bahçe Kapısı sell, by and large, the same goods as in Byzantine times. Citing a poem by the Byzantine author Ptochoprodromus (1115–66), Schrader lists the local delicacies detailed in Greek, only to conclude that little has changed in the eight hundred years since: "While the political relationships have shifted, on the level of trade Byzantium-Stambul is still connected to the lands that once saw it as their capital city with proud admiration."[65]

Even sections of *Constantinople* that detail shifts in demographics of specific neighborhoods do not vilify one group over another or attribute these shifts to Ottoman conquest. The section entitled "Perschembe Basar," for example, describes the neighborhood of Galata. Once a predominantly Christian neighborhood inhabited by Dominicans, Galata was settled by Moriscos after their expulsion from Spain in 1609. Descendants of Spain's Muslim population, most Moriscos were forced to convert to Christianity by royal decree in the sixteenth century. Following a 1566 edict, which forbade the Moriscos of Granada to speak their language and follow their own cultural customs, a general revolt ensued. Due to their supposedly "unassimilable" nature, Moriscos were then deported en masse by royal decree between 1609 and 1614.[66]

Schrader describes Moriscos as renewing the memory of Maslama by bringing the call to prayer back to the Galata neighborhood. This reference to Maslama ibn Abd al-Malik is significant; a prominent Arab general of the eighth century, he led several campaigns against the Byzantine Empire.[67] But it is not this history that Schrader evokes. Rather, he points to the history of the Inquisition and the foremost role that Dominicans played within it. As an ecclesiastical tribunal established by Pope Gregory IX, the Inquisition sought to suppress heresy, at times by drastic measures such as torture. Starting in 1231, the Dominican Order received papal commissions to carry out inquisitions across Western Europe. While many other actors were involved, including bishops and members of other Christian orders, the Dominicans were both the "primary authors and circulators of anti-heretical and inquisitorial literature" and those who most actively enforced inquisitions on the ground.[68] Schrader's example of the demographic shifts in a specific Constantinople neighborhood thus does not point to barbaric

Muslim traditions but, on the contrary, to a history of persecution under-taken in the name of Christianity.

As even these select examples demonstrate, Schrader's essays on Constantinople challenge the historic portrayal of the Ottoman Empire as a fundamental threat to Christian Europe. As such, his writing also works against the depiction of Ottomans as a barbarian "other," upon which this narrative was predicated. But how does this largely historic focus of Schrad-er's Constantinople essays tie back into his translation of Halide Edip's *The New Turan* and his late-career engagement with the discourse of humanism? I return here to Schrader's essay "Turkish Culture" in which he describes Ottoman divan poets Fuzûlî (1494–1556) and Bâkî (1526–1600) as funda-mentally Hellenistic in nature: "An age-old artistic culture emanates from such works, the immorality of which represents the height of aesthetic inspi-ration. Everywhere in them, one finds sensualism reminiscent of antiquity and the Renaissance, a ripe fruit of the southern sun and the luminosity of the Mediterranean shore."[69] Schrader's move to revalue Ottoman divan poetry—a genre he had disparaged twenty years prior as fossilized and unoriginal—is part and parcel of his call for the Ottoman Empire to rekin-dle its relationship to the Mediterranean realm, and in particular to its Arab and Persian neighbors, in the wake of World War I. His further articula-tions of a Mediterranean civilization and cultural heritage[70] recall Halide Edip's vision of a decentralized Ottoman state that would also appeal to Arabs and Persians.

Whereas Schrader had deemphasized this aspect of *The New Turan* in his 1916 framing of the novel, "Turkish Culture" arguably rearticulates Halide Edip's utopian vision for the future on different terms. Notably, Schrader's move to revalue Ottoman divan poetry in 1920 also entails a rethinking of his approaches to both language reform and translation. In his earliest articles, Schrader expressed the need to "free" Ottoman Turk-ish from Persian and Arabic vocabulary in order to forge an authentic form of a purer modern Turkish. In doing so, he reiterated a philologist-Orien-talist critique, which not only viewed Ottoman Turkish as unnecessarily difficult but also treated the hybridities of Ottoman Turkish as an imped-iment to the creation of a national and thus also a "native" language for the Turks. On the contrary, Schrader asserts in 1920 that the question of language purity is not a reflection of quality. He points rather to the spirit (*Geist*) and composition of a work, arguing in turn that "we Germans" must take the *aesthetic* quality of Oriental texts into consideration.[71] On the most basic level, Schrader's emphatic use of "we" suggests an implicit criticism of his own disregard for questions of language and form when translating a text like *The New Turan*. But what are the deeper implications of this late-career valuation of the aesthetic? If, in regard to divan poetry, attention to aesthetic quality inevitably involves attention to the intricacies and hybridities of Ottoman Turkish itself, then to what extent does an article like "Turkish Culture" also call for a reinvestment in the very terms of hybridity? Such an investment would not only run counter to the logic of ethnic nationalism but also to Schrader's philological training in German scholarly Orientalism, which sought to draw clearly demarcated lines between a *Volk*, an ethnicity, and a given geographic area.

In conclusion, I argue that Schrader's inward-facing criticism in a text like "Turkish Culture" is not merely an anomaly of his late career. Schrader's literary essays on Constantinople—which were published as a collection in 1917—also evidence his investment in the multiethnic and multilingual makeup of the Ottoman Empire, as opposed to the racial underpinnings of ethnic nationalism. Written between 1911 and 1916—which also spans the time between Halide Edip's composition of *The New Turan* and Schrader's German translation of it—Schrader's Constantinople essays hint at the violent and destructive qualities of ethnic nationalism precisely via his criticism of the Europeanization process. Whereas Schrader identifies racial consciousness as a positive form of self-determination learned from Europe in his introduction to *Das neue Turan*, his Constantinople essays suggest otherwise. Without offering an explicit critique of ethnic nationalism, they do provide the basis from which such a critique could ultimately take shape.

Notably, Schrader's Constantinople essays are not free of Orientalist tropes. For example, while he composed these essays largely during World War I, Schrader tends to shy away from the violence of the contemporary moment through an attempt to relegate the Ottoman Empire to the past. This is doubly significant, as many essays first appeared in the feuilleton section of the *Ottoman Lloyd*, which otherwise reported heavily on the political situation. At times, Schrader even expresses an explicit desire for Constantinople to exist outside of time. The opening essay, "A Winter Morning in the Neighborhood" ("Ein Wintermorgen in der Mahalle"), describes the district of Çukurbostan as if covered in a mantel of silence, separate from and indifferent to the political events unfolding around it. And yet even as the text makes this claim, it contradicts itself via the delivery of newspapers to the local coffeehouse. The essay then imagines local men gripping these papers, reading about the destruction of Serbia in the war.[72]

Schrader's depiction of the Egyptian Spice Market employs a similar structure, in that it first sets an idyllic scene, only to then bring this scene into the present. He describes the market as a secretive and half-dark place from which the scents of Arabia come forth like poetry.[73] Detailing the different spices that are sold here, Schrader then notes how knowledge of and belief in the efficacy of herbal remedies is slowly abating because of the influence of European culture and Western medicine. While accurate in its conclusions, this passage borders on the nostalgic, mourning the loss of a traditional world in the face of modernization.

Yet Schrader's depiction of the threat of Europeanization goes beyond the form of imperialist nostalgia described by Renato Rosaldo, in which colonialists long for the traditional form of a now-colonized culture, without acknowledging their own role in altering precisely that which they seek to preserve.[74] While Schrader laments a loss of cultural specificity caused by the Ottoman Empire's increased interactions with Europe, his writing also challenges an essentialist portrayal of "Turkish" tradition. This tension is particularly palpable in Schrader's essays on the *meddah*, an oral storyteller who often performed in coffeehouses or at Ramadan festivities. In emphasizing the *meddah*'s typically virtuosic use of his voice, Schrader points specifically to the polyphonic quality of the empire that was performed on the stage. Often knowledgeable of several languages, *meddahs* would generally imitate diverse accents within their performances. Citing the performances of Aşkı Efendi, Schrader recalls one instance in which he first impersonated an Anatolian man, then a Ladino-speaking Jew, followed by an older Turkish woman, and finally a Greek mariner.[75] Schrader's depiction of the *meddah* thus highlights a traditional Turkish art form that testifies to the multiethnic character of the empire rather than some quality understood to be fundamentally Turkish. In his praise of the *meddah* as an artist with an unusual discernment toward human life, Schrader notes that these performances are no longer valued by an Ottoman Turkish literary elite that has embraced European literary forms such as the short story and the novel. If Schrader laments the negative impact of Europeanization on the art of oral storytelling, he also laments the specific threat that Europeanization poses to the *diversity* of its subject matter.

Notably, Schrader's depiction of Europeanization at the turn of the century—which is part and parcel of a sociocultural modernization process he otherwise lauds—stands in contrast to other essays that demonstrate the numerous ways in which Constantinople was historically already European. In an essay entitled "Baroque and Rococo" ("Barok und Rokoko"), for example, Schrader walks his readers along the Byzantine city walls toward the district of Fener and calls attention to building facades from yet another time period. Schrader describes the baroque windows and doors bearing the spirit of the Italian architect Bernini as "witnesses of another world."[76] While these houses are products of the eighteenth-century Levant, Schrader likens both their style and their location on the shores of the Golden Horn to the canals of Venice.[77] For him, this is but one sign of the longstanding history of exchange between the Ottomans and the Venetians, which in turn affected both the Ottoman Turkish language and its forms of artistic expression. In particular, he points to two stock figures of the *commedia dell'arte*,[78] Arlecchino (Harlequin) and his mistress Colombina, who made their way into traditional Turkish folk theater (*orta oyunu*). A second essay on carnival celebrations in Constantinople similarly attests to the effects of Italian culture in the city, at the same time that Schrader notes the subtle ways in which Muslim tradition has also affected this Christian celebration.[79]

These essays and others dealing with the time period *prior* to the nineteenth century portray Ottoman interactions with Europe as testament to the *diversity* of histories and traditions that find home in the city of Constantinople. On the contrary, essays focusing more closely on the turn of the century detail a different, destructive quality of the contemporary Europeanization process. Europeanization emerges here as a threat to a form of Ottoman—as opposed to more strictly Turkish—cultural specificity, which is itself grounded in the multiethnic, polyphonic quality of the empire. This threat is strikingly similar to that of ethnic nationalism, which proved deadly for minorities of the empire during World War I. As such, Schrader's Constantinople essays prefigure his postwar criticism of Turanism's investment in a specifically Turkish race in important ways.

On the surface, Schrader's 1920 suggestion in "Turkish Culture" for the Ottoman Empire to rekindle relationships to its Arab and Persian neighbors appears to advocate for the return to an era prior to the onset of Europeanization. And yet, similar to the manner in which his essay "A Winter Morning" contradicts its initial relegation of the empire's constituents to the past by bringing the narrative into the immediate present, "Turkish Culture" also looks toward the future. It does so by articulating the futility of searching for clear-cut origin stories—such as the myth of Turan or the pre-Ottoman origins of the Turkish race—in the past. By focusing rather on the aesthetic value of a genre like divan poetry, it provides an incipient basis for a critique of European Orientalist philology and Turkish nationalism alike. Moreover, Schrader's move to resituate Ottoman Turkish culture in the Mediterranean does not simply entail a turning away from Europe. Rather, by articulating the Hellenistic nature of Persian and Ottoman divan poetry, Schrader articulates a form of humanism that is indebted to ancient Persia as much as to ancient Greece. In doing so, he also decenters Europe as the so-called origin of humanism. Against diverse assertions of origins and authenticity so central to philology, ethnic nationalism, and humanism alike, the kind of Mediterranean alliances Schrader mentions in "Turkish Culture" hold the potential to articulate a more complex form of Turkishness, one that is closely in line with the politically liberal and democratic vision of Turanism that Halide Edip had already imagined for the future in 1911.

PART 3

Sabahattin Ali

Theorizing World Literature from
Early Republican Turkey

CHAPTER 5

A Prelude in Potsdam
World Literature as Translational Multiplicity

"Following boundless gratitude to Allah the everlasting, the worship of whom is a necessity, the reason for the composition of this lengthy travelogue is to be proclaimed."[1] So unfolds the story of a young man who has accrued such high levels of debt that he is forced to escape his hometown of Yozgat and the tyranny of his creditors. As luck would have it, he encounters an official from the Ministry of Education, who urges him to sit for a government exam. Upon successful completion, he qualifies to study abroad in *Frengistan*, or "the land of decadent infidels."

This unlikely beginning of the modernist Turkish author Sabahattin Ali's "The Comprehensive Germanistan Travelogue" ("Mufassal Cermenistân Seyâhatnâmesi," 1929) already points to the humorous mixture of biographic, fictitious, contemporary, and historical references with which he deftly crafts his narrative. Ali received a prestigious four-year governmental grant to study literature, philosophy, and the German language in Berlin and Potsdam at the age of twenty-one. One of several modernizing and secularizing initiatives undertaken by the fledgling Republic of Turkey, this grant program aimed to foster the reorientation of Turkish culture toward Western Europe, by educating a new intellectual youth in its languages and cultures. Ali was one of fifteen select individuals sent abroad for this purpose.[2] Originally composed as a letter to friends back home, Ali's travelogue goes on to detail his departure from the historic Sirkeci train station in Istanbul; his journey through Bulgaria, Serbia, Hungary, and Czechoslovakia; and his arrival in, and first impressions of, Germany.

Alongside biographical references are numerous jarring historical markers. The opening praise to God is but one example of how Ali stylized his letter through generic conventions of the *seyahatname*, a form of travelogue penned throughout the Islamic world since the Middle Ages. Ali's use of exaggeration and fabrication—for example in reference to his debts—recall more specifically the seventeenth-century *seyahatname* of Evliya Çelebi (d. 1682), through which the genre received canonical status.[3] The term *Frengistan*—meaning "the land of the Franks"—dates to a similar time frame. Used in the Ottoman Empire through the seventeenth century, it refers to any land perceived as Christian in Western or Latin Europe.[4] Ali's decision to refer to present-day Germany through the outdated term *Frengistan* is central to the humor of his pseudohistorical travelogue, which culminates in the description of a "modern" New Year's Eve celebration in Potsdam and Ali's "accidental" kiss with a young libertine woman (*fâcire-i mel'ûne*) on the street.[5]

Compounding the specific historic references in Ali's travelogue— of which there are numerous examples—is his use of the Perso-Arabic script in the prominent Ottoman handwriting style of *riq'a*. Ali composed his travelogue, dated to 1929, just one year after the letter revolution (*harf devrimi*), which replaced the Perso-Arabic script of Ottoman Turkish with a slightly modified Latin alphabet and prohibited any further use of the old script in public documents.[6] Signaling a symbolic break with an Islamic Ottoman past, the letter revolution was central to the ideological reorientation of the new secular republic toward Western Europe. While Ali never intended his letter for publication, his use of the Perso-Arabic script—which would be outlawed even in private correspondence just one year later— serves as a forcefully comical provocation to the very modernizing reforms that enabled his travels to Potsdam. By describing his experiences in the "modern" city of Potsdam via the specific historic genres and mediums of Ottoman Turkish, his letter produces a deliberately estranging mismatch of form and content.[7] Within this context, language in particular emerges as a site of conflict via the triangulation of an outdated form of Ottoman Turkish, the German language, and a notably absent modern Turkish.[8]

Ali does not simply translate his experiences abroad into an outdated form of Ottoman Turkish. It is rather the intricacies of Ali's Ottoman Turkish that expose Potsdam as a site of translation for his modernist imagination. Translation thus emerges as a productively unsettling, omnidirectional movement that underscores the hybridity of Germanness and Turkish-ness alike. Such omnidirectionality gains historical significance amid the diverse modernizing reforms in early republican Turkey—including the letter revolution and the grant program Ali participated in—which fueled a conception of the "West" as a fixed and stable entity toward which Turkey could orient itself. In the space of Ali's travelogue, Potsdam emerges rather as an unstable and thus disorienting force.

As such, Ali's travelogue also provides a prescient alternative to concep-tualizations of world literature that would emerge in Turkey in the following decade. While "world literature" gained visibility as a named entity with the initiation of the state-sponsored Translations from World Literature series (Dünya Edebiyatından Tercümeler) in 1940, the term *cihan edebi-yatı* was already in use during the 1930s. Uniting the different usages of this term is a persistent—if at times implicit—coding of world literature as European, vis-à-vis a nationally imagined Turkish literature. Most often used to describe European classics translated *into* Turkish, world litera-ture thus also served as a key point of reference for other Westernizing cultural reforms that were underway. In contrast to the idea of world liter-ature *in translation*—which emphasizes the act of transferring an intact European literature into the Turkish literary-cultural realm—Ali points to the elements of translation already at work in German culture, as one so-called origin of world literary classics. Ali achieves this through a form of self-translative Turkish, which I contend presents an early theorization of Turkish literature *as* world literature. This understanding of world litera-ture is not premised on the translation of world literary classics into Turkish or on the "arrival" of Ali's travelogue on the international market. Rather, world literature emerges within the translative, transcultural encounters of Ali's letter as a productively disorienting and destabilizing force, which confounds the one-way directionality of terms like Westernization and modernization, as well as of translation itself.

PHONETIC TRANSLATION CONTRA PHONETICISM

Movements to reform the Perso-Arabic script to better suit the sounds of Ottoman Turkish date to the mid-nineteenth century. Questions regard-ing the purpose, form, and implementation of script reform continued to preoccupy statesmen and intellectuals alike through the demise of the Otto-man Empire.[9] Following the foundation of the modern Republic of Turkey, the ruling Kemalist party instituted diverse secularizing and modernizing reforms over and against its Islamic Ottoman predecessor. Aimed at forging a national Turkish character that identified itself as European, significant structural reforms included the abolition of the Caliphate and the Şeriat court system (1924), the centralization of a new secular system of education (1924), the adoption of the European calendar and the twenty-four-hour day (1925), and the introduction of a new civil code modeled on the Swiss system (1926). As both a mode of national expression and the primary medium through which Western concepts could be conveyed to the Turkish populace, language was situated in the cross fires of these historically momentous changes. By the late 1920s, script reform had gained ever-increasing centrality to the state's modernizing mission.

At the forefront of debates on language reform was the perceived inadequacy of the Perso-Arabic alphabet to represent the sounds of Turkish. The Perso-Arabic script contains a number of consonants that are superfluous to Turkish but were necessary to maintain in the language for the purpose of writing Arabic and Persian loanwords. On the flipside, the Perso-Arabic script contains only three vowels, in comparison to Turkish's eight.[10] As a result, single words were often represented through divergent spellings; at times, words with radically different meanings also shared the same spelling. Perhaps the most famous example of the latter appears in the verbs *ölmek* (to die) and *olmak* (to be), which would be rendered the same on the page (اولمق). As a result, contextualized reading was of central importance to the process of interpretation.

On the surface of language reform was thus the desire to adopt a new script free of such ambiguities. In 1926, an official Language Council (Dil Heyeti / Dil Encümeni) was tasked accordingly with studying the applicability of the Latin alphabet to the Turkish language. After nearly two years of deliberation, the council delivered a forty-one-page Alphabet Report (Elifba Raporu) to the republic's founder, Mustafa Kemal. Among the core components of this report was the concern that "the new letters do not generate any ambiguity [*iltibas*] among the sounds they represent." In its outline of a national phonetics (*millî fonetika*), the report thus recommended that each sound have an individualized form of representation. Rather than utilize the digraphs *ch* and *sh*, for example, it called for the adaptation of diacritical markings such as ç and ş to produce one-to-one corresponence between individual letters and sounds.[11]

In order to achieve such a strictly phonetic alphabet, the council recommended adopting diacritics from several European languages, including

French (*â, î, û, j, y*), German and Hungarian (*ö* and *ü*), and Romanian (*ş*). A slightly modified Latin script was then presented as a "native" element of national Turkish culture, despite its clearly mediated origins. This entailed a strategic recoding of the Perso-Arabic script—which served as a symbolic sociohistorical connector to Islam and the Ottoman Empire—as both illegible and alien.[12] On the surface, this depiction of the new script as "native" took recourse to the practicalities of pronunciation; yet in reality, it signaled a paradoxical reorientation of Turkish society toward Western Europe. Closely in line with other reforms that signaled a civilizational shift from East to West—such as the adoption of Western numerals, the Gregorian calendar, the metric system, and the top hat—the romanization of the alphabet provided a central, visible marker of Turkey's Europeanness.[13] And yet, premised on the need for legibility, language reform strategically obscured the "inherent mediacy" of the new Latin script in order to uphold an essentialized, selfsame understanding of Turkishness.[14]

Sabahattin Ali composed his travelogue in 1929, just one year after the Law Concerning the Adoption and the Application of Turkish Letters (Türk Harflerinin Kabul ve Tatbiki Hakkındaki Kanun, November 1, 1928) dictated that all public signs, newspapers, and magazines be printed in the new script starting December 1, 1928. The law further required that *all* correspondence—both public and private—be undertaken in the new script starting June 1, 1930.[15] As I show in the following, Ali's letter flies in the face of this governmental attempt to control its citizens' use of language at the level of the private sphere. Whereas script reform marked an attempt to *control* ambiguity, Ali leverages the script and vocabulary of Ottoman Turkish to *generate* ambiguity on multiple levels. Consider, for example, the following passage: "According to Hayrullah Molla Bey, a contemporary etymologist, the word Potsdam consists of the words *put, sedd*, and *ümm. Put,* as is known, is a shrine found in the churches of the infidels in the form of Christian portraits and statues; *sedd* means to close, cover or conceal; *ümm*, or mother, here means the Mother Mary. Altogether, by means of cubism, it means: 'O Mother Mary, cover the idols!'"[16] While seemingly absurd at its outset, this comic refraction of Potsdam through the vocabulary of Ottoman Turkish also presents a highly sophisticated form of phonetic translation. Simply put, phonetic translation disregards the meanings of words to focus instead on the proximate sounds of languages. It is in this manner that *Potsdam* becomes *Putseddümm.* And yet this phonetic transformation is enacted by a *mullah*, whom Ali otherwise describes as a "contemporary etymologist." The ironies of this small detail run deep: As the study of the history of words, etymology engages in a search for origins. On the most basic level, Ali thus suggests that we search for the "origins" of Potsdam outside of German geography and language, in the realm of Ottoman Turkish. This is of course a counterintuitive suggestion in 1929, amid the promulgation of a Europe-oriented modern Turkish language over and against the image of an outdated Ottoman Turkish.

Ali's very gesture toward the origins of words also presciently prefigures the most radical stage of language reform in the modern Republic of Turkey. Marked by attempts at excising all Persian and Arabic vocabulary from the language, reforms of the 1930s also sought to forge a more essential or "pure" form of modern Turkish (*öz Türkçe*), in part by recovering pre-fourteenth-century words of Turkic origin that had fallen out of usage. Whereas 1930s language reformers sought to "uncover" and uphold an essential form of Turkishness in the modern era, Ali employs a fictional *mullah* to undertake a fundamentally different endeavor. In the transformation of *Potsdam* to *Putseddümm*, Ali mimics the typical Turkish pronunciation of a word with a difficult consonant cluster by breaking up *tsd* with the vowel *e*. In doing so, he also approximates the sound of the German word *Potsdam* in the sounds of Ottoman Turkish. The result is a kind of phonetic or surface translation that is not bound by issues of fidelity. Rather than seek to render the "essential" meaning of a German word in Turkish translation, the sound-play of phonetic translation reveals the arbitrariness of language itself. In short, this process of phonetic translation does not take the "original" meaning of a word into consideration but rather allows new meanings to emerge where the proximate sounds of different languages meet.

In the context of the travelogue, for example, Ali utilizes the sounds of *Put-sedd-ümm* to refer to the thick layer of snow covering the statues in public parks. But *Putseddümm* also points more generally to Ali's agency as cultural interpreter. In his rewriting of the word, Ali not only reveals that the "origins" of Potsdam lie outside of itself, in the Ottoman Turkish language; he further posits that these "origins" are themselves translative. In short, he performs a kind of etymology contra etymology, which reveals the impossibility of any search for "pure" linguistic origins. In doing so, he also embraces a form of phonetic translation contra phoneticism. Whereas the adoption of a purely phonetic Turkish alphabet in 1928 aimed to eradicate ambiguity, Ali's phonetic translation of Potsdam amplifies it.

Phenomenology describes orientation as a question of starting points. Husserl, for example, describes the body as the zero-point of orientation from which the world unfolds.[17] Alfred Schutz and Thomas Luckmann write further, "The place in which I find myself, my actual 'here,' is the starting point for my orientation in space."[18] On the contrary, Ali's phonetic translation of Potsdam questions the very concept of hereness, suggesting that "here" can never exist completely separate from "there." As the history of phoneticism in early republican Turkey attests, the contours of Turkey's "here" were closely tied to the Westward direction it sought to face, thus granting a paradoxical stability to Europe's "there" in the process. Contra this history, the dislocated sounds of *Putseddümm* are generated in and through a process of phonetic translation that does not take recourse to etymological origins but that instead highlights the interdependence, and thus also the instability, of both "here" and "there."

In this manner, the word *Putseddümm* speaks back to the title of Ali's travelogue. Derived from the word *Cermen*, meaning Teutons, the fabricated place name *Cermenistan* recalls the Germanic peoples who inhabited Northern Europe from approximately the third to the ninth century. By refering to present-day Potsdam through this pseudohistorical name, Ali caricatures the essentialization of contemporary cultural identies through recourse to historical predecessors.[19] More pointedly, by joining *Cermen* with the Persian suffix *-stan*, meaning "land," Ali suggests that the contours of German culture may also be shaped by aspects of the Persian language, which have in turn been absorbed into Ottoman Turkish.

The place name *Cermenistan* points further to the intricacies of Ali's language, which consistently generates humor through cultural indicators that rely on linguistic and historical knowledge. In this light, one of the most humorous lines of Ali's letter is the proclamation that he has "made every effort to avail [himself] of simple language,"[20] so as to avoid overtaxing his readers. The ironies of this line cannot be lost on contemporary readers of modern Turkish, who would find it nearly impossible to access Ali's language. Even in transliteration, contemporary readers would need training in the grammar and vocabulary of Ottoman Turkish to make sense of its complexities. Indeed, already in 1929, Ali's use of ironic understatement points to the significant changes Ottoman Turkish had undergone across the nineteenth century. As such, his reference to "simple language" offers a pointed commentary on one of the consistent goals of language reform in the republican era: the desire to forge a modern Turkish language that was simpler, more streamlined, and thus also more "legible" than its Ottoman Turkish predecessor. This accusation of illegibility was tied to an Orientalist perception of the Ottoman Turkish language as difficult and therefore also untranslatable. On the contrary, Ali's travelogue forges a form of self-translative Turkish by playing with the very terms of legibility.

Reflecting on the journey to Germany, for example, Ali writes: "At the border to Hungary, upon fully comprehending that we were in Europe, we began to admire the signs of civilization."[21] Typical of the travelogue's outdated language, he uses the Ottoman Turkish word *umrân* to refer to civilization rather than the more contemporary *medeniyyet*. With the Arabic root '-m-r, *umrân* refers to prosperity or the flourishing of civilization. Related to the word for architect (*mimar*), it also references the creation of buildings or the structures of civilization. Yet in Ali's travelogue, this official entrance into European civilization references the Great Hungarian Plain. Long before the train enters the city of Budapest, Ali expresses astonishment not at the architectural beauty of Europe but at the utter monotony of its landscape: the train passes for hours through wide-open plains, with no sign of human civilization in sight. Here again Ali endorses a kind of etymology contra etymology. While the meanings of *umrân* point to architectural wonders as signs of civilization, architecture as an actual signpost of orientation is absent in the Great Hungarian Plain. In an era of Europeanizing reforms in early republican Turkey, Ali's use of the term *umrân* is thus productively disorienting, in that it points to the paradoxical problem of orienting oneself toward something in its absence.

Once in Germany, Ali raises a similar question through a second instance of phonetic translation. He describes a group of young Germans engaged in a humorous "dance" (*raks*), which he terms *pat bî-nâz*. This word is a phonetic play on *patinaj*, the Ottoman Turkish term for ice-skating, which is itself derived from the French word *patinage*. Whereas the cognate *patinaj* has the same etymological origin as *patinage*, Ali's neologism *pat bî-nâz* allows new meanings to arise through the proximity of the sounds of French and Ottoman Turkish. *Pat* serves as an onomatopoeic sound that expresses a thud or fall to the ground. The Persian preposition *bî*, which is commonly used with a noun to produce a negative prepositional phrase, is then paired with *nâz* to literally mean "without conceit."[22] Together, the phrase *pat bî-nâz* offers a humorous portrayal of inexperienced ice-skaters: "In line with the name of the dance," Ali writes, "they would skid to the ground with a thud, only to reemerge with ease and hasten toward an unknown direction."[23]

This curious reference to an "unknown direction" ties into the very term *pat bî-nâz*. More than an instance of witty word play, Ali's neologism adds to the ironic tone of his letter. As a European form of entertainment, ice-skating had become a sign of modernity and progress in turn-of-the-century

Constantinople, in that it provided a new form of public social interaction between men and women. At the same time, the relative (in)ability to ice-skate served as a metaphor for one's adaptability to the modern era. Quite on the contrary, Ali's depiction of clumsy German skaters in 1929 recalibrates the coordinates of cultural orientation.[24] It suggests that taking Western European standards as a point of reference does not necessarily engender a clear-cut process of self-orientation but may rather lead one in "unknown directions" to deeper, messier processes of cultural disorientation.

As with *umrân*, the phrase *pat bî-nâz* also points to something that it is not: falling rather than skating. Again, the ingenuity of this phrase hinges on the intricacies of Ali's language, which utilizes aspects of the Ottoman Turkish language that would soon be deemed "foreign" to it amid language purification policies in the following decade. These policies, which sought to craft a pure form of modern Turkish (*öz Türkçe*), were informed by the European practice of Turkology. Itself embedded within the philologically minded field of Orientalism, Turkology treated the Ottoman Turkish language as a conglomerate of essentially separate Turkish, Persian, and Arabic elements. It furthermore propagated the idea that Turkish had been progressively altered, and thereby diluted, by Arabic and Persian influence across the centuries. Under this premise, linguistic modernization went hand in hand with a process of nationalization, which required separating out the distinct linguistic parts of Ottoman Turkish in order to identify what was essentially Turkish.[25]

Amid such nationalist language policies, Ali's sophisticated writing points instead to the fundamental hybridity of the Ottoman Turkish language in which these assumedly separate parts cannot be so easily separated from one another. Whether through Arabic-based vocabulary, such as *umrân*, or the Persian suffix *bî*, Ali reveals these elements of his language as integral to the effects of his narration. Far from being unoriginal or derivative to a more streamlined form of modern Turkish, Ali's travelogue is original precisely in its playfulness and creativity. The ingenuity of the narrative hinges on the intricacies of Ali's Ottoman Turkish, which prove that translative ambiguity does not hinder but enhances the very possibilities of expression. In the face of attempts to contain and delimit Ottoman Turkish amid the historic reorientation of Turkish culture toward Europe, Ali thus produces a language that cannot be contained.

This kind of uncontained writing provides the grounds for an alternative vision of world literature than would otherwise emerge in the decades to come. While Turkish scholars utilized terms for world literature in close

relationship to the translation activity of the 1930s and 1940s, world literature designated almost exclusively the translation of Western European
classics into Turkish. Against this understanding of world literature in
translation—which suggests the one-way movement of texts from a fixed
point of (European) origin into the Turkish cultural realm—Ali's travelogue presents an open-ended conception of translation as the power to
traverse time frames and cultural spaces.

CONCEPTUALIZING WORLD LITERATURE IN EARLY REPUBLICAN TURKEY

As early as 1932, Agâh Sırrı Levend employed a specific term for world
literature in his monograph *Lessons from the History of Literature Until the
Tanzimat Era* (*Edebiyat Tarihi Dersleri: Tanzimata Kadar*).[26] This encyclopedic historical overview of literary history contains alternating chapters
on "world literature" (*cihan edebiyatı*) and either pre-thirteenth-cen-
tury "Islamic literatures" or post-thirteenth-century "Turkish literature."
While Levend does not reflect on the meanings of the term, his schematic
organization points to a clear distinction between "world literature" and
religiously and culturally specific Islamic and Turkish literatures, respectively. Used exclusively in reference to French, Italian, Spanish, German, and
English literatures from the Renaissance to the nineteenth century—with
discussion of select pre-Renaissance authors and Russian authors from the
nineteenth century onward—"world literature" is furthermore coded as a
decidedly European affair. This distinction is validated by İnsel Publishing
House's World Literature series (Cihan Edebiyatı Serisi), which ran from
1945 through at least 1951, publishing predominantly European literature.
Aside from one translation of the American author Helen Grace Carlisle,
the series maintained a strong focus on Italian literature, with additional
translations from French, English, Russian, and Romanian.[27]

In contrast to these rather static applications of the term, Melahat
Özgü offers a brief theoretical reflection on world literature in her 1938
essay "Goethe's Persona in World Literature" ("Göte'nin Cihan Edebiyatındaki Şahsiyeti"). Following an introduction to Goethe's life and work—in
which she highlights his inherent genius and the timeless quality of his
oeuvre—Özgü argues that Goethe's world literary persona manifests itself
at the point where divergent ways of seeing his work intersect.[28] It is the

position of this site of intersection, she writes, "that ultimately determines [Goethe's] persona in world literature."[29]

This depiction of world literature as a mode of dynamic interpretation that can nevertheless secure a stable form of positionality belies a tension that weaves its way through Özgü's entire essay. She describes world literature as a spiritual domain or sphere from within which poets address not only their own people but all peoples of the world. Identifying this form of address as a gift, Özgü then argues that the entrance of one poet's voice into another national sphere changes that nation, gives it shape, and completes its shortcomings. Rather than lead to a loss of individuality, this interaction engenders a process of clarification, enlightenment, and maturation. It is through such spiritual actions, she argues, that world literature becomes effective. This dynamic process that Özgü describes is nevertheless suspiciously limited to a canon of classic authors who have gained entrance into—and thus also secured a place for themselves within—a delimited sphere. While Özgü describes world literature as a phenomenon encompassing all of humanity, the nations and authors she mentions by name are exclusively European:

> Poetry is a yield for a specific people but also for the world. In other words, its roots are on a nation's soil, but its summit may rise, indeed rise so high that the domain in which it is situated broadens out to such an extent that it enters into the domains of literature and humanity. It is for this reason that poetry is a language understood by all nations. Whether it be Homer, Dante, Shakespeare, Cervantes, Raccine, Dostoyevsky, or Ibsen; regardless of the blood flowing in their veins—whether Greek, Italian, English, Spanish, French, Russian, or northern blood—those who hear the voice of poetry, in other words everyone who is human, will hear a piece of their own soul.[30]

Here, Özgü describes a process of broadening out from the level of the national to that of the universal, which in turn renders poetry accessible to all of humankind. Achieving universality is thus akin to entering into the sphere of world literature. While Özgü does not explicitly exclude Turkish literature from this sphere, the authors and nationalities she chooses to cite closely align with Levend and the World Literature series' presentation of European literature *as* world literature. Indeed, there are no references to

Turkish literature within the scope of Özgü's essay. Özgü's understanding of a delimited sphere of world literature is furthermore based on a form of positionality: only once the poet has secured a stable position in the sphere of world literature can he orient himself toward others and engage in a productive process of exchange. Engendering clarification and enlightenment, this exchange serves in turn to affirm one's own self-positionality.

In contrast, Ali's travelogue points to a more radical form of mutual transformation, which occurs through processes of *dis*location and *dis*orientation. The place names *Cermenistan* and *Putseddümm*, for example, dislodge Germany and Potsdam, respectively, from their meanings as designations of specific geographic positions. As a meeting point for the German and Ottoman Turkish languages, they serve instead as a site from which new meanings can emerge. Rather than achieve a form of stable positionality vis-à-vis one another, these languages thus produce translative instability in their encounter.

The instability engendered by Ali's travelogue differs sharply from other theories of translation in 1930s Turkey that underscored the concepts of entirety and completeness. İsmail Habib Sevük (1892–1954) and Hilmi Ziya Ülken (1901–1974), for example, both underscored a concept of "complete translation," which was closely tied to both language reform and emergent definitions of world literature at the time. The desire to forge a "pure" form of modern Turkish in the 1930s was premised on an understanding of Turkish culture as an essential whole in and of itself. Sevük and Ülken's conceptions of "complete translation" stem from a similar premise: the existence of an intact corpus of European literary classics that could be translated into Turkish in its entirety.

In early republican Turkey, these different conceptualizations of wholeness converged around an emergent understanding of world literature as a universalized European literature that was imagined to be fundamentally separate from a national Turkish one. The project of language reform, which also aimed to forge a modern Turkish capable of conveying the concepts of Western civilization, ultimately served the goal of successfully transferring "world literature" into Turkish via literary translation. On the contrary, Sabahattin Ali's travelogue provides the grounds for an alternative vision of world literature that is not premised on the concepts of wholeness or transfer. Contra the premise of two distinct cultural-linguistic entities brought into contact via translation, Ali's travelogue reveals translation to be a mutual process of transformation that underscores the hybridity of language itself. This in turn lays the groundwork for a conception of world literature-*as*-translation rather than the dominant republican investment in world literature-*in*-translation.

COMPLETE TRANSLATION

Ülken produced the first full-length book dedicated to the question of translation in the republican era: *The Role of Translation in Periods of Awakening* (*Uyanış Devirlerinde Tercümenin Rolü*, 1935). For Ülken, national awakening coincides with a nation's entrance into a larger universal concept of civilization that nevertheless carries contradictory undertones. While Ülken identifies "one single civilization," he also attributes dynamic processes of multiplication and expansion to it.[31] Here, Ülken contrasts what he terms open and closed civilizations, suggesting that those civilizations that did not maintain contact with and allow themselves to be influenced by outside factors ultimately withered and dried up. That Ülken cites Ottoman civilization as "closed" here is an illuminating example of how he viewed republican Turkey's contact with the "West" as more thorough and comprehensive.[32]

Openness, for Ülken, is embodied by processes of translation,[33] and he identifies major translation movements in periods of national awakening across historical civilizations, from ancient Greece and Egypt to Romantic Germany and beyond. Yet it is ultimately through this very contrast between openness and closedness that Ülken is able to depict *Western* civilization as universal: "The most important characteristic of Western civilization is the fact that it was founded on a historical culture, which attempts to take into account multiple perspectives, including all of the civilizational moves that were born and disappeared before it."[34] In short, Western civilization is capable of universality precisely because it remains open to and thus encompasses *all* the particularities of civilizations that have come before it. In Ülken's terms, then, a Turkish national awakening involves the production of a specifically Turkish national language and culture via processes of translation that are explicitly tied to the goal of Westernization. He identifies the Tanzimat era as a shift in orientation from East to West, which then culminates in the republican era with a complete awakening and what he terms a "complete transfer of civilization."[35]

This rhetoric of completeness ties back into the title of the translation series in which Ülken's monograph appeared: Complete Translations of Yesterday and Tomorrow (Dün ve Yarın Tercüme Külliyatı).[36] Emphasizing a *complete* corpus of translations, the title of this series refers beyond a core canon of past works—or even a comprehensive selection of contemporary authors—to an ideological encapsulation of the unwritten works of *tomorrow*. With this title, Vakit Publishing House echoed a general sentiment among leading intellectuals of the time: the need for a systematized program of translation in the republican era.

Ülken also emphasizes systematicity in his monograph: in contrast to translation activity in the Tanzimat and post-Tanzimat eras, which Ülken describes as "scattered" and "haphazard,"[37] he stresses the need for a "conscious, organized, and complete" contemporary translation movement that would encapsulate all of the great classics and contemporary works of art and philosophy.[38] The underlying assumption here, that a complete translation of "Western" literature and culture is indeed possible in the modern republican era, relies on a specific image of the "West" as a fixed and stable entity toward which Turkey could orient itself. Such stability stands in clear tension to the openness Ülken otherwise underscores as so necessary for civilizational evolution.

While Ülken's conception of the "West" is not geographically delimited in this 1935 work,[39] his 1946 essay "East and West" ("Şark ve Garp") clearly asserts that the West is indeed Europe. He argues here that Europe achieved the status of a rational and universal civilization via the process of colonization, which allowed European values to spread beyond its continent to the entire world. "To Westernize," he concludes, is thus "to transition from a closed to an open civilization. To say that we are Western or that we will become Western is to say that we have participated in a rational and universal world civilization."[40]

Ülken's statement here is in line with what Tarık Zafer Tunaya has termed the wholist approach toward Westernization. Whereas partialists like Ziya Gökalp maintained that only the scientific and technological advancements of Western civilization should be adopted in order for Turkey to develop its own cultural and moral basis, wholists such as Ülken called for the adoption of Western civilization in its entirety.[41] As is evident from Ülken's diverse writings, his wholist approach necessarily relied on a conceptualization of the West as a complete and whole entity. While debate certainly existed in this realm, the early republican state also took a wholist approach toward the Westernization process, with the belief that it could not simply adopt certain elements from the West but needed to initiate a full-scale Westernization movement.

The discourse surrounding translation in the 1930s and 1940s participated in this rhetoric via its insistence on a systematic and comprehensive translation movement that could counter the perceived lack of conscious selection processes in the late Ottoman era. Among other factors, this persistent emphasis on systematicity led to what Fırat Oruç terms a "strategic universalization of the West," or the idea that "Western civilization represented the great synthesis, even the totality, of all previous civilizations." In short: "modern European culture subsumed [previous ones] in a new 'universal' paradigm. Europe, therefore, was not a particular civilization among others, but the absolute signifier and measure of the universal."[42]

Such universalization is evidenced in another significant series: Translations of World Authors (Dünya Muharrirlerinden Tercümeler Serisi), launched in 1937 by Remzi Publishing House. On a semantic level, this series' choice of the word *dünya* for "world" links it to the state-funded Translation Bureau, which was established in 1940 to produce its signature Translations from World Literature series. *Dünya* was also the preferred term for the 1938 translation series initiated by Suhulet Publishing House, Translations of World Classics (Dünya Klasiklerinden Tercümeler).[43] The emphasis these series place on the classics as universal works of literature, together with their specific translation records, presents a Eurocentric take on the term "world" that aligns with the publishing history of the Translations from World Literature series, at least in its initial phase from 1940 to 1946.[44] From among 467 titles translated in this time frame, twenty-three (approximately 5 percent) were Eastern classics; these consisted mainly of Arabic and Persian texts.[45] In short, the series placed a heavy emphasis on Western literature, including Greek and Latin classics.[46]

Beyond the level of semantics, the Translations of World Authors series was closely linked to the Translation Bureau of the 1940s.[47] The bureau was the brainchild of several intellectuals, including Sabri Esat Siyavuşgil (1907–1968), Hasan Ali Ediz (1905–1972), and Hasan Ali Yücel (1897–1961).[48] Many of its writers and translators also went on to work for—and in the case of Yücel, direct—the Translations from World Literature series. Active for thirty years, the World Authors series roughly converged with and ran parallel to the World Literature series run by the state. Responsible for the publication of several journals—including *Kalem*, *Oluş*, and *İnsan*—Remzi also served as an important precursor to the Translation Bureau, which produced the journal *Translation* (*Tercüme*). This journal served as an important forum for debate regarding translation methods and new terminology, as well as a site for shorter translations to appear alongside their originals. Finally, as the chief editor of *İnsan*, which was a leading publication on the topic of Turkish humanism, Hilmi Ziya Ülken was also the first to announce the idea of a Turkish renaissance in the explicit terms of Westernization: "today we are engaged in a Renaissance in the truest sense. We are joining the world anew. Western methods will guide us in re-discovering ourselves."[49]

Remzi expressed similar sentiments in its official advertising material. In the back matter to a detailed catalogue from 1939, the publishing house provided a series of bullet-point-like answers to the self-posed question of what purpose its translation series had set out to fulfill. Above all, Remzi identifies translation as a source of enrichment for a national culture, the success of which is predicated upon the translation of the most beautiful and famous works of Western literature into Turkish. In doing so, Remzi also addresses the question of orientation, via the express purpose of "giving our literature a new direction."[50] Without explicitly employing the rhetoric of completeness, Remzi does identify its series as different from the others preceding it, owing to its carefully planned structure. The desired result is a library of quality yet inexpensive translations: with the cost of a book at approximately fifty *kuruş*, Remzi underscored accessibility as one of its fundamental purposes.[51] This need for affordable books was also one main recurring argument on the part of Turkish intellectuals in support of state intervention in the publishing industry and an express goal of the Translation Bureau.

While the paratextual material used to advertise the World Authors series did not explicitly emphasize completeness, other texts published by Remzi Publishing House did. İsmail Habib Sevük's arguments in *European Literature and Us: Translations from the West* (*Avrupa Edebiyatı ve Biz: Garpten Tercümeler*, 1940), for example, bear a striking resemblance to those expressed by Ülken five years earlier. In this survey of translation history from Greek and Latin antiquity to the present, Sevük aligns the process of translation in republican Turkey with the goal of Westernization, which he explicitly links to Europe. Like Ülken, Sevük also prefers translation to the process of learning a foreign language. In order for Turks to arrive at a state of "complete Europe" (*tam Avrupa*), he argues, they must first engage in "complete translation" (*tam tercüme*).[52] Such a transformation can only occur once Turks have achieved the highest level of proficiency in their *own* language, at which point European values might be properly reflected in Turkish via translations.

Sevük demonstrates here a desire to textualize Europe. On one hand, textual participation in European values holds the potential to dislocate the concept of "Europe" from a specific geographic location and expose it

to stratified levels of meaning-making: "A European nation is not necessarily one that is found on European geography. A European nation is
one that has first transferred the fundamental works of antiquity, namely
Greek and Latin, and then also the fundamental books of other European
nations into its own language."[53] On the other hand, this process of dislocation is premised on the *entire* translation of Western antiquity. Whereas
dislocation in Ali's travelogue, for example, points to the fundamental
incompleteness of German and Ottoman Turkish via their encounter with
one another, Sevük utilizes the metaphor of dislocation to undergird the
imagined completeness of the European literary canon.

Taking stock of the translations covered in his own historical survey,
Sevük does recognize the impossibility of "complete translation" on a practical level. He nevertheless describes his own work as *close* to complete,
dismissing his own oversights as insignificant. What exactly is at stake
in Sevük's refusal to acknowledge the incompleteness of his own undertaking? In contrast to Ülken's more expansive understanding of Western
civilization in his 1935 work, in 1940 Sevük already presents a more concep-
tually bounded understanding of the West as Europe, which is imagined as
complete in and of itself. It is the very boundedness of Europe that in turn
allows Sevük to imagine a complete corpus of translations in the republican era. On one hand, these two aspects of his argument complement one
another, in that only a stable and unchanging Europe could be translated
into the Turkish cultural realm unchanged. On the other hand, while the
image of a complete Europe was meant to ensure the success of large-scale
Westernizing reforms, it ultimately reinforced the idea that Europe was
distinctly separate from the new Turkish nation-state.

TRANSLATIONAL MULTIPLICITY

In the context of persistent emphasis on translational completeness and
European universality, Ali's turn to cubism as the unlikely extension of an
Ottoman *mullahs'* etymological interpretation of Potsdam gains pointed
significance. Consider, once again, the following passage: "According to
Hayrullah Molla Bey, a contemporary etymologist, the word Potsdam
consists of the words *put*, *sedd*, and *ümm*. *Put*, as is known, is a shrine
found in the churches of the infidels in the form of Christian portraits and
statues; *sedd* means to close, cover or conceal; *ümm*, or mother, here means
the Mother Mary. All together, by means of cubism, it means: 'O Mother

Mary, cover the idols!'" As an art form in which the subject is abstracted and represented from different perspectives, cubism allows a viewer to occupy multiple positions vis-à-vis a given subject, thus rendering the subject as inherently multiple. In short, it destabilizes the viewing practice, in that it enables numerous forms of perspectival orientation simultaneously.

By tracing the etymological "origins" of the place name Potsdam to the Ottoman Turkish words *put-sedd-ümm* by means of cubism, Ali insists on the need to view Potsdam as inherently multiple, from a position that is also inherently multiple. Within Ali's intricately crafted travelogue, translation provides the grounds on which this practice may proceed. As such, Ali's turn toward cubism embraces a very different conception of openness than that of Ülken. For Ülken, the openness of Western civilization is based on its ability to successfully incorporate the perspectives of all previous civilizations, through which it is in turn rendered universal; this universalized image of the West is complete in and of itself and thereby also a stable point of reference for the Turkish nation-state. On the contrary, Ali shows how the meanings of Germany/*Cermenistan* and Potsdam/*Putsed-dümm* transform in their contact with Ottoman Turkish. Rather than an absorption of Ottoman Turkish into German, or a translation of German *into* Ottoman Turkish, the transformation of these place names presents an open process of mutual becoming. Translation as such does not simply bring two otherwise separate and intact languages into contact but reveals rather their fundamental, if at times surprising, interconnectedness.

This process is also different from İsmail Habib Sevük's concept of "complete translation," which is premised on a bounded understanding of Europe and its literary canon. Closely tied to the actual agendas of translation initiatives of the 1930s, concepts such as "complete translation" were central to a nascent understanding of world literature as European literature in Turkish translation. Amid diverse republican Westernizing reforms, translation rhetoric thus provided clear grounds for orientation. It posited a stable external reference toward which Turkish culture could orient itself, at the same time that the externality of this reference delineated Turkishness as a distinct and separate cultural realm.

Whereas this mode of orientation demands a one-way process of translation *from* Europe *into* the new Turkish nation-state, Ali's travelogue enacts a dynamic, omnidirectional translation practice that stems from the instability of the cultures and languages in question. Enabling a form of multiperspectival orientation that cannot be delimited, omnidirectional translation thus reveals culture itself to be inherently multiple. Multiplicity stems, in turn, from the intricacies of Ali's Ottoman Turkish language, which take recourse to "outdated" genres, vocabularies, and grammatical structures to render "modern" experiences on the page. In the surprising absence of modern Turkish, Ali's travelogue thus asks what it might mean to "properly reflect" Western values in that language. Rather than dwell on the perceived insufficiencies of a modern Turkish language under reform, Ali flaunts the intricacies of Ottoman Turkish to reveal the depths of its expressive capacity. The resulting mismatch of form and content not only destabilizes the process of cultural encounter but also that of reading, thus rendering the text open to unknown future interpretations.

This openness of Ali's travelogue resonates strongly with Gayatri Chakravorty Spivak's call for a "loosening" of the terms that make up world literature. In contrast to efforts to clearly define "world" and "literature," she conceives of world literature as an event to come.[54] In other words, world literature has not necessarily already happened in a manner that can be easily defined and does not delineate a set of authors or texts. World litera-ture points rather to the active power of texts—and texts in translation—to project a future that is still open to imagination and interpretation. Ali's travelogue projects a similar vision of world literature through its approach to translation as a disorienting rather than orienting force. In this work, translation does not orient itself toward an original that it comes after. Instead, translation moves backward and forward across times and places to imagine an inherently open future in which new and creative meanings may emerge.

CHAPTER 6

Silencing the *Ansatzpunkt*
World Literature as Radical Interrelationality

Lamenting at once "the fateful coalescence" of cultures and the seeming "superabundance of materials, of methods, and of points of view" in the nascent postwar era of decolonization, Erich Auerbach proposes the concept of the *Ansatzpunkt*—or point of departure—in his 1952 essay "Philology of World Literature" ("Philologie der Weltliteratur").[1] Faced simultaneously with the decline of a tacitly Eurocentric worldview and the impossibility of doing justice to the vast components of a world literature that might actually encompass the world, Auerbach turns to the small and the specific. In place of sweeping categories such as the Baroque or the Romantic, he calls attention to the level of the sentence or the syntactic sequence. Exact and objective, Auerbach writes, the *Ansatzpunkt* should form "an organic inner part of the theme," with a role so eminently clear, it is able to "speak for itself."[2] Only in this way can it form a "handle"[3] from which to seize the object under analysis, its specificity opening inquiry into a broader universal synthesis. If chosen correctly, the *Ansatzpunkt* thus has a "radiating power,"[4] the interpretation of which enables a movement outward. Encompassing a region greater than itself, this radiating movement in turn provides a form for viewing, dealing with, and ordering world history.

In this chapter, I ask what it might mean to take up narrative gaps as an *Ansatzpunkt* for considering the interrelationship of the modernist author Sabahattin Ali's work as a novelist and a translator. How might a textual silence "speak for itself" or radiate outward? And what implications might this have both for Auerbach's understanding of world literature in the post-war era and for diverse Turkish intellectuals' usage of the term nearly a decade prior? In answer to these questions, I turn to key narrative gaps in Heinrich von Kleist's *The Engagement in Santo Domingo* (*Die Verlobung in St. Domingo*, 1811) and Ali's final novel, *The Madonna in the Fur Coat* (*Kürk Mantolu Madonna*, 1943). Ali's translation of *Engagement* (*San Domingo'da Bir Nişanlanma*)—which first appeared in 1940 in the journal *Translation* (*Tercüme*)—incidentally coincided with the serialization of *Madonna*; both texts were subsequently published in book format in 1943.[5] In my analysis of the narrative gaps in each text, I argue that the radiating power of this *Ansatzpunkt* lies precisely in its refusal to allow for a clearly defined synthesis. Rather than provide the groundwork for orderly analysis, the narrative gap as *Ansatzpunkt* exerts a destabilizing and disorienting force.

This force gains significance within the historical context of the 1940s—during which Auerbach incidentally held a position at Istanbul University—amid sweeping humanist reforms aimed at the orientation of Turkish culture toward Western Europe. Responsible for some 1,247 publications—including Ali's rendition of *Engagement*—the state-sponsored Translations from World Literature series formed one core pillar of these reforms.[6]

Together with the publication history of Translations from World Literature, this chapter considers the viewpoints of other leading Turkish intellectuals in the 1940s to show how world literature (*dünya edebiyatı* or *cihan edebiyatı*) was coded as decidedly European. This understanding of world literature was in turn premised on a more general conceptualization of Western civilization as a synthesizable whole. In line with larger Turkish humanist reforms of the time, Translations from World Literature sought to transfer assumedly universal Western values into the Turkish language and culture, through an orderly and systematic translation movement on a grand scale.

In sharp contrast, my focus on Sabahattin Ali allows for the emergence of a vision of world literature that is premised on the messy interrelationship of his own writing and his translation practice. In a moment of societal reorientation toward Western Europe, Ali shows how translation can serve as a productively disorienting force. Whereas world literature in translation was meant to serve as a coordinate of cultural orientation in 1940s Turkey, Ali's work suggests rather that world literature is about a form of (inter)relationality, which places the stability of each side of the literary exchange into question. As such, it also upends Auerbach's understanding of world literature in the postwar era. Whereas the world historical synthesis Auerbach still longed for in 1952 necessarily depended on the existence of stable component parts, the interrelationship of *Engagement* and *Madonna* betrays the fundamentally hybrid character of both Germanness and Turkishness. Converging on—and radiating outward from—narrative gaps in each text, this interrelationship conveys the unstable positions of translator/translated and source/target, thereby upending the premise of cultural originality itself.

EARLY REPUBLICAN HUMANIST REFORMS

During his tenure as minister of education (1940–46), Hasan Ali Yücel sought to create a Turkish renaissance through the numerous humanist reforms he worked to put in place. These reforms introduced central tenets of classical Western education, with the aim of producing a common frame of reference for Turkey and the West.[7] Modeled on classical secular humanism, reforms emphasized Greek and Roman antiquity as the basis of contemporary European culture. Yet while Turkey sought to situate itself within a Greco-Roman cultural model in order to emphasize its fundamental Europeanness, reforms simultaneously utilized a model of universal humanism for the purpose of developing a modern national-cultural Turkish identity. Consider, for example, the following speech delivered by Yücel on the role of the newly founded state conservatory in Ankara:

> [TURKISH HUMANISM] is a free understanding and sensitivity which appreciates human work without any exception and does not limit it with time or location. Our hearts will feel nothing but only respect and admiration for any work—no matter from which nation—which brings a new thought and feeling to humanity. We do not express this respect and admiration with a theoretical approach, but by performing, experiencing and making them our own. The author may not be one of us, the composer can be from another nation. But it is we who understand and perform the words and sounds. This is why the plays and operas performed by the State Conservatoire are ours. They are Turkish and national.[8]

Yücel expresses here a contradictory form of timeless, universal humanism that can both transcend sociocultural and historical differences and be appropriated for a specifically national purpose. While Yücel underscores the fundamentally open quality of humanist works, the plays, operas, and concerts staged by the Ankara State Conservatory at this time were almost entirely European.[9] Yücel is confident that these works can become fundamentally Turkish through the act of performance.

Similar goals informed the establishment of other institutions within the humanist reform process: village institutes, for example, trained teachers in classical and Western European languages but also aimed more generally to raise literacy levels in Turkey. The state-sponsored Translation Bureau was established in 1940, with the goal of systematically translating the great works of Greco-Roman antiquity and contemporary European literatures, while also helping the modern Turkish language forge uniquely national modes of expression. And the establishment of a national library in 1946 solidified the nation's ongoing emphasis on literacy, while also serving as a central unifying institution that could house translations of the Western European classics alongside numerous new dictionaries of the Turkish language.

These reforms were preceded by a sweeping overhaul of the Darülfünun, the first institution of higher education in the Ottoman Empire modeled on the European university system.[10] On July 31, 1933, the Darülfünun was closed by legal decree, after which the institution officially reopened its doors as Istanbul University one day later. With this symbolic name change, the state signaled its goal of restructuring the university on the example of the nineteenth-century Humboltian model of education. The reform process was enabled largely by German-Jewish academic refugees who had lost their university positions under the conditions of National Socialism and were subsequently forced into exile.[11] While this historic restructuring came at the expense of numerous Turkish academics who lost their positions in the process, it did also lead to new and innovative collaborations between Istanbul and Ankara, both within academia and without. The approximately 130 refugees from Germany who lived and worked in Turkey between 1933 and 1945 engaged in diverse collaborative projects. To name only a select few: Leo Spitzer and Erich Auerbach each served as chair of the Department of Western Languages and Literatures at Istanbul University before taking up academic positions in the United States; Georg Rohde collaborated with Hasan Ali Yücel on the state-funded Translations from World Literature series; Paul Hindemith helped found the Ankara State Conservatory, where Carl Ebert would later direct the Ankara State Opera company with Sabahattin Ali as interpreter; and Rudolf Nissen served as

chair of the Medical School at Istanbul University, where he trained Turkish physicians and professors.[12]

To date, scholarship on this time period has focused largely on the
figures of German-Jewish exiles Spitzer and Auerbach and their later significance for the development of comparative literature in the United States in
its contemporary form. Whether it is depicted as a site of intellectual isolation[13] or a hotbed of worldly linguistic exchanges,[14] scholars such as Edward
Said, Aamir R. Mufti, and Emily Apter all credit Istanbul for producing the
conditions under which a new kind of comparative philological scholarship with a global scope could emerge. Whereas Istanbul serves mainly as
a backdrop for these scholars, Kader Konuk provides a multifaceted analysis of the city—and of the Turkish humanist reforms more generally—in
her reading of Erich Auerbach's *Mimesis: The Representation of Reality
in Western Literature* (*Mimesis: Dargestellte Wirklichkeit in der abendlän-
dischen Literatur*, 1946). Working against the standard framework of exilic
studies that figure *Mimesis* as a product of intellectual isolation, Konuk
understands exile as a "condition of multiple attachments,"[15] suggesting
the need to consider the historicity of the exile's experience, as well as the
material conditions of his or her existence. As Konuk's reading of *Mimesis*
nevertheless reveals, Turkey functions *ex negativo* within Auerbach's text;
it is through the omission of Turkish literature in this foundational work
of contemporary comparative literature, she argues, that the concept of a
"bounded" Judeo-Christian world can emerge.[16]

While itself a significant rewriting of the history of German-Jewish exile
in 1930s and 1940s Turkey, Konuk's research thus also lends weight to Nergis
Ertürk's claim that Turkish literature and scholars have largely remained
an "absent presence" in the scholarship on this particular moment and in
the field of comparative literature more generally. Through the example of
Ahmet Hamdi Tanpınar—a prominent modernist author and literary historian who participated in the humanist reform process—Ertürk shows how
the field of Turkish literature has grappled with questions of comparabil-
ity with Europe since at least the 1850s, long before the arrival of European
academic exiles on the scene.[17]

More recently, Fırat Oruç has called renewed attention to the role played
by Turkish scholars in the humanist reform process. If, as he argues via
reference to Apter, a "volatile crossing" or "two-way collision" did occur
in Istanbul between European philological humanism and conservative
Turkish language politics, then we must attend equally to both sides of
this collision.[18] This involves a serious examination of the conservative

language politics that undergirded Turkish humanist reforms. Oruç turns here to Azra Erhat, a prominent translator from ancient Greek who first studied and later took up a position in the Romanology Seminar at Istanbul University. While central to an expansion of the expressive capacity of modern Turkish in the aftermath of language reform, Erhat also provided an "ideological legitimation for . . . essentialist nationalism."[19] Similar to Spitzer, Erhat's investment in new practices of philology—which sought to break down the barriers between literature and linguistics—was tied to an organicist approach to language. Yet her belief that language should evolve according to its everyday usages also harbored the desire to eradicate an "obsolete" and "fossilized" idiom of Ottoman Turkish that was not in line with a new national consciousness.[20]

My focus in this chapter on Sabahattin Ali provides a different point of contrast to the scholarship on German-Jewish exiles in 1930s and 1940s Turkey. Ali was a foremost expert on German literature, although he never occupied an academic position. From outside the confines of Istanbul University, Ali's literature and translations enact their own volatile crossings, albeit not in the name of Turkish nationalism. Whether in his private letters, fictionalized memoirs, or translations, Ali's writing reflects critically on the meaning of the Turkish-German relationship vis-à-vis Turkish humanist reforms and the specific image of Europe upon which they were modeled. If previous scholarship has pointed extensively to German-Jewish émigrés' reflections on the ultranationalist context in Turkey, this chapter then asks how a contemporary Turkish modernist author imagined Germany and Germanness in order to reflect further on the conflicted meanings of Turkishness. Nowhere is this critical potential of Ali's legacy more evident than in the interstices of his novelistic writing and his translation practice. In the following, I thus introduce the premise and goals of the state-sponsored Translation Bureau and the Translations from World Literature series that Ali helped put into action, in order to more clearly address the manner in which his roles as translator and author crossed and informed one another.

WORLD LITERATURE IN TRANSLATION

Alongside other diverse modalities of translation, the Turkish state enacted an extensive translation project in 1940 under the direction of minister of education Hasan Ali Yücel and the German-Jewish émigré Georg Rohde.

With support from the state-funded Translation Bureau, the Translations from World Literature series ran through 1966, although its most productive period was undeniably under the tenure of Yücel, who stepped down in 1946 amid accusations of communist affiliations.

Well versed in Islamic mysticism and the classics of Persian literature in particular, Yücel did not conceive of a fundamental difference between "East" and "West." He underscored literature as rather the embodiment of a common human spirit (*insan ruhu*).[21] Looking back on his career, for example, Yücel wrote of the Translations from World Literature series that: "In our opinion it was necessary to not limit ourselves to ancient Greece as a source but to go even further back, and also to other realms; wherever there is a trace or a work that carries its own meaning for the human spirit, we need to include these within the broadest conception of humanism that embraces all of humanity. We achieved this through the publication of classics with the Ministry of Education. Plato's dialogues appeared alongside Confucius, Rūmī, and Sa'dī's works, and together with this sensibility a Turkish consciousness was born."[22] While indicative of Yücel's own worldview, the sentiment of this statement did not come to full fruition in the actual program of translation published by the World Literature series, particularly in the period from 1940 to 1946, during which Yücel served as minister of education. During this time period, the discourse of humanism was closely associated with the translation of Western classics into Turkish, with a heavy emphasis on the works of ancient Greece. Yücel himself expressed exactly this in his opening speech for the First Turkish Publishing Convention in 1939. Emphasizing the need for Turkey to "mobilize" for a widespread translation movement, he urged the country to translate the great works of the "civilized world" in order to become "a distinguished member of the Western cultural and intellectual community."[23] Over a period of multiple years, Yücel's call for a comprehensive and concrete program of translation that could serve as the basis of Turkish education was strongly supported by leading authors and intellectuals of the time. Figures such as Ahmet Hamdi Tanpınar, Yunus Kâzım Köni (1903–1957), and Yaşar Nabi Nayır (1908–1981) all emphasized the need for state intervention in order to make quality and affordable literature in translation available to an undereducated public with little disposable income.[24]

The overwhelming public support for this translation project gains significance within the historical trajectory of this book: The Tanzimat era (1839–76) of the Ottoman Empire initiated a "radical shift of semiotic orientation,"[25] during which new European-inspired genres were introduced into the Ottoman Turkish sphere via translation. The introduction of a systematized program of translation in the 1940s represented an attempt to both solidify this societal reorientation toward Western Europe and simultaneously deem the efforts of Tanzimat and post-Tanzimat scholars as insufficient. In short, the Translations from World Literature program aimed at a *successful* form of societal reorientation that was deemed to have been only inconclusively attempted in the past.

Closely in line with the agenda of 1930s private translation initiatives, this state-sponsored series solidified an already widespread conception of world literature as European literature in translation. The series' emphasis on systematicity further demonstrates an attempt to fulfill previous calls for a "complete" translation of European literary classics in order to engender a Turkish renaissance in the present. This pervasive rhetoric of completeness was in turn central to the universalization of the "West" in early republican Turkey.[26] Broadly understood as a synthesizable whole, Western civilization's imagined values were then understood as transferable into the Turkish cultural realm via a process of problem-free translation.[27]

Convened in May of 1939, the First Turkish Publishing Convention aimed to establish the structure through which to realize this goal of a systematic program of translation. Committees consisting of authors, intellectuals, journalists, publishers, and educators were established to assess and report on the state of seven categories, including translation.[28] Sabahattin Ali served as one of twenty-seven members on the translation committee,[29] which took the first major step in realizing Yücel's vision by producing an initial list of 294 works to be translated into Turkish.[30] This list, which formed the basis for the Translation Bureau's signature Translations from World Literature series, consisted overwhelmingly of Western European classics. The largest section contained more than one hundred works of French literature, followed by English (forty-two), Greek and Latin (thirty-eight), German (thirty-four), Russian (thirty), and select titles from Italian, Spanish, Northern European, and American literatures. In contrast, the complete list contained only seven works by "Eastern" authors.[31] Accordingly, works of non-Western literature comprised a mere 5 percent of the translations undertaken for the series through 1946.[32] As such, this list strongly reflects the vision of a translation program that would enable Turkey to participate in the history of Western thought and thereby become an active, independent member of Western society and civilization.

Following the successful establishment of a temporary translation committee (*Tercüme Heyeti*), a permanent bureau was established in 1940 under the direction of Nurullah Ataç. Sabahattin Ali served as one of seven permanent board members for this bureau, as well as editor and translator of German texts until 1944, when he was put under surveillance for suspect political activity.[33] In her assessment of the bureau's activities and reception during this time period, Şehnaz Tahir Gürçağlar views the establishment of this institution as central to other statist republican reforms in the fields of economics and culture. Within this political climate, she argues, authors tended to view state involvement in the publishing industry at large as both natural and necessary.[34]

Ali's good friend and fellow translator Melahat Togar describes, in particular, Ali's enthusiasm for the translation project and recalls the excitement and dedication with which he approached his work at the bureau. Her description of this phase in Ali's life as a "happy period" (güzel dönem) is a reminder of the positive effects state intervention had in the publishing industry: It initiated the extensive Translations from World Literature, as well as other series. It also led to the establishment of a bureau where authors came together to grapple with questions of how to translate great works of literature into a newly reformed modern Turkish language that was still struggling to establish its own vocabulary and modes of expression.

Ali clearly supported the Translations from World Literature project. Yet his own fiction and translations complicate the paradigms of European universality, civilizational transfer, and smooth translatability that were so central to republican translation rhetoric and humanist reforms, thereby acting as a force of critical intervention from within this series. My reading of Ali in this light is informed by the fact that he was put under surveillance in 1944 for suspect political activity and shortly thereafter removed from his positions at the Translation Bureau and state conservatory. In an extremely tempered letter to Yücel dated December 14, 1945, Ali expresses both his grief and indignation at this decision. While underscoring his enthusiasm for humanist reforms at large, Ali suggests that his position as a government employee at the Translation Bureau and his identity as a writer had become incompatible.[35] In conclusion, Ali states the real and formidable fear of one day no longer being able to feed his family on the meager salary of an independent author. Yet only when he had lost all hope in the prospect of following his political convictions would he return to the state's door. "Until then," he writes, "I will try to make a living with my pen."[36] Implied here is a "living" that does not conform to state standards.

The inherent contradiction of interests Ali expresses between his identities as a state employee and an author in 1945 leads me to reconsider the socially critical potential of his literary output during the years he was employed at the Translation Bureau. As a tragic love story, Ali's final novel, *Madonna*, fell under the radar of state censorship and continues to be read in a largely apolitical light. In the following sections I show how, on the contrary, this novel is closely tied to Ali's translation activity for the bureau. In particular, the myriad connections between *Engagement* and *Madonna* open up an alternative vision of world literature from that officially endorsed by the state.[37] Unlike the statist conception of world literature as European literature in translation—which served in turn as a stable coordinate of cultural orientation for the still-fledgling modern Republic of Turkey—Ali's final novel points to a vision of world literature as a form of radical interrelationality and thereby also instability. Whereas the state-sponsored series figured world literature as a knowable, synthesizable, and transferable entity, Ali's writing figures world literature as a process of confronting the unknown. Converging on and radiating outward from the narrative silences in each text, the specific relationship of *Engagement* to *Madonna* points toward the futility of orienting the (national) self through translation. Translation constitutes rather a form of encounter that underscores both the hybridities of the self and any external references one might orient oneself toward.

IDENTITIES IN CRISIS

Ali was an active translator prior to his involvement with the Translation Bureau. By the first publishing convention in 1939, he had clearly established himself as an expert on German literature and culture.[38] While it is impossible to determine the exact role Ali played in selecting works for the Translations from World Literature series, it is safe to assume he had significant influence with regard to the German portion of this list. The initial selections from German literature included standard Enlightenment (Goethe, Lessing, Schiller), Romantic (Hoffmann, Chamisso, the Grimm brothers), and realist (Keller) authors. The inclusion of several works by Heinrich von Kleist is not surprising, considering his canonical status at the time of the publishing convention. Yet the placement of his texts within a translation series meant to generate a comprehensive humanist reform movement in Turkey raises larger discursive questions that are also pertinent to Ali's involvement with the bureau. In the introduction to each text published within the World Literature series, Yücel describes literature as an embodiment of the humanist spirit. Here—and in other public statements and publications—he underscores the value of translation activity as a means of participating in humanist civilization, strengthening the Turkish educational system, and enriching Turkish readers' level of perception in the world:

> The first understanding and feeling of the spirit of humanism starts with the adoption of works of art which are the most concrete expression of human existence. Among art forms, literature is the richest in terms of the intellectual elements of this expression. Therefore, when a nation repeats the literature of other nations in its own tongue, or rather in its own conception, it increases, reviews and re-creates its intellect and power of understanding. . . . The richness of a nation's library in this respect indicates a higher level of comprehension in the world of civilization. Consequently, to administer the activity of translation in a careful and systematic manner, is to strengthen the most important aspect of Turkish education, to serve its development and expansion.[39]

Yücel viewed humanism not as an end in itself but as a tool to both expand and strengthen a Turkish national literary consciousness. Within this endeavor, translation is posited as both a repetition of another nation's ideas and a unique form of recreation. As such, it constitutes one method of participating in what Yücel describes here as the "world" of civilization. This formulation is in line with Yücel's understanding of translation activity as a method of underscoring the commonalities, rather than points of division, between East and West. And yet on other occasions, Yücel did locate the concept of civilization as intrinsic to the West, which was underscored by the emphasis placed on Western classics in the World Literature series.

What would it mean to translate Kleist's *Engagement* into both Yücel's more capacious vision of humanism and the actual program of translation endorsed by the World Literature series? While Ali describes Kleist as a Romantic in the introductory remarks to his translation, Kleist's literature does not easily fit into any specific literary movement. His work offers, rather, a provocative and inconclusive exploration of topics central to the experience of modernity, such as the inauthenticity of the self, the psychology of national belonging, and anticolonial struggle. Kleist's grueling everyday experiences in the Prussian military (1792–99) exposed him to the contradictions of enlightened humanism at a young age. Two years after his decision to leave the service, his famous "Kant crisis" (1801) marked a crucial turning point in his career at which he began to doubt his earlier investment in the Enlightenment ideals of autonomy, reason, and progress and develop in its place a radically skeptical view of the world.[40] Further informed by his experience of the French Revolution, its violent disruption of established power relations, and the period of political instability that followed, Kleist's diverse textual production reveals the tensions and paradoxes of Enlightenment rationalism and eighteenth-century humanist discourse.[41] Whether intentional or not, the inclusion of Kleist's short stories and dramas within the Translations from World Literature series thus contains the potential to subvert a republican investment in the ideals of humanist discourse and their presumed value for Turkish society. Among Kleist's texts included in this series,[42] Ali's decision to translate *Engagement* is notable for several reasons, from the relevance of the turbulent political context and cross-cultural modes of belonging it evokes to the subtle but unmistakable Kleistian references within *Madonna*.

Through its focus on the continued practice of slavery in the French colony of Saint-Domingue following the French Revolution, Kleist's novella takes as its background the contradictions of a race-based colonial order. Set at the tail end of the Haitian Revolution (1791–1804)—the first successful slave revolt in the Western Hemisphere—*Engagement* takes up the issues of race, gender, class, and nationality within a complex matrix of colonial power relations. The Turkish translation of this text thus presents a critical force of disorientation in a cultural-historical moment that otherwise aimed at the successful orientation of Turkish society toward the West.

In her article "Hegel and Haiti" (2000), Susan Buck-Morss expounds upon the significance of the Haitian Revolution, which exposed inherent contradictions between thought and practice with regard to the concept of freedom in eighteenth-century Western political philosophy. While freedom was broadly viewed by Western philosophers as a natural and inalienable right, to whom exactly did the category apply, and how? Definitions of British liberty as the protection of property, for example, legitimized the owning of slaves as a form of moveable property.[43]

Americans furthermore utilized slavery as a metaphor for injustice in reference to the process of taxation without representation, while the justification for actual slavery was upheld by the Constitution.[44] These are all examples of how a "political metaphor of freedom took root at precisely the time that the economic practice of slavery—the systematic, highly sophisticated capitalist enslavement of *non*-Europeans as a labor force in the colonies—was increasing quantitatively and intensifying qualitatively to the point that by the mid-eighteenth century it came to underwrite the entire economic system of the West."[45]

A foremost producer of sugar—which was in high demand in eighteenth-century France—Saint-Domingue was home to a drastically increasing number of slaves across the course of the eighteenth century, their numbers reaching well above five hundred thousand.[46] The staggering weight of these numbers testifies to the glaring incompatibility of the colonial slave trade with European theorizations of freedom. Yet even in the aftermath of the French Revolution—which espoused equality and universal freedom at home—the practice of slavery in Saint-Domingue was not ultimately ended through actions of the French state but rather via the 1794 armed revolt of Black Saint Dominguans, who demanded the universalization of abolition across the French colonies.[47] Buck-Morss describes the period that followed as a limit case, or a period of time in which universalist principles of the Black Jacobins in Saint-Domingue "surpassed the metropole in actively realizing the Enlightenment goal of human liberty."[48]

The success of the Haitian Revolution was briefly overturned in 1802, when Napoleon reinstituted slavery on the island in an attempt to ensure French hegemony across its colonies. Kleist's *Engagement* takes place in the aftermath of Napoleon's 1802 decree, during which Black Jacobins sought to violently eliminate whites from the island. Following General Jean-Jacques Dessalines's decisive defeat of French forces in the Battle of Vertières in 1803, a Swiss family attempts to make their way across the island to escape from the city's port. After hiding his extended family in the wilderness, the character Gustav von der Ried seeks provisions and shelter from the plantation of Congo Hoango, a leader of the slave revolt, who is currently not at home. It is here that Gustav comes into contact with the "Mulattinn" Babekan and her "Mestize" daughter Toni. Through their conversations, we learn that Toni was born in France to a French father who denied his paternity. We discover further that Congo Hoango and Babekan force Toni to lure in white travelers—who are comforted by the relative whiteness of her skin—in order to then trap and murder them. While Toni is initially complicit in this plot, she is seduced by Gustav and henceforth considers herself "betrothed" to him following an unarrated moment of sexual union from which the story takes its title.[49] When Congo Hoango returns unexpectedly, Toni ties up her betrothed in order to feign allegiance to the Black rebel cause. Gustav misreads this as an act of betrayal and shoots

Toni in the chest as soon as he is unbound. Upon realizing his mistake, Gustav then shoots himself in the mouth. In a series of tumultuous events, Gustav's family members then manage to escape without him to Switzerland, where they erect a monument in the memory of Gustav and Toni's love.

In the introduction to his translation, Ali offers not a narrative summary but rather a brief history of the European colonization of Haiti. Beginning with Spain's "discovery" of the island in 1492, Ali then describes the Fench occupation of its Western side in the seventeenth century and the events of the Haitian Revolution. Noting the near annihilation of the island's native population by 1533,[50] Ali details Spain's decision to enslave peoples from Africa in order to continue its agricultural pratices in the Carribean. While noting the significant "mixing" of races from the seventeenth century onward, Ali notes that Black and biracial subjects did not enjoy the same rights as whites but were rather subject to "terrible treatment.[51] In his discussion of the Haitian Revolution, Ali specifically notes how the French Revolution inspired slaves to demand their own freedom. In doing so, he also points to the limits of European universalism and Enlightenment categories such as freedom. He then goes on to detail the following turbulent time period in which Blacks were granted equal rights only to then see those rights rescinded. In the few sentences that directly address *Engagement*, Ali notes how the novella appears to conform to popular European portrayals of the Haitian Revolution, which viewed the slave revolt as an act of brutality against the white population.[52] In conclusion, Ali nevertheless argues that Kleist *does* expose the tyranny endemic to white colonials' brutal treatment of the African slave population, which led to the Haitian Revolution.[53] Ali's use of the word *zulüm*—meaning oppression, persecution, or tyranny—points to the second page of Kleist's novella; here Kleist uses the word "tyranny" (*Tyrannei*) to describe the process of "wresting" slaves from their homelands.[54]

Contemporary scholarship is conflicted about the extent to which Kleist's novella allows for a complex coming to terms with the power dynamics of racism and colonialism in the nineteenth century. In an early treatment of race in *Engagement*, for example, Sander Gilman reads the novella as a response to the aesthetics of Blackness in eighteenth-century theories of perception. Among others, Gilman cites Edmund Burke, who viewed darkness as a source of terror that could lead to the sublime. Noting Burke's anthropomorphization of blackness as a Black subject to be feared, Gilman shows how his writings also raised the question of how the Black subject could tolerate the sight of himself. This question came to a head in the writings of Kant, who argued that the Black subject could tolerate himself due only to the fact that he was void of aesthetic sensibility.[55] In his reading of *Engagement*, Gilman reads Gustav as a character who resorts to a rigid and historically determined aesthetics of Blackness. Whereas Toni declares herself to be white in the final pages of the novella—and thus also buys into the same rigid system of belief—Gustav relegates her to her reality as Black in order to sustain his predetermined assumption of her betrayal. Despite the rigidity of these characters' assumptions, Gilman reads the tragic ending of *Engagement*, "as an indictment of a system of aesthetics outmoded and rejected by the beginning of the nineteenth century."[56] For Gilman, Kleist's novella thus reveals its tragic ending to be the result of faulty universal belief systems.

In a more recent reading of the novella, Vance Byrd takes an intersectional approach. Highlighting the "intercategorical complexity" of Kleist's characters, Byrd notes how their actions are informed by factors as diverse as age, gender, sexuality, property ownership, and colonial status. As a result, characters' subject positions are constantly shifting in accordance with the specific situation and relationship they find themselves within.[57] Across the arc of the novella, this serves to both produce ambiguities and erase the brutalities of slavery and colonialism. In the opening pages of *Engagement*, for example, we learn how Congo Hoango's former master, Herrn Guillaume von Villeneuve, first grants him freedom, then appoints him as overseer of the plantation and "provides" him with Babekan and Toni in place of a more conventional marriage. In his narration of this sequence of events, Kleist reverts to the language of racial stereotpyes to differentiate Congo Hoango from his white master. Villeneuve is described as showering his former slave with benefactions (*Wohltaten*), whereas Congo Hoango is refered to as dreadful (*fürchterlich*) and ferocious (*grimmig*) and his desire for revenge as inhuman (*unmenschlich*). Despite the vocabulary of this opening section, the act of granting Congo Hoango his freedom is not simply a beneficious act. As Byrd aptly shows, manumission is an act that can never be reciprocated; what appears at first to be an act of gratitude is thus actually one of domination, as Congo Hoango becomes indebted to his prior master.[58] In his reading of the novella's ending in particular, Byrd views the memorialization of Toni and Gustav in Switzerland as a rewriting of their story, which "erases the historical and political circumstances that surrounded their murder/suicide" and exchanges their "intercategorical ambiguity [for a] single status."[59]

As just these two competing interpretations reveal, *Engagement* is a text ripe with contradictions. In the following, I focus specifically on the significance of translating these contradictions into the context of the humanist reforms in 1940s Turkey. By highlighting key tensions between the content and mode of Kleist's narration, I first demonstrate how Ali's translation picks up on these tensions, in order to then examine their repercussions in his final novel, *Madonna*. Ali's translation of *Engagement*, I argue, raises pointed questions about the role and purpose of translations from Western European literatures into Turkish at that time. Whereas Turkish humanist reforms sought to forge a uniquely Turkish national identity via the contradictory emulation of a projected European universality, *Engagement* does not uphold a universal European identity or a patriotic expression of Germanness. It reveals, rather, the fracture lines of both European and German identities at the turn of the century. As such, I argue that *Engagement* did provide Ali the means with which to challenge prevailing paradigms of universality in early republican Turkey.

Kleist composed *Engagement* in 1811, following Napoleon's occupation of German lands in 1806. In this regard, it is significant that Gustav is neither German nor French but rather Swiss.[60] As a member of the French army and a citizen of a country that was also occupied by France, Gustav plays a double role: he is both a victim and a perpetrator of French imperialism, who passes for the enemy within the slave revolt. Read in this vein, the introduction of *Engagement* into the Turkish literary canon in the 1940s has subversive implications regarding the historically important role Germany in particular played for key Turkish reformers of the early twentieth century. Nineteenth-century German humanism and philology provided an important model for the Darülfünun, to the extent that faculty worried it was becoming too German. İsmail Hakkı Baltacıoğlu (1886–1978), a professor of pedagogy who later became president of the university, feared a form of foreign infiltration: he warned against the dangers of remaining German (*Alman kalmak*), appearing German (*Alman görünmek*), and working in German (*Almanca çalışmak*).[61]

In contrast, the leading architect of Turkish nationalism, Ziya Gökalp, understood the German model as crucial for both a successful restructuring of the university and the establishment of a Turkish national consciousness. In his 1916 article "The Question of Education" ("Maarif Meselesi"), Gökalp argues that a German national conscience (*millî vicdan*) came into being via the rejection of French cultural dominance. Just as Germans could not discover their essential character while striving to imitate the French, he concludes, neither could a Turkish national literature come into being with-out excising a lingering Persian and more recent French influence. While Gökalp strictly warns against all forms of cultural imitation, he suggests that Turkish literature should follow the German example in establishing its own national preferences and tastes.[62]

A story such as *Engagement* complicates the idea of what it means to follow a "German" model. While it can be read in response to the French occupation of Germany, it in no way posits an authentic German national character. On the contrary, its tragic interracial love story—populated by characters who cannot be clearly defined along racial or national lines, regardless of their own attempts at self-characterization—engages in processes of cultural translation that undermine its potential to represent a unified understanding of Germanness.[63]

The question of what it means to translate such racial and cultural hybridities into the heightened nationalism of 1940s Turkey takes on new meanings within the translation rhetoric of this time period. Already in 1935, Hilmi Ziya Ülken's concept of "complete translation" (*tam tercüme*) perpetuated an image of the West as a fixed, monolithic entity that could be translated at face value. In 1940, İsmail Habib Sevük developed a concept of Europe as complete (*tam Avrupa*), which designated a canon of timeless world literary texts. According to Sevük, textual participation in European civilization was premised on the "entire" translation of Western antiquity. As such, the rhetoric of completion and entirety predicated a republican belief in the smooth translatability of Western European values into the repub-lican context.[64] Notably, while significant debate existed on the method and practice of translation, almost all Turkish intellectuals of the time called for a systematic translation movement that could counter "haphaz-ard" and "disorganized" translation practices of the past. This emphasis on systematicity underscored again an investment in completeness vis-à-vis both Europe and the Ottoman past. As a text riddled with question marks, narrative gaps, and misreadings, *Engagement* upends this investment in systematicity and indeed our very ability to treat a text—let alone Euro-pean or more vaguely defined "Western" values—as a semantic whole.

SAN DOMINGO'DA BIR NIŞANLANMA AND RAIF'S INNER WORLD

The fatal attraction between Gustav and Toni develops within a complex matrix of colonial power relations and racial tensions. Ordered by her mother to lull the fugitive Gustav into a false sense of security, Toni never-theless sympathizes with and is drawn to him.[65] In an initial attempt to test her loyalty, Gustav also finds himself enamored by Toni's youthful coun-tenance and likens her to his deceased beloved. What follows is a crucial, unnarrated moment in which an implied sexual encounter marks a turn-ing point for the story. Toni and Gustav's physical union is marked by a textual absence that simultaneously points to an unspoken speech act of engagement from which the story takes its title.

Following a tearful embrace, Kleist writes: "Was weiter erfolgte, brauchen wir nicht zu melden, weil es jeder, der an diese Stelle kommt, von selbst lies't."[66] ("There is no need to describe what then happened, as everyone who has come to this point can read it for himself.") In the spirit of the *Ansatzpunkt*, this moment of nonnarration clearly has a radiating power within *Engagement*'s textual unfolding. It leads to a series of crucial misreadings that ultimately incite Gustav to accuse Toni of prostitution and betrayal. In a moment of confusion, he shoots her in the chest, just below the cross pendant he had offered to her as a sign of their engagement. Upon realizing his mistake, Gustav shortly thereafter commits suicide by shoot-ing himself.

In asking what it means to translate a moment of nonnarration, I turn to Ali's rendition of this passage into Turkish: "Bundan sonra ne olduğunu söylemeye lüzum yok çünkü buraya kadar gelen herkes alt tarafını kendiliğinden okur."[67] A literal translation of this passage would read: "There is no need to say what happened next, because everyone who has come this far can figure out the rest." Ali's use of *alt tarafı* (after all) in the accusative form, *alt tarafını*, nevertheless calls attention to the phrase's potential spatial implications, suggesting a meaning such as subtext—or literally "underside."[68] This would open up the meaning of this phrase to something like "everyone who has come this far can read the subtext for himself." It is of course impossible to know if Ali intended this particular meaning. The ambiguity of this passage nevertheless attests to the histor-ical juncture in which Ali was writing, during which the newly reformed Turkish language was still very much in flux. Just as acts of translation were central to the establishment of a new discursive center for Turkish soci-ety, translators played a crucial role in defining the parameters of the new language by both testing and expanding its limits of expression.

The ambiguity of meaning encapsulated by the phrase *alt tarafını* also opens up a commentary on what it means to read the ambiguous and contradictory nature of Kleist's text as a whole. It points to the existence of textual layerings that work both with and against one another. *Engagement* is marked by myriad textual inconsistencies. These range from semantic issues (such as missing, misplaced, or open-ended quotation marks) to orthographic differences in character names (Gustav is alternately referred to as August) and contradictory narrative information. Congo Hoango, for example, is said to raze his master's plantation to the ground in the initial slave revolt, only to then inhabit its main house several pages later. Much more than potential mistakes or flaws, such inconsistencies point to a heightened level of semantic ambiguity. They set up situations in which the narrative drives characters' actions on the surface, even while such actions undermine the very meaning of the language in which they are expressed.

Ali's translation of another key scene in *Engagement* clearly draws out the semantic ambiguity of Kleist's German. Following their implied sexual encounter, Gustav gives Toni a necklace with a cross pendant. Ali's translation of this "engagement gift"—which attests to an otherwise unspoken engagement—as a *nişan hediyesi*[69] conveniently plays on the double meanings of *nişan* as both "engagement" and "target." Indeed, the place where the cross lies on Toni's chest marks the spot where Gustav shoots her later in the story, after he misreads her actions as a sign of betrayal.

Given that *nişan* was the standard word for engagement at the time, this is certainly a unique coincidence. Yet this does not detract from the double meanings *nişan* accrues in the context of Ali's translation, which amplifies the ambiguities of Kleist's novella. As such, this single word *nişan* embodies Ali's own reflections on the act of translation: "The language of a work of art, as opposed to that of other written works, is a living being. In the course of translation and the transfer of its words' meanings, this life perishes, leaving only a chain of dead words behind. The real translator can give this lifeless matter a new life in the language it has been transferred to. . . . The translator must not forget that he has undertaken a debt of consciousness and a serious responsibility toward the author of the work in question, and the public he wants to present the work to."[70] Here Ali figures the initial act of linguistic transfer (*nakil etmek/nakletmek*) as one that literally takes the life of a living work of art. Real translation, he argues, cannot remain at the level of transfer but must then enliven the dead words of the literary text. This is the ethical responsibility of the translator to both the author and the public.

In the context of *Engagement*, the text's "new life" in translation is provocative on several levels. Other leading intellectuals, such as İsmail Habib Sevük, argued for translating literary classics into Turkish over the learning of foreign languages. But couched within this argument was the assertion that European values could only be properly reflected in translation once Turks had gained the highest level of proficiency in their own language.[71] This is but one key example of how debate often centered on the perceived inability of the Turkish language to properly convey European values. In the context of *Engagement*, a word such as *nişan* shows, on the contrary, how Turkish could accurately reflect the contentious and ambiguous qualities of the "classics" rather than some essential quality they were otherwise imagined to represent. If, in the case of *Engagement*, such ambiguities serve to ultimately place the universality of European concepts such as freedom into question, Ali's translation also undermines a republican era tendency to universalize a broadly construed "West" in order to then forge a uniquely Turkish national identity via the translation of such concepts into Turkish.

The nonnarrated sexual union between Gustav and Toni presents another critical instance of contradiction in the German text, in that it asks us to read a moment of nonnarration. Andreas Gailus analyzes this aspect of the text as an "unmooring" of language, or a paradoxical situation in which we are asked "to *stop* reading the text, stop reading the semantic and typographical signs of absence and discontinuity the text puts before us."[72] In support of this argument, Gailus argues that we cannot overlook Kleist's use of outmoded typography: the verb *lies't* (in place of *lieset*, to read) contains a contractual elision that marks the very gap the passage asks us to ignore and thus runs counter to the sentence in which it is embedded. In short, the text foregrounds its own incompleteness by pointing to potential events that occur outside the frame of narration. In the following, I read this moment of nonnarration as an *Ansatzpunkt* for exploring the complex relationship of *Engagement* to *Madonna*.

Madonna details the experiences of its main character, Raif, in Weimar-era Berlin, where he is sent by his father to learn the soap trade. While in Berlin, Raif falls in love with the German-Jewish woman Maria, whom he first encounters in the form of her self-portrait at an exhibition of contemporary artists. *Madonna* depicts the development of their relationship in loving detail over the span of multiple conversations and monologues. Maria and Raif's feelings for one another then come to a head at a frenzied New Year's Eve celebration, following which Maria suddenly declares her love for Raif. An implied sexual encounter takes the form of a gap in the narration, which marks both the apex and temporary breaking point of their relationship. It leads to a silence between the lovers, who find themselves at a loss for words in one another's presence. These double silences in the text address a problem of referentiality. Feeling suddenly estranged from Raif, Maria repeatedly attempts but finds herself unable to explicitly refer to their moment of sexual union.[73]

In considering the relationship of these sexual encounters to one another, it is notable that *Engagement* and *Madonna* employ markedly different methods of narration. In his introduction to the translation, Ali accurately describes *Engagement* as a text that hinges on the power of the event (*vaka*); it is in the carrying out of key events that the complex and contradictory nature of Kleist's characters comes to the fore.[74] *Madonna* is, on the contrary, a text driven by descriptive detail, long conversational passages, and the psychological development of its main characters. Considering the otherwise divergent nature of these texts, what does it mean for *Engagement* and *Madonna* to converge precisely on a narrative gap?

In answering this question, I argue that *Madonna* also contains an inverted counterpart to the textual elision of Raif and Maria's sexual encounter: the text of Raif's dairy, which records the story of his youth in Weimar-era Berlin and which we receive, word for word, as the internal narrative of *Madonna*. At the close of the external narrative that opens the novel—in which the narrator and Raif slowly become friends through their positions at a local bank—Raif becomes deathly ill. After asking the narrator to retrieve a small black notebook from his work desk, Raif then pleads with him to throw it into the fire of his stove. Raif's desire to have this notebook destroyed—an act that would silence his own transcultural life story—points us back to both the moment of textual silence that marks his relationship with Maria and the crucial narrative elision in *Engagement*. In defiance of Raif's request, the narrator opens the notebook. Taking in the large and disorderly (*iri ve intizamsız*) handwriting, the narrator notices first the date—June 20, 1933—and then the opening sentence. In a rush, he then states, "*alt tarafını* okuyamadım"[75] (my emphasis) to suggest that he could not read the lines below. This literal use of the phrase *alt tarafını* to refer to the spatial makeup of the page sets up another connection between Ali's translation of *Engagement* and *Madonna*. Metaphorically, it also points to the layers and depths of Raif's life story, which the narrator will eventually internalize through the practice of reading.

Within *Madonna*, the act of reading Raif's life story is nevertheless incommensurate with knowing or even getting to know Raif in a more casual sense. Reading is figured not as a process of filling in the gaps but rather as a process of being confronted with gaps. As a counterpoint to the nonnarrated moment of Raif and Maria's sexual encounter, the text of Raif's notebook figures the act of reading as a cross-cultural encounter that can take us into the realm of the unknown. Ali already introduces this kind of reading practice on the first page of *Madonna*, when the narrator comments on the mundane qualities of Raif's appearance, only to then state that in order to truly know a person, we must first delve below the level of the external: "We never entertain the thought that they might have ... a whole internal universe of their own making. What if we stopped assuming that, just because they don't express their inner world to others, they're not living a fulfilled life? The fundamental desires of human curiousity would stoke in us a need to satisfy our wonder, and we'd suddenly be able to see things we didn't at all suspect, to discover a complexity we never thought existed."[76] In the process of delving below the surface, however, the narrator does not discover some essential aspect of Raif's character. It leads him rather to multiple levels of disorder. At work, for example, the narrator discovers a quick sketch Raif has made of their mutual boss. The complexity and depth of this sketch suddenly lead him to perceive the multiple contrasts (*tezatlar*) that make up Raif's character.[77] These contrasts are replicated in spatial terms during the narrator's first visit to Raif's house. Whereas Raif's in-laws have carefully staged the parlor with expensive items to lend the room a more bourgeois feel, his own bedroom is described as surprisingly chaotic: clothing, dirty dishes, and empty medicine bottles fill every corner, leaving no space for the narrator to even find a seat.[78] Toward the close of the frame narrative, the narrator then reflects on how even the simplest of human beings may have a magnificent (*müthiş*) and complex (*karışık*) soul,[79] a comment I can only read in relation to the character of Raif. Ali's use of the word *karışık* here could imply a number of attributes, including mixed up, disorderly, or even hybrid. To read Raif's life story, I argue, is to be confronted with precisely these disorderly and hybrid qualities of his character.

In this regard, it is notable that Raif is coded as outdated within *Madonna*. Rather than the European-influenced *bey*, meaning mister, Raif is referred to with the outdated Ottoman title of respect *efendi*. Within the modern Ankara bank where he works as a translator, he is figured as both out of place and out of sync with the times. In this way, Raif also stands in contrast to metaphors of Ankara as the new capital of modern Turkey. Publications of the early republican era represented Ankara as both the heart and the mother of the new nation because of its geographic centrality and its symbolic status as a capital city that was built at the founding of the republic. The newness and cleanliness of Ankara was contrasted with portrayals of Istanbul as old-fashioned and unclean, and the order of Ankara's streets was pitted against the chaos of the historic capital city of the Ottoman Empire.[80] Raif's place of residence on the outskirts of Ankara upends this image of an orderly capital city: making his way to Raif's house on foot, the narrator passes through narrow neighborhoods with damaged sidewalks, only to finally discover Raif's house standing alone among piles of sand and rocks.[81] At the same time, the figure of Raif does not represent a nostalgic approach to the pre-republican era. His childhood memories are marked rather by the turbulence of the Balkan Wars, World War I, and the Turkish War of Independence.

The messiness and complex nature of Raif's inner character stands in critical contrast not just to the projected orderliness of the modern republic but also to the image of Europe itself. Upon arriving in Berlin, Raif eagerly explores its museums, parks, and cafés, only to quickly be overcome by a feeling of despair. Observing Berlin's wide streets and masses of people but also smaller details like the smiles on women's faces as they lean against their companions, Raif ultimately concludes, "Europe! So what?" and thus declares the world (*dünya*) to be an essentially boring place.[82] This naïve utterance—based on the localization of Europe in Berlin—draws a comic equivalence between Europe and the world. Whereas the Translations from World Literature series largely presented "world" literature as European, and thereby partook in the strategic universalization of a more loosely defined "West," here Ali aligns Europe with the "world" only to question a republican desire to emulate it in translation.

In the face of such disenchantment, Raif turns to books. With the help of a dictionary, he begins to read the Russian classics in German. Devouring this literature, Raif feels as if a new world were opening before his eyes, as the books he reads give sudden meaning to his life. Raif's reading practice echoes his childhood, during which he also devoured the classics of Russian and French literature in translation, much to the chagrin of his father, who would turn the lights out on Raif at night. For the young Raif, reading was a means of discovering other worlds in order to escape the realities of war-torn Turkey in the aftermath of World War I. While literature provides Raif with the initial means to overcome his boredom with Europe as an adult, the literature of his childhood is thus figured as the very *source* of this disenchantment as well. Upon first arriving in Berlin, Raif remarks on the incommensurability of his childhood textual experiences of Europe with the realities of this actual city: "Ultimately, this was just another city. A city with wider streets—much cleaner, and with blonder people. But there wasn't much about it that would make a person swoon in awe. For my part, I was still . . . unaware what kind of a thing the Europe of my dreams really was, and how much the city I was now living in lacked, in comparison to that image. . . . It hadn't yet dawned on me how the mind can conjure the most improbable projections."[83] Raif's response ties into Sabahattin Ali's own personal history and his position as a translator for the state. Ali's closest friends recall his unbridled passion for reading—sparked in part by the diverse literature he discovered via the German language. While Ali broke off his studies in Germany after only one and a half years, his experiences abroad made an indelible impact on his life and work. The German language did not serve as a point of departure solely into German literature and culture; Ali also read the great works of Russian literature—such as those by Gogol, Tolstoy, Turgenev, Chekhov, and Gorky—in German translation and translated works of antiquity— such as Sophocles's *Antigone*—into Turkish from German. In contrast to a reductive textualization of Europe as an essentialized idea, Ali's textual experience of Europe attests to a mutual and omnidirectional mediation of literatures through their international circulation and translation. Similarly, in *Madonna*, I read Ali's textualization of Europe as a testament to the power of Raif's imagination and the fact that literature is never a direct reflection of reality. If Turkish intellectuals such as Hilmi Ziya Ülken and İsmail Habib Sevük textualized Europe in order to underscore its universality, Raif's localized disenchantment with Berlin exposes the projection of a universal Europe as fantasy.

CIVILIZED ENCOUNTERS, IMPURE MIXTURES

If, in Ali's terms, to translate is to bring a text to life in a new language, he does so, precisely by exploring new semantic ambiguities—like those of *alt tarafı* and *nişan*—that highlight the textual surfaces and substructures of Kleist's novella.[84] Just as *Engagement* asks us to read a moment of nonnarration, the kind of translation Ali endorses is closely tied to the ability to read through the double meanings and potentially contradictory layers within a given text. As such, Ali's translation practice enacts the kind of double dislocation Theo Hermans describes as "thick translation," whereby concepts in both the source and target languages are unhinged from their apparent meanings. Hermans builds here on Clifford Geertz's notion of "thick description," which resists universalizing tendencies by actively reflecting on the interpretive and constructivist nature of an ethnographer's observations. In recognizing that acts of translation, interpretation, and description play out in the same discursive space, Hermans's concept of "thick translation" resists the imposition of categorical definitions. In working from the bottom up—rather than from the top down—"thick translation contains within it both the acknowledgment of the impossibility of total translation and an unwillingness to appropriate the other through translation even as translation is taking place."[85]

In conclusion, I argue that through intertextual references within *Madonna* that are tied to his translation of Kleist, Ali foregrounds and invites a similar process of reading as cross-cultural interpretation. Following the implied sexual encounter in *Madonna* and Maria's expression of her inability to love another human being, Raif wanders blindly through the streets of Berlin until he reaches the southernmost limits of the city. In a key turning point for the novel, he finally takes notice of his surroundings. On the shore of Berlin's Wannsee, he recognizes the spot where Kleist and his lover, Henriette Vogel, had committed suicide in 1811, a date that incidentally also marks the publication of *Engagement*.

This famous suicide pact—in which Kleist first shot his lover and then himself—serves not as a clear point of reference for Raif and Maria's relationship but rather as a bitter point of inversion. In contrast to Maria's assertion that two people can never really become one, Raif imagines the lovers Heinrich and Henrietta, with a bullet through the temples and chest, respectively, their blood streaming and mixing into a single pool at his feet.[86] In a self-deprecating fantasy, he imagines first calling Maria, then shooting himself in the head, so that he might listen to her saying his name as he lies, dying, in a pool of his own blood. Only in this way would she "understand that, to the end of her days she would never forget me, that I'd bound myself to her memory with my blood."[87]

The manner in which Kleist committed suicide is also eerily reminiscent of the suicide in *Engagement*, in which Gustav first murders Toni by shooting her in the chest and then kills himself out of remorse with a bullet through the head. Indeed, Raif's bitter fantasy also recalls the image of Toni writhing in her own pool of blood at the close of Kleist's novella. This intertextual reference, together with Ali's multiple visual references to blood, leads me to consider the stakes of Raif and Maria's intercultural relationship in *Madonna*. While this novel is consistently read as a tragic love story, scholarship has not questioned the significance of Raif and Maria's specific backgrounds to the development of the narrative. Yet in one of their first excursions together, Maria brings Raif to the Botanical Gardens in Berlin, where she compares the strange and uprooted plants it houses to her Jewish ancestors.[88] Through this conversation, we learn that Maria's father was a Jew born in Prague, who converted to Christianity before she was born. It seems no coincidence that Maria shortly thereafter describes her mother as "a Protestant of pure German blood."[89] How is this depiction of Maria as the child of an interracial couple—replete with its reference to "pure" German blood—potentially related to the *mixing* of blood in the crucial scene where Raif envisions Kleist's suicide? In other words, how is Raif's fantasy of his own union with Maria—in which she becomes bound to him in memory by blood—also the projection of an impure mixture and a commentary on the kinds of hybridities and interracial couplings Kleist employs in *Engagement*?

Ali's recourse to the rhetoric of purity offers a clear reference to the racial politics of National Socialism at the time of *Madonna*'s publication in the early 1940s. Raif's notebook is furthermore composed in June of 1933, a year that marked the official end of the Weimar Republic and Adolf Hitler's systematic consolidation of power. With regard to these historical implications, I return again to the question of what it means for Ali to translate the key moment of nonnarration in *Engagement*, which marks the implied sexual union between Toni and Gustav. In addition to the text of Raif's black notebook, I suggest that this moment of nonnarration finds a second inverted counterpart at the close of *Madonna*'s internal narrative through the event that finally leads Raif to document his life in Berlin. A chance encounter with Frau von Tiedemann, owner of the boarding house where Raif lived in Berlin, leads him to discover the existence of his ten-year-old daughter. Described as "thin," "still," and "silent,"[90] this girl serves as a ghostly physical testament to Raif's relationship with Maria, whom he now learns passed away shortly after giving birth.

The moment of nonnarration that marks both Gustav and Toni's and Raif and Maria's sexual encounters is translated into the silence of this small child. Whereas the love story in *Engagement* reveals a crisis in German identity in the face of French imperialism prior to the establishment of the German nation-state, Ali gestures, through this child, to the colonial power structures within which Raif's relationship to Maria is embedded in the twentieth century. Frau von Tiedemann—who is incidentally Maria's cousin—reveals that she is traveling through Ankara en route to Berlin along the Berlin-Baghdad Railway. Her Prussian husband, Herr Döppke, whom she describes as a colonial merchant,[91] is now involved in the date trade in Iraq. Recalling her husband's previous experience with the date trade in the German colony of Cameroon, Raif notes perplexedly that Baghdad is not a German colony. To this, Frau von Tiedemann replies in condescendingly generalized terms: "My husband specializes in the produce of warm contries."[92]

In contrast to the kind of cultural essentialization Frau von Tiedemann expresses here, *Madonna* highlights the hybridities of both Turkishness and Germanness via its interrelationship with *Engagement*. This relationship goes far beyond a simplistic form of cross-referencing. It points rather to translation, interpretation, and reading as intricately connected processes of epistemological destabilization. These connections crystalize around moments of narrative elision, which I read as an unlikely *Ansatzpunkt* from which to approach the specific interrelationship of *Engagement* and *Madonna*. More generally, my readings demonstrate the inextricable connection between Ali's translation practice to his work as author. They reveal that, for Ali, translation was not a secondary activity tied to the simple transfer of an external textual entity into a new linguistic and cultural realm. It was rather an act of creation with powerful, radiating consequences.

Whereas in 1952, Auerbach depicted the radiating power of the *Ansatzpunkt* as a means toward viewing, dealing with, and ordering world history, the linked narrative silences in both *Engagement* and *Madonna* point to a messy, radiating power that is not ordering or synthesizing in nature. This radiating power runs counter to the Translations from World Literature program enacted by the Turkish state, which was premised on a general conceptualization of Western civilization as a synthesizable whole. Whereas this series sought to orient Turkish society toward Europe through the translation of "world" (albiet largely European) literature into Turkish, Ali shows that "world" literature was already intricately connected to "Turkish" literature. This interconnection does not serve, however, as a clear coordinate of orientation. On the contrary, it manifests itself as a process of deep reading that leads us to confront the unknown.

Epilogue

Approximately one hundred years after the initiation of the Turkish Library (Türkische Bibliothek) by German Orientalist and Turkologist Georg Jacob in 1904, the Robert Bosch Foundation launched a twenty-volume translation project of the same name in 2005.[1] Separated by two world wars, an extensive history of Turkish postwar labor migration to West Germany, and the era of globalization, these libraries may seem worlds apart: Ever unsure of funding, Jacob produced each translation in his series as if it were the last. The contemporary Turkish Library was, on the contrary, backed by the Robert Bosch Foundation, the Swiss publisher Unionsverlag, and a 1.58 million euro budget.[2] Riddled with footnotes and parenthetical information, Jacob's series was clearly a scholarly enterprise, its translations circulating mainly within the confines of academia. While the contemporary Turkish Library also struggled to find a readership,[3] it strove to be reader friendly and undertook diverse promotional events, such as reading tours and exhibitions, in order to reach the broadest possible audience.

Despite these key differences, striking continuities are discernable across the century that divides these two libraries. While markedly dissimilar in their translation styles, the contemporary Turkish Library was also headed by two Turkologists: Erika Glassen (University of Freiburg) and Jens Peter Laut (University of Göttingen).[4] In his remarks on the Turkish Library, Laut notes the series' high academic standards;[5] Glassen in turn describes it as an important resource for Turkology departments in particular.[6] While Glassen's intentions for the library were clearly much broader than this, her comments underscore a long-standing practice of translating from (Ottoman) Turkish for specifically academic purposes. They perhaps inadvertently recall the history of an earlier Turkish Library and the significant role philologically minded Turkologists, such as Jacob, played in the assertion of an "authentic" Turkish culture in the transition from a multilingual and multiethnic empire to a Turkish nation-state imagined as monolingual.

Boasting accuracy and fidelity, Jacob expressed the desire to "allow Turkish texts to speak for themselves" in translation. By treating source texts—together with the cultural realm he presumed them to represent—as stable and intact entities, Jacob upheld an understanding of translation as a simplistic mode of reproduction. This viewpoint was underscored in diverse framing materials, which underscored a static image of an "authentic" Turkish cultural realm in need of preservation amid seismic processes of Europeanization in the late Ottoman Empire. Yet the series' simultaneous insistence on translation as one key method of preservation conveniently ignored the important role translations from European source texts had played in initiating a new kind of experimental modern Turkish literature. More importantly, it disregarded the role projects such as the Turkish Library played in asserting this modern literary realm as essentially "Turkish" in the first place.

On the contrary, editors Glassen and Laut pay careful attention to the diversity of styles, genres, and political orientations represented by the contemporary Turkish Library. Texts included in this series range from late Ottoman novels to lyric poetry and from short stories to essays from across the twentieth and twenty-first centuries. Promotional materials nevertheless belie the sociological intentions behind the Turkish Library's inception: The Robert Bosch Foundation describes the library as "presenting milestones of Turkish literature from 1900 to the present," in order to "help the German reader penetrate deeper into the intellectual world of today's Turkey."[7] In her summation of the library's intentions, Glassen further articulates the main goals of the project. Literature, she argues, is eminently suited to present to a German readership the diverse intellectual processes that have formed modern Turkey. Reading Turkish literature in translation, she concludes, can enable readers to better grapple with the specific question of whether or not Turkey belongs to Europe.[8]

Glassen's comments are timely: the launch of the Turkish Library in the summer of 2005 occurred just months before Turkey's application for full membership in the European Union.[9] Turkey joined the Council of Europe in 1949 and the European Economic Community in 1987; it was later recognized as a candidate for full membership in the European Union in 1999. Membership negotiations have nevertheless been continuously stalled and in recent years have come to a complete standstill. While the reasons for this are multifaceted, Turkey's contested status as the single potential Muslim-majority country in the European Union has played a consistently important role in public aversion to its membership. Similarly, while the twenty-first century has brought new forms of critical engagement with Turkish literature and culture, ossified Orientalist stereotypes of Turkey as traditional, as an Islamic Other, or as merely peripheral to conceptions of Germanness and Europeanness persist in the public imaginary.

In the face of such stereotypes, the contemporary Turkish Library selected texts that exemplify the "dynamic cultural and societal changes" that have defined modern Turkish history since the nineteenth century. In Glassen's words, the conceptualization of the Turkish Library was based on the following premise: Turkey's historical "renunciation of its own Eastern tradition," which occurred through a "permanent process of Westernization."[10] While at times gesturing toward Eastern traditions and values, Turkish literature is, in Glassen's estimation, fundamentally caught up in, and thus also constitutive of, the Westernization process. As a primary site of expression for the ensuing conflict between individual and society, literature operates in a field of tension marked by both the crisis of and the search for a new "Turkish" identity.[11]

In contradistinction to this fundamentally dynamic understanding of Turkish (literary) history, the Turkish Library aimed to systematically select texts in order to provide a complete picture (*Gesamtüberblick*) of modern Turkish literature within its limited number of volumes.[12] This emphasis on systematicity was born in part out of necessity. The library sought both to represent previously untranslated literature and to supplement the previously subjective selection of translations from Turkish into German. In order to achieve these goals, Glassen and Laut divided texts into three main categories. The first category includes texts that in some way capture the pulse of their time and have since attained the status of a "classic." Deeply connected to their specific historical contexts, these texts were carefully chosen to represent different decades, generations, and intellectual approaches from across the twentieth century.[13] The second category contains works by younger authors and aims to portray contemporary trends in Turkish literature since 1980. Addressing lyric poetry, essays, and short stories, the third category is made up of five anthologies.

While this approach allows for an impressive breadth of texts, the library's emphasis on systematicity and completeness runs counter to Glassen's dynamic depiction of Turkish literary history. It furthermore recalls another major translation project of the twentieth century: while significantly different in subject matter, the conceptualization of the Turkish Library exhibits striking similarities to the Translations from World Literature series (1940–66) funded by the Turkish government. While the contemporary Turkish Library only produced a fraction of translations in comparison to the Translations from World Literature series, each proposed to fill a gap in translation history through recourse to a program of systematicity. Director and editor Erika Glassen furthermore described the project of the Turkish Library as a form of cultural transfer (*Kulturtransfer*),[14] which strongly echoes the early republican Turkish understanding of translation and its belief in the smooth translatability of Western European humanism into the Turkish context as part of the larger Turkish nation-building project.

More pointedly, Glassen describes second- and third-generation Turkish-German youth as in search of their "cultural roots" or "original homeland" and thus as one target audience for the twenty-first-century Turkish Library.[15] Glassen addresses here the children and grandchildren of Turkish citizens who first came to the Federal Republic of Germany in the 1960s. Following the rapid recuperation of its economy in the postwar era, West Germany initiated bilateral labor agreements with a number of countries in order to ameliorate labor shortages; Turkish workers were first recruited in 1961 and continued to receive short-term work visas up until the 1973 recruitment ban (*Anwerbestopp*). For diverse reasons, large numbers of Turkish "guest workers" decided to remain in West Germany following this ban and, to date, people of Turkish descent constitute the largest ethnic minority in unified Germany.[16]

In the terms of this book, Glassen suggests that the Turkish Library might provide coordinates of cultural orientation for generations of children and grandchildren who were born and raised in Germany but continue to be linked to this history of migration in the public imagination. This suggestion replicates the fallacies that Germany is not a "homeland" for Turkish-Germans and that Turkey might serve as both a primary and a *stable* point of reference for increasingly diverse Turkish-German communities. This raises a plethora of questions relevant to this book: What might it mean for Turkish-Germans to orient themselves toward a presumably stable Turkish homeland? And what, exactly, might they learn from literature-in-translation about their "own" heritage?

Phenomenology assumes that in orienting ourselves toward a stable external referent, we in turn verify our own position in space and time, thus reinforcing the self as the zero-point of orientation. Yet much more than solidify the position of Turkish-Germans, the texts presented in the Turkish Library destabilize both sides of this hyphenated identity. Going far beyond the diversity of texts provided by Jacob and his colleagues, the twenty-first-century Turkish Library boasts a wealth of previously untranslated materials. Ranging from Halit Ziya Uşaklıgil's turn-of-the-century *Forbidden Love* (*Aşk-ı Memnu*, 1900 / *Verbotene Lieben*, 2007) to Ahmet Hamdi Tanınpar's epic depiction of Istanbul in *A Mind at Peace* (*Huzur*, 1949 / *Seelenfrieden*, 2008) and from Leyla Erbil's central text of Turkish feminism *A Strange Woman* (*Tuhaf bir Kadın*, 1971 / *Eine seltsame Frau*, 2010) to Murat Uyurkulak's *Revenge* (*Tol*, 2002 / *Zorn*, 2008), which presents an unofficial history of Turkey since the 1950s from the perspective of the revolutionary left, the contemporary Turkish Library confronts its readers with the complexities and contradictions of the modern Turkish literary landscape.

Sizing up the project in 2011, Ingo Arend accurately described the library as a unique archive of polyphonic and diverse texts, the likes of which has never before been available in German.[17] Indeed, even individual volumes, such as *From Istanbul to Hakkâri: A Round Trip in Stories* (*Von Istanbul nach Hakkari: Eine Rundreise in Geschichten*, 2005), aim to capture a diversity of representations. Incorporating depictions of Turkey from the Mediterranean to the mountains of Anatolia, the Turkish Library describes this anthology of short stories as "a literary tour guide through the diversity of peoples, ways of life, and landscapes" in twentieth- and twenty-first-century Turkey.[18] Dealing furthermore with issues such as gender, individualism and society, existentialism, war and revolution, and the role of Istanbul in modern Turkish literature, the twenty-first-century Turkish Library as a whole uncovers the very contradictions of Turkish literary modernity that make it the unlikely exemplification of an originary "home" culture. If anything, a project such as this reiterates that however the translators or editors seek to orient their readership, the translations themselves hold the power to point in different, more contradictory directions.

By accessing the Turkish Library in translation, readers experience the ruptures and transitions that mark modern Turkish literature through the German language. Unlike contemporary debates on migration and *Leitkultur*, which assert a one-way process of integration predicated on the successful and correct acquisition of the German language, the Turkish Library initiates a more complex process of negotiation between German and (Ottoman) Turkish. Rather than uphold some specific understanding of Turkishness, the medium of the German language propels the multiple processes of translation punctuating Turkish literary history into a new temporal and linguistic context.

These multiple tensions inherent to the contemporary Turkish Library recall its early twentieth-century predecessor. In particular, the question of the Ottoman Empire and Turkey's relative "Europeanness" forms a red thread connecting one series to the other. While Jacob and his colleagues repeatedly emphasize the Europeanizing tendencies of modern Ottoman Turkish literature, for example, his Turkish Library as a whole clearly differentiates the Ottoman Empire from Europe. This is most evident in the series' philological approach to translation, which sought to explicate every aspect of its source texts through the use of footnotes, glosses, and prefaces. Even more than uphold the linguistic difficulty of Ottoman Turkish, this approach gestured toward an impermeably foreign quality of source materials, which required extensive explanation for a German readership. Despite the series' self-professed instrumentalist approach—which upheld translation as a simple process of one-to-one reproduction—the first Turkish Library thus proved incapable of providing an unmediated window into Ottoman Turkish culture for its receiving audience. On the contrary, translators themselves became implicated in the Ottoman modernization process by rendering works of modern Ottoman Turkish literature into a Central European language.

Projects like the twentieth- and twenty-first-century Turkish Libraries exemplify the diverse modes of orientation at work in all translations. While framing materials in particular often seek to orient readerships in a specific direction, translations themselves subject texts to new and unexpected references, thereby opening them to new potential interpretations. As such, translation is never a neutral enterprise but rather carries deep ethical implications. In the words of Esra Akcan, "translation is the very medium that exposes not only the formal but also the epistemological and ethical dimensions of cultural interactions."[19] It reveals inequalities, geopolitical tensions, and psychological anxieties, while also enabling new forms of cultural interaction.

While attending to the tensions and anxieties undergirding the specific German–(Ottoman) Turkish relationship, it is this productive and enabling force of translation that I have sought to emphasize throughout the case studies in this book. The diverse translations, literature, essays, scholarship, and journal articles I examine do not exist in a vacuum. On the contrary, they are deeply connected to the histories of German Orientalism and (Ottoman) Turkish modernizing reforms from which they emerged. The specific archive I have assembled attests not only to deep interconnections between these two histories but also to myriad other forms of German–(Ottoman) Turkish interconnection, which provide the grounds from which to rewrite the basic premises of Orientalism and Westernization, respectively. This involves an interrogation of the terms of orientation on multiple levels: Through my focus on figures such as Johann Wolfgang von Goethe and Friedrich Schrader, I suggest that "Western" Orientalists cannot so easily orient themselves vis-à-vis their subject matter or fixate the "East" in space and time in order to ensure their own secure position outside of it. At the same time, I have shown how "Eastern" authors, such as Sabahattin Ali, upend the assumption that Westernizing reforms in the modern Republic of Turkey might take the "West" as a stable point of reference for the purposes of cultural orientation. As the complex relationship between his own novelistic and translation practices attest, the Turkish and European literary spheres of his time were both deeply interconnected and equally marked by cultural hybridities that did not conform to clear-cut coordinates of orientation. On the contrary, his translation practice did not necessarily orient itself toward a presumed "original" that it followed in space and time. Like the numerous other translations analyzed in this book, they constitute instead a creative act with the power to renegotiate the very terms of originality by linking diverse traditions, times, and places via their omnidirectional trajectories.

Notes

1. The author in question is Vâsıf-ı Enderunî (1771–1824).

2. For an excellent discussion of the history of the term *züppe*, see Gürbilek, "Dandies and Originals," 609, 626.

3. Tanpınar describes *Carriage* as a "köksüz gölgeler kitabı" and refers to Bihruz Bey as "az mevcut bir insandır." Tanpınar, *XIX. Asır*, 442.

4. "Bütün roman bir şakaya benzer." Ibid., 444.

5. Tanpınar writes, "Görülüyor ki Ekrem Bey, *Araba Sevdası*'nda gençlik senelerinin kronolojisini yapmak istemişti. Hiçbir muharrir yoktur ki, kendi neslinin hikâyesini bir defa olsun yapmasın." Ibid., 441. He later adds, "Zaten kitap, yer yer devir tenkidiyle bu çağ psikolojisi arasında sallanır." Ibid., 443.

6. Tanpınar writes, "Bu romanda izahı biraz güç olan tek mesele kitabın roman bünyesine uygun ilk Türk eseri olmasıdır." Ibid., 441.

7. "Bir Türk romanı niçin yoktur?" ("Why is there no Turkish novel?"). Tanpınar, "Bizde Roman I," 33.

8. Tanpınar uses the word "yokluk" in the forms "yokluğu" and "yokluğundan." Ibid., 33, 34. He also describes Turkish literature as weak, barren, and anemic in this essay. For a discussion of Tanpınar's fixation with authenticity, see Moran, *Türk Romanına Eleştirel Bir Bakış*, 242.

9. "Müşterek vasıfları cemiyet ve hayatımızla Türk insanı ve onun mes'eleleriyle olan alâkasından gelen ve beraberinde taşıdığı hava ile birbirine en uzak nümûnelerinde bile bir bütünlük gösteren bir Türk romanı." Tanpınar, "Bizde Roman I," 33.

10. "Kendimize, kendi hayatımıza, mazimize, zenginliklerimize dönmek." Tanpınar, "Millî Bir Edebiyata Doğru," 82. Through the concept of return, Tanpınar sought to salvage specific aspects of the past for an explicitly Kemalist form of Turkishness in the present. To this end, Tanpınar's narrow understanding of Turkishness does not account for the complexity of the nineteenth-century literary landscape, which also involved non-Sunni Turcophone communities, including writers of Armeno-Turkish and Greek-scripted Ottoman Turkish. For an insightful discussion of how Tanpınar's scholarship has shaped and limited subsequent approaches to the study of nineteenth- and twentieth-century Turkish literature, see Mignon, "Tanpınar Kadar," 133–46.

11. For a discussion of Tanpınar's approach toward synthesis, see Göknar, "Ottoman Past," 648.

12. For a comprehensive discussion of the terms of belatedness in relation to the Turkish novel, see Gürbilek, "Dandies and Originals." For a discussion of belatedness in relation to the terms of translation, see Seyhan, *Tales of Crossed Destinies*, 8.

13. Novels were not always translated directly from European languages. In 1864, for example, Ahmet Lütfi Efendi translated *Robinson Crusoe* from Arabic into Ottoman Turkish. The first novels written in Ottoman Turkish were furthermore published in the Armenian script. Mignon, "Tanpınar Kadar," 143.

14. Göknar, "Ottoman Past," 648.

15. Husserl describes the body as "the bearer of the zero point of orientation, the bearer of the here and the now." Husserl, *Ideas*, 61.

16. While underscoring Turkishness as an inherently hybrid construction, this book also pays heed to the important role translations played in defining the contours of Turkishness in cultural, linguistic, and national terms. In this sense, my reference to a "Turkish" history of translation deserves further explanation. In the early twentieth century, the words "Turk" and "Turkish" were reclaimed from their status as derogatory terms for uneducated peasants and rendered into a designation of pride (see Arnakis, "Turanism," 25). By referring to a "Turkish" history of translation in this book, I gesture both toward this process and toward the contested nature of an essentialized understanding of Turkishness that emerged in the twentieth century. While recognizing that the adjective "Turkish" includes a broader set of

nineteenth-century authors—including those writing in Armeno-Turkish and Greek-scripted Ottoman Turkish—this book focuses on the scholarship and translations of Ottoman Turkish authors writing in the Perso-Arabic script. My depiction of a "Turkish" history of translation from the mid-nineteenth through the mid-twentieth century furthermore runs counter to the dominant narrative in which 1923 marks a fundamental breaking point with the Ottoman past. Early republican Turkish authors sought at times to vehemently distinguish themselves from Ottoman Turkish literary norms, while simultaneously searching for pre-Ottoman Turkic predecessors. I seek, on the contrary, to emphasize continuities between translation activity in the late Ottoman Empire and the modern Republic of Turkey.

17. Ahmed, "Orientations," 551.

18. Ibid., 544–45.

19. "(In ermangelung der Magnetnadel) aus einer bekannten Weltgegend die übrigen, namentlich die östliche zu finden suchen." Quoted in Stegmaier, *Philosophie der Orientierung*, 61.

20. Tymoczko, *Translation in a Postcolonial Context*, 140.

21. Emmerich, *Literary Translation*, 2.

22. Emphasizing the transformative power of translation, for example, Lawrence Venuti describes it as a process through which "the source text becomes the site of multiple and conflicting interpretations." Venuti, "Hijacking Translation," 198. In her work on bilingual cities, Sherry Simon further notes the nonneutrality of translations, describing them instead as "events which sustain or transform social and literary interrelations." Simon, *Cities in Translation*, 3.

23. Emmerich, *Literary Translation*, 2.

24. Ibid., 2, 29.

25. As of 2019, TEDA (Translation and Publication Grant Programme of Turkey) had funded 2,389 translations in total. "Statistics TEDA," TEDA, Republic of Turkey Ministry of Culture and Tourism, https://teda.ktb.gov.tr/EN-252217/statistics-teda.html.

26. The Turkish Library translation series was augmented by a traveling exhibit and pedagogical materials to support the teaching of Turkish literature in German high schools.

27. In 2008, to coincide with Turkey's presence as guest of honor at the Frankfurt Book Fair, 139 translations were undertaken. Özkan, "Turkish Literature," 5–6. Scholarly opinion on the significance of this increase in translation activity remains contested. Translator Wolfgang Riemann describes the years following 2008 as a "success story" for Turkish literature. Riemann, "How Has Turkish Literature." Simge Yılmaz argues, however, that the number and kind of recent translations from Turkish have not led to an increased interest in Turkish literature for the German-speaking public. Yılmaz, "Under the Shadow," 68. Furthermore, in her detailed study of the Turkish Library (2005–10), Christine Dikici notes that many of the volumes in this series did not make it past a first edition. Only select titles by contemporary authors such as Hasan Ali Toptaş, Ahmet Ümit, and Murathan Mungan were relatively successful; these German translations garnered prizes, led to paperback editions, and were accompanied by reading tours. Dikici, *Die Rezeption*, 135–44. Dikici nevertheless recognizes the significance of recent translation activity, which has finally rendered a more representative picture

of the broad spectrum of Turkish literature into German. Ibid., 103.

28. Stephan-Emmrich and Schröder, "Introduction," 43. This quotation is in reference to the concept of transtemporality. The connection to translation is my own.

29. Ahmed, "Orientations," 554.

30. Ibid., 29.

31. Evin, *Origins*, 9–10. In 1871, the Chamber was taken over by the Ministry of Foreign Affairs, at which point it served as a school for young Ottoman writers and statesmen. Berk, *Translation and Westernisation*, 29. For a concise history of the emergence and development of the Translation Chamber, see also Findley, *Bureaucratic Reform*, 133–36.

32. The Tanzimat was proclaimed on November 3, 1839, with the Imperial Script (Hatt-ı Hümayun). It ended with the institution of the first constitutional era in 1876 and the introduction of the first (short-lived) parliamentary regime.

33. It is important to acknowledge that modernizing reforms—particularly in the realm of the military—were undertaken prior to the Tanzimat era. The Tanzimat era nevertheless initiated a new level of conscious and sustained Westernization in the history of the Ottoman Empire. Berk, *Translation and Westernisation*, 14.

34. Evin, *Origins*, 12. Evin states that "the late nineteenth-century intelligentsia looked almost exclusively to the French realist and naturalist novel as their model, and eventually singled [these] out as the most advanced form of prose fiction." Ibid., 19.

35. Holbrook, *Unreadable Shores*, 20.

36. Due to the specific nature of the German–(Ottoman) Turkish relationship at the core of this book, I have

chosen to highlight here translation activity from European languages. For an insightful and rich discussion of multidirectional translation networks within the Ottoman Empire, see Charrière and Ringer, introduction to *Ottoman Culture*, 5–8.

37. Mithat, *Felâtun Bey ile Râkım Efendi*.

38. Gürbilek, "Dandies and Originals," 612. Jale Parla goes even further to argue that the voices of *Carriage* do not "belong" to anyone; the result is a fundamental lack of communication in which characters neither understand themselves nor others. Parla, *Babalar ve Oğullar*, 108.

39. Gürbilek, "Dandies and Originals," 612.

40. Alternately, Jale Parla describes Bihruz's attempt to translate a French poem into Turkish as representative of a "mimetic crisis that Ekrem perceived was engendered by the cultural and linguistic chaos of his times." Parla, "Car Narratives," 538.

41. See Ekrem, *Araba Sevdası*.

42. Ekrem, *Bütün Eserleri III*, 264.

43. For an in-depth discussion of the manner in which divan poetry was coded as "difficult," see Holbrook, *Unreadable Shores*, 21–22.

44. Ekrem, *Leidenschaft in Çamlıca*, 80. Caner's translation maintains select French phrases in quotation marks, such as "Jardin" and "á la mode." Ibid., 26. In the majority of cases, however, she elects for a German phrase, such as the replacement of *syej* (*siège*) with *Kutschblock*. Ibid., 28. In some cases, Caner opts for a German cognate, such as *Promenade*, to replace the Turkish transliteration of the French term. Ibid., 26.

45. I borrow this reference from Susanne Zantop, who writes, "The battle against French 'imperialism' during the Napoleonic Wars promoted a sense of identification with the colonized underdog, and hence fantasies replete with compassion and self-pity." Zantop, *Colonial Fantasies*, 8.

46. Seeba, "'Germany: A Literary Concept,'" 354. Seeba cites here an exemplary line from Friedrich Schiller's *Wilhelm Tell* (1804)—"Wir wollen sein ein einzig Volk von Brüdern" (We want to be united as one people of brothers)—as a "fictional battle cry for national unity" that was referred to in 1870 during the Franco-Prussian War, in the aftermath of the 1918 revolution, and during the Third Reich, among other moments in history. Ibid., 354–55.

47. Berman, *Experience of the Foreign*, 11–13.

48. Quoted in ibid., 40.

49. Quoted in Louth, *Hölderlin*, 26.

50. My understanding of German and Turkish translation histories as inherently comparative is inspired by Nergis Ertürk's work on Walter Benjamin and Ahmet Hamdi Tanpınar. Ertürk reads each author's depiction of a language in crisis not simply as a modernist theme but as a structural condition of the modern. She thus engages in a method of comparison that provides a "supplementary vision of literary modernity in which neither Europe nor Turkey stands for the telos of the modern; rather, each of these placeholders diffuses into the other in a partial narrative of two simultaneously entwined and disparate histories of language in crisis." Ertürk, "Modernity and Its Fallen Languages," 43–44. This approach works against center-periphery models that emphasize a

Euro-American modernity and its "outside" by revealing the inherently comparative nature of both the German and Turkish literary fields. Whereas Ertürk utilizes the concept of comparativity to place German and Turkish authors who historically "missed" one another in conversation, this book examines the diverse forms of German–(Ottoman) Turkish *contact* engendered in and by translation.

51. Within the field of Comparative Literature, Turkish is most often deemed a "minor" language, and in the terms of world systems theory—which has informed several scholars of world literature in the twenty-first century—Turkish certainly qualifies as "peripheral." For an example of the application of world systems theory to the concept of world literature, see Moretti, "Conjectures." See also Casanova, *World Republic of Letters*.

52. While German is not always at *the* center, it is safe to assume that German qualifies in most theories of world literature as a major—or a central—European language.

53. Ahmed, *Queer Phenomenology*, 112.

54. Ibid., 113.

55. Said, *Orientalism*, 5.

56. Ibid., 7.

57. Ibid., 41.

58. While Bihruz is referred to with the modern mode of address, *bey* (Mr.), Naîm is coded as old fashioned through the more traditional *efendi* (sir, gentleman). *Efendi* was historically used to address princes, members of the clergy, government officials and members of the military, as well as generally learned people, such as teachers and students.

59. Ibid., 322.

60. The entire line of poetry in question is *"Bir siyeh-çerde civandır"* (S/he is a swarthy youth).

61. The Arabic letter in question is ‏ح‎ (jīm); the Persian letter in question is ‏چ‎ (che). Ekrem writes out jīm as (‏جيم‎) to emphasize that it needs to be read as a pronunciation of an Arabic letter.

62. Ertürk, *Grammatology*, xii.

63. Ibid., 32.

64. On the concept of Ottoman interculture, see Paker, "Translation as *Terceme* and *Nazire*," 120–43; Selim S. Kuru, "The Literature of Rum," 548–92; Walter Andrews, "Starting Over Again," 15–40. On the manner in which Persian absorbed Arabic, see Gould, "Inimitability Versus Translatability," 83.

65. Holbrook, *Unreadable Shores*, 19.

66. Gibb wrote this for an *Encyclopedia Britannica* entry in 1911. Quoted in ibid., 19.

67. Paker, "Terceme, Te'lif ve Özgünlük Meselesi," 42.

68. Ibid., 38.

69. Ibid., 53–54.

70. Ibid., 58–59; "kendine özgünlük," "başkasına benzemezlik," quoted in ibid., 57. According to Namık Kemal, a text must display an "individuality of its own" and the characteristic of "dissimilarity to others" in order to serve as a literary model.

71. Ertürk, *Grammatology*, 75–76.

72. Mutman, *"Carriage Affair,"* 249.

73. Ibid., 250.

74. Ertürk, *Grammatology*, 60.

75. Ibid., 58.

76. For an insightful discussion of the terms of translatability in this novel, see Levih, "How Not to Translate," 43–45.

77. Even-Zohar, "Laws of Literary Interference," 56.

78. "Literarische Gefangenschaft." Hachtmann, *Die türkische Literatur*, 8.

79. Said, *Orientalism*, 3.

80. Ibid., 19.

81. Marchand, *German Orientalism*, 13.

82. Schleiermacher, "Different Methods," 49. "Entweder der Uebersezer läßt den Schriftsteller möglichst in Ruhe, und bewegt den Leser ihm entgegen; oder er läßt den Leser möglichst in Ruhe und bewegt den Schriftsteller ihm entgegen." Schleiermacher, "Ueber die verschiedenen Methoden," 218.

83. For discussion of these terms, See venuti, *Translator's Invisibility*.

84. Schleiermacher, "Ueber die verschiedenen Methoden," 228–29:

Zuerst, daß diese Methode des Uebersezens nicht in allen Sprachen gleich gut gedeihen kann, sondern nur in solchen die nicht in zu engen Banden eines klassischen Audrukks gefangen liegen, außerhalb dessen alles verwerflich ist. Solche gebundene Sprachen mögen die Erweiterung ihres Gebietes dadurch suchen, daß sie sich sprechen machen von Ausländern, die mehr als ihre Muttersprache bedürfen; hiezu werden sie sich wol vorzüglich eignen; sie mögen sich fremde Werke aneignen durch Nachbildungen oder vielleicht durch Uebersezungen der andern Art: diese Art aber müssen sie den freieren Sprachen überlassen, in denen Abweichungen und Neuerungen mehr geduldet werden, und so daß aus ihrer Anhäufung unter gewissen Umständen ein bestimmter Charakter entstehen kann.

85. Berman, *Experience of the Foreign*, 144.

86. Zantop, *Colonial Fantasies*, 7.

87. Ibid., 6–7.

88. Kontje, *German Orientalisms*, 5.

89. As examples, Kontje cites Johann Friedrich Blumenbach's *Über die natürlichen Verschiedenheiten im Menschengeschlechte*, Georg Wilhelm Friedrich Hegel's *Vorlesungen über die Philosophie der Geschichte*, Christoph Meiners's *Grundriß der Geschichte der Menschheit*, and Immanuel Kant's essays "Von den Verschiedenen Rassen der Menschen" and "Bestimmung des Begriffs einer Menschenrasse." Ibid., 3–6, 245.

90. Ibid., 6.

91. Mani, *Recoding*, 52–53, 61–62, 68–69, 81.

92. Mufti, *Forget English!*, 104–5.

93. Ibid., 104.

94. Ibid., 80.

95. Ibid., 19.

96. Ibid., 20 (emphasis in original).

97. Many thanks to Duygu Ergun for conducting a thorough search with WorldCat and various online booksellers for existing editions of the novel.

98. I agree with Özlem Berk Albachten that modern editions of Ottoman Turkish texts should be described as intralingual translations, even though they are rarely labeled as such. Older texts that have been rendered into modern Turkish are most commonly referred to as "simplified" (*sadeleştirilmiş*), "Turkicized" (*Türkçeleştirilmiş*), "arranged" (*düzenlenmiş*), or "prepared for publication" (*yayına hazırlanmış*). These terms mask the often ideological and political motivations behind the "updating" of texts for newer generations of readers. Berk Albachten, "Turkish Language Reform," 165–80.

99. Damrosch, *What Is World Literature?*, 4.

100. Ibid., 4.

101. Apter, *Against World Literature*, 27.

102. Apter argues for an understanding of untranslatability "not as pure difference in opposition to the always translatable . . . but as a linguistic form of creative failure." Ibid., 20. She gestures here toward the work of Barbara Cassin, who describes *intraduisibles* as concepts that give rise to ceaseless linguistic inventions through the never-ending processes of imperfect translation they demand. Untranslatability thus does not intend to uphold essential, insurmountable differences between languages but calls for the constant negotiation of difference as it attests to the radical heterogeneity of language itself. Nevertheless, the rhetoric of untranslatability in and of itself is a poor fit with Turkish literary history and, in particular, with the articulation of modern Turkish literature in the late nineteenth century.

103. Andrews, "Ottoman Lyrics," 6.

104. Spivak, *Aesthetic Education*, 472.

105. Ibid., 459.

106. The original reads, "jeder muss jetzt dazu wirken, diese Epoche zu beschleunigen." Quoted in ibid., 461.

107. Said, *Orientalism*, 20 (my emphasis).

108. The emphasis here on orientation is my own interpretation of Said's argument.

109. Said, *Orientalism*, 222.

CHAPTER 1

1. Goethe began work on the *Divan* in 1814 and the first edition was published in 1819. A second, slightly expanded version was published in 1827.

2. This collecton is overseen today by the Klassik Stiftung Weimar.

3. Keudell, *Goethe als Benutzer*, 151.

4. Ibid., 151.

5. Ibid., 153. The author in question is Jalāl al-Dīn Rūmī, who is more commonly known as Mevlânâ in Persian and Turkish and as Rūmī in the West.

6. Ibid., 163. Goethe also owned a copy of Georg Forster's 1791 translation of the Sanskrit play *Śakuntalā*, Joseph von Hammer-Purgstall's 1813 translation of Ḥāfeẓ's poetic divan from Persian, and Wilhelm von Humboldt's 1826 translation of the Bhagavad Gita from Sanskrit. Mani, *Recoding*, 53–54.

7. "Auf die orientalische Poesie und Literatur [ist] überhaupt Rücksicht genommen . . . ja, die türkischen Dichter sind nicht außer Acht gelassen." This quotation is from an unsent letter to Goethe's publisher Cotta. Goethe, *Goethes Werke*, 415.

8. Mangold-Will, *Eine "weltbürgerliche Wissenschaft,"* 30, 45.

9. Kontje, *German Orientalisms*, 5.

10. "Uns [hat] geographische Lage [und] politische Verfassung . . . den eklektischen Karakter verliehen, womit wir das Schöne, Gute und Vollkommene . . . uneigennützig um sein selbst willen erforschen, sammeln und so lange ordnen sollen, bis etwa der Bau des menschlichen Wissens vollendet da steht, —oder unsere Rolle gespielt ist und künftige Menschenalter die Steine, die wir zusammentrugen, zu einem neuen Gebäude brauchen." Forster, "Vorrede des Uebersetzers," xxv.

11. Mufti, *Forget English!*, 59.

12. Numerous German Romantic authors—including the Schlegel brothers, Otmar Frank, Joseph Goerres, Arthur Schopenhauer, and Georg Friedrich Creuzer—looked to the Far East, and in particular India, for inspiration.

13. Mani, *Recoding*, 68.

14. See ibid., 52, 69, 70. See also Mufti, *Forget English!*, 102.

15. While the *Fundgruben* was an academic journal, its subtitle—"bearbeitet durch eine Gesellschaft von Liebhabern" ("edited by a community of enthusiasts")—highlighted the nonacademic status of its editors.

16. Von Hammer-Purgstall, "Vorrede" (1809), iv.

17. "Vielfältige unmittelbare Berührung mit dem Orient." Ibid., iii.

18. *"Die drey Sprachen"* (emphasis in original). Von Hammer-Purgstall, "Vorrede" (1811), n.p.

19. Katharina Mommsen is a notable exception. Her book *Goethe und Diez* documents the relationship between these two men and uncovers the individual poems in Goethe's *Divan* that were inspired by Diez's translations. Her work has been an invaluable resource for me in writing this chapter.

20. Petritsch, "Wiener Turkologie," 25.

21. Ibid., 26.

22. Other important diplomats who studied at the academy include Ignatz von Brenner-Felsach, Ignaz Lorenz von Stürmer, Franz von Ottenfels-Gschwind, and Bartholomäus von Stürmer. Ibid., 31. Thomas von Chabert, who also graduated from the academy, undertook the first translations from Ottoman Turkish into German in 1800. His collection of divan poetry by Latifî and Çelebi is titled *Latifi, oder biographische Nachrichten von vorzüglichen türkischen Dichtern, nebst einer Blumenlese aus ihren Werken.*

23. Mangold-Will, *Eine "weltbürgerliche Wissenschaft,"* 47.

24. Polaschegg, *Der andere Orientalismus,* 220–21.

25. Andrea Polaschegg states for example that, "Die türkische Dichtung fand . . . kaum deutsche Übersetzer, Verleger und Leser." Ibid., 220. Petra Kappert describes Ottoman Turkish literature in the era of Goethe and the Romantics as "terra incognita," noting that it had few admirers or translators. Kappert, "Vom Übersetzen," 213.

26. Fleischer is otherwise known as the cofounder of the German Oriental Society. Both Georg Jacob and Martin Hartmann studied under Fleischer. For more on this, see Stein, "Zur Geschichte," 45. Jacob went on to establish and edit the twenty-six-volume translation series the Turkish Library (Türkische Bibliothek, 1904–29) and to publish a multiregional history of shadow theater from China to the Ottoman Empire. Hartmann went on to become a foremost scholar of Islamic studies. While his scholarship focused heavily on Arabic sources, he also wrote on modern Turkish poetry and published a candid reflection on his experiences in Constantinople during the aftermath of the 1908 Young Turk Revolution. See Hartmann, *Dichter der neuen Türkei*; Hartmann, *Unpolitische Briefe.*

27. These factors were exacerbated by the multiethnic makeup of the Ottoman Empire. Polaschegg, *Der andere Orientalismus,* 220–23.

28. "Eines Übermaßes an Gegenwärtigkeit." Ibid., 223.

29. Andrews, "Ottoman Lyrics," 5.

30. Bobzin, "Friedrich Rückert," 69.

31. Said, *Orientalism,* 73 (my emphasis). This special status does not render the Ottoman Empire or the modern Republic of Turkey any less "Oriental" throughout the spectrum of Said's scholarship. In "Secular Criticism," for example, Said argues that the strength of Auerbach's *Mimesis* comes from his

"critically important alienation from [Western cultural tradition]" and his state of "Oriental, non-Occidental exile and homelessness." Here Istanbul is treated as the capital of a historic empire that represents the quintessential antithesis of European humanism. Said, *World*, 226.

32. In the introduction to *Memoirs of Asia*, Diez writes, "Ich habe mich zwar nie anders als blossen Liebhaber ansehen dürfen, der nur aus Verlangen nach Erkenntniss seine eigene Wissbegierde zu befriedigen gesucht." Diez, *Denkwürdigkeiten*, 1:xvi.

33. Mangold-Will, *Eine "weltbürgerliche Wissenschaft,"* 50–51.

34. According to Franz Babinger, Diez enjoyed the company of Polish, Russian, and Hungarian colleagues during his legal clerkship in Magdeburg; Diez picked up these languages largely through regular conversations with these colleagues. Babinger, "Ein orientalischer Berater," 85.

35. Diez received word from his friend and colleague Christian Wilhelm von Dohm (lawyer, diplomat, author) that Friedrich the Great had dismissed Ambassador Christian Friedrich Gaffron in Constantinople and that the position was to be filled. Diez wasted no time in applying, even though he was not well qualified for the position. A sudden downturn in Friedrich the Great's health nevertheless afforded Diez an extra eight weeks to study French intensively with a private tutor before interviewing for the position. Diez was also particularly lucky that only one other applicant was in the running. Ibid., 86–89.

36. Margoliouth, "Turkish Diplomacy," 46. See also Shaw, *Between Old and New*, 45–47.

37. In 1876, for example, Diez was raised to the position of envoy extraordinary (a rank below that of ambassador), which bestowed more authority upon his opinions. Ibid., 47.

38. Gronau, *Christian Wilhelm*, 112–13.

39. "Mein Schiff ist seit vorgestern von Türken nicht leergeworden, welche zu mir gekommen sind, um zu weinen und Abschied zu nehmen. Alle haben nur diese Worte im Munde: ein solcher Gesandter, wie der, war niemals hier, und es wird auch kein zweiter nach ihm kommen. Genug für mein Herz!" Ibid., 112.

40. Diez later moved to Kolberg and then Berlin. Balcke, "Heinrich Friedrich von Diez," 189.

41. "Gräber der morgenländischen Handschriften." Diez, *Denkwürdigkeiten*, 1:xv.

42. Ibid., 1:xxii–xxiii. While Diez does not mention it, it is worth noting the most famous example of such literary contact: Antoine Galland's first, and extremely influential, translations (1704–17) of *1001 Nights* into French were based on an Arabic manuscript brought to Paris from Constantinople by French-Ottoman diplomat Marquis Nointel.

43. "Sprecher der Morgenländer." Diez, *Denkwürdigkeiten*, xvii.

44. Babinger, "Ein orientalischer Berater," 93–94.

45. I draw here on Arif Dirlik's insightful discussion of the Orientalized Westerner. Dirlik, "Chinese History," 390.

46. "Vor den Worten den Geist des Orients nicht sehen können." Ludwig, "Briefwechsel," 32.

47. Mangold-Will, *Eine "weltbürgerliche Wissenschaft,"* 50.

48. Bett, "Pyrrhonian Skepticism," 404.

49. "Der Zweifler entscheidet nicht absolut, weil er nicht weiß auf welcher Seite Wahrheit ist. Ich aber suche keine Wahrheiten, und leugne daß es dergleichen gebe und geben könne. Die Unterschiede, die man macht, als Wahrheit, Irrthum, Vorurtheil, Falschheit etc. hebe ich auf, und bringe alles auf das Wort Ideen zurück, die sich jeder nach seiner Art macht." Mauvillon, *Mauvillons' Briefwechsel*, 107–8. For a more detailed discussion of Diez's relationship to Pyrrhonian skepticism, see Gibson, "Changing States," 24–27.

50. Ibid., 116. "Jeder kann sich Welt und Menschen nur vorstellen, wie er sie sieht, und jeder sieht sie nur nach Verhältniss des Orts, wo er gestanden, nach Art der Geschäfte, welche er getrieben, und nach Maasse der Erkenntniss und Erfahrung, welche er sich erworben." Diez, *Buch des Kabus*, 1.

51. "Die eigenen Büche der Asiaten bleiben daher immer das sicherste Mittel, uns von ihren Sachen zu unterrichten." Diez, *Denkwürdigkeiten*, 1:xiii.

52. Ibid., 1:xix.

53. For more on this topic, see Gibson, *Changing States*, 60–83.

54. Said, *Orientalism*, 20.

55. Goethe expressed this idea in a letter to Cotta from May 1815. Cited in Mommsen, *Goethe und Diez*, 79.

56. Goethe, *West-östlicher Divan*, 220.

57. Schwarz, *Der Orient und die Ästhetik*, 148.

58. "Eine virtuelle Situation der Gleichzeitigkeit." Bhatti, "Der Orient als Experimentierfeld," 122.

59. Goethe, *West-East Divan*, 206. "Die kostbarsten und niedrigsten Waren im Raume [sind nicht] weit gesondert, sie vermischen sich in unseren Augen,

und oft gewahren wir auch die Fässer, Kisten, Säcke, worin die transportiert worden." Goethe, *West-östlicher Divan*, 221.

60. "Reisender" and "Handelsmann." Ibid., 166.

61. Almond, *History of Islam*, 79–88.

62. Mommsen, *Goethe und die Weltkulturen*, 246–52.

63. Goethe, *West-östlicher Divan*, 25.

64. Ibid., 24–25.

65. My interpretations of the following are indebted to the careful work of Katharina Mommsen, who first identified the Ottoman Turkish source texts for numerous poems in Goethe's *Divan*.

66. Goethe uses the verb *vorrücken*. Goethe, *West-östlicher Divan*, 359.

67. Goethe, *West-East Divan*, 175. "Wer das Dichten will verstehen, / Muss ins Land der Dichtung gehen; / Wer den Dichter will verstehen, / Muss in Dichters Lande gehen." Goethe, *West-östlicher Divan*, 163.

68. Goethe, *West-East Divan*, 4.1–4. "Lasst mich nur auf meinem Sattel gelten! / Bleibt in euren Hütten, euren Zelten! / Und ich reite froh in alle Ferne, / Über meiner Mütze nur die Sterne." Goethe, *West-östlicher Divan*, 10.1–4.

69. Ibid., 361.

70. Ibid., 364.

71. Cited in Louth, *Hölderlin*, 26.

72. Humboldt began this translation in 1796. For an insightful discussion of Humboldt's process of revision, see Mendicino, *Prophecies of Language*, 62–93.

73. "Erweiterung der Bedeutsamkeit und der Ausdrucksfähigkeit der eigenen Sprache." Humboldt, "Einleitung," xvii.

74. "Das unbestimmte Wirken der Denkkraft zieht sich in ein Wort

zusammen, wie leichte Gewölke am heitren Himmel entstehen." Ibid., xv–xvi.

75. Berman, *Experience of the Foreign*, 155; Humboldt, "Einleitung," xix.

76. Goethe, *West-östlicher Divan*, 270.

77. All materials from Goethe's personal archive related to the *Divan* have been reproduced in Bosse, *Meine Schatzkammer*. All archival materials cited in this chapter can be found in this source.

78. "Die sittlichen Sternbilder / Kabus und Oguz / fest im Auge." Bosse, *Meine Schatzkammer*, 518.

79. "Dem sittlichen Pend-Nameh des Firadeddin." Ibid., 517. Goethe was familiar with this work by way of Antoine Isaac Silvestre de Sacy's translations published in *Fundgruben des Orients*.

80. Goethe first encountered these poems via William Jones's English translation in 1783, when he was inspired to translate some of the material into German; he later encountered Anton Theodor Hartmann's 1802 translations of these poems in 1815. Ibid., 176.

81. Anke Bosse describes them as a *Navigationspunkt*. Ibid., 523.

82. Diez, *Denkwürdigkeiten*, 1:161.

83. Diez uses the phrase "national Zeugnisse." Ibid., 162. Goethe's reformulation reads as "Sprichwort bezeichnet Nationen." Quoted in Mommsen, *Goethe und Diez*, 103.

84. Goethe, *West-östlicher Divan*, 60.12–13.

85. Goethe, *West-East Divan*, 66.1–2.

86. The Ottoman Turkish reads, "Deniz olup taşma, elinden gelemeyecek işe dolaşma" (my transliteration). Diez, *Denkwürdigkeiten*, 1:196. A literal translation of this would read: "Don't

overflow like the sea, don't get tangled up in an affair you are not able to take on."

87. Goethe, *West-East Divan*, 82.1–4. "'Die Flut der Leidenschaft, sie stürmt vergebens / Ans unbezwungene, feste Land.' / Sie wirft poetische Perlen an den Strand, / Und das ist schon Gewinn des Lebens." Goethe, *West-östlicher Divan*, 68.1–4.

88. Haque, "From the Desert to the City," 233.

89. Goethe, *West-East Divan*, 1.1–12. "Nord und West und Süd zersplittern, / Throne bersten, Reiche zittern: / Flüchte du, im reinen Osten / Patriarchenluft zu kosten! / Unter Lieben, Trinken, Singen / Soll dich Chisers Quell verjüngen. / Dort, im Reinen und im Rechten, / Will ich menschlichen Geschlechten / In des Ursprungs Tiefe dringen, / Wo sie noch von Gott empfingen / Himmelslehr in Erdesprachen / Und sich nicht den Kopf zerbrachen." Goethe, *West-östlicher Divan*, 7.1–12.

90. Mommsen, *Goethe und die arabische Welt*, 92.

91. Müller-Sievers, *Desorientierung*, 16–18.

92. "Aus ital. orientare, franz. orienter, trans. u. reflexiv (in ermangelung der Magnetnadel) aus einer bekannten Weltgegend die übrigen, namentlich die östliche zu finden suchen, dann überhaupt in eine gegend, in einen raum, in eine lage oder ein verhältnis sich zurechtfinden." Quoted in Stegmaier, *Philosophie der Orientierung*, 61.

93. "Dem Osten zuwenden." Ibid., 55.

94. Goethe, *West-East Divan*, 86.1–4. *"Ich gedachte in der Nacht, / Daß ich den Mond sähe im Schlaf; / Als ich aber erwachte, / Ging unvermutet die Sonne auf"* (italics in original). Goethe, *West-östlicher Divan*, 71.

95. "In dem Türckischen Reiche ist Selimus Kayser worden, nachdem er seinen Vatter Baiazet umgebracht und seinen Bruder Zizimus verjaget hatte." Mommsen, *Goethe und die Weltkulturen*, 243.

96. "Traum-Tag- und Sonne-Mond-Symbolismus." Henkel, "Bildermodulation," 257.

97. Goethe, *West-East Divan*, 94.1–4. "Die Sonne kommt! Ein Prachterscheinen! / Der Sichelmond umklammert sie. / Wer konnte solch ein Paar vereinen? / Dies Rätsel, wie erklärt sichs? wie?" Goethe, *West-östlicher Divan*, 77.1–4.

98. Ibid., 92.1–4, 93.23–24.

99. Goethe, *West-East Divan*, 104.1–5. "Bist du von deiner Geliebten getrennt / Wie Orient vom Okzident, / Das Herz durch alle Wüsten rennt; / Es gibt sich überall selbst das Geleit, / Für Liebende ist Bagdad nicht weit." Goethe, *West-östlicher Divan*, 86.1–5.

100. "Wenns von dir bis zur Geliebten so weit seyn sollte als vom Orient zu Occident: / so lauf nur, o Herz! denn für Liebende ist Bagdad nicht weit." Diez, *Denkwürdigkeiten*, 2:232. Diez does not provide the original text for this particular scene.

101. Holbrook, *Unreadable Shores*, 14.

102. Andrews, "Ottoman Lyrics," 8.

103. See Pizer, "Johann Wolfgang von Goethe," 9; Nicholls, "'Goethean' Discourses," 174–77.

104. Quoted in Strich, *Goethe and World Literature*, 349–50. "Denn eben diese Bezüge vom Originale zur Übersetzung sind es ja, welche die Verhältnisse von Nation zu Nation am allerdeutlichsten aussprechen und die man zur Förderung der vor- und obwaltenden allgemeinen Weltliteratur vorzüglich zu kennen und zu beurteilen

hat." Quoted in Strich, *Goethe und die Weltliteratur*, 370.

105. Damrosch, *What Is World Literature?*, 7.

106. See Strich, *Goethe und die Weltliteratur*, 372.

107. Eckermann, *Gespräche*, 223.

108. "Gemeingut der Menschheit." Ibid., 224.

109. Nicholls, "'Goethean' Discourses," 173.

110. Cheah, *What Is a World?*, 38.

111. See, for example, his remarks from January 31, 1827, in which he upholds the ancient Greeks as the ultimate model. Eckermann, *Gespräche*, 225.

112. "Europäische, das heißt Weltliteratur." Quoted in Strich, *Goethe und die Weltliteratur*, 29. Goethe composed this list in relation to volume 6:3 of the journal *Über Kunst und Alterthum*, which was published in 1832. The original title was simply *Weltliteratur*.

113. Quoted in Strich, *Goethe and World Literature*, 350. "Wenn wir eine europäische, ja eine allgemeine Weltliteratur zu verkündigen gewagt haben, so heißt dieses nicht, daß die verschiedenen Nationen voneinander und ihren Erzeugnissen Kenntnis nehmen, denn in diesem Sinne existiert sie schon lange, setzt sich fort und erneuert sich mehr oder weniger. Nein! hier ist vielmehr davon die Rede, daß die lebendigen und strebenden Literatoren einander kennenlernen und durch Neigung und Gemeinsinn sich veranlaßt finden, gesellschaftlich zu wirken." Quoted in Strich, *Goethe und die Weltliteratur*, 370–71.

114. Berman, *Experience of the Foreign*, 55.

115. Strich, *Goethe und die Weltliteratur*, 29–30.

116. Pizer, *Idea of World Literature*, 27.

117. Mani, *Recoding*, 62.

118. Ibid., 64–65.

CHAPTER 2

1. Kaplan, *Klâsikler Tartışması*, 64–69.

2. Goethe, "Literarischer Sanscülottismus," 198.

3. "Hinderte doch den Deutschen als Deutschen sich früher zu entwickeln." Ibid., 200–201.

4. Quoted in Strich, *Goethe and World Literature*, 350. "Sodann bemerke, daß die von mir angerufene Weltliteratur auf ich, wie auf den Zauberlehrling, zum Ersäufen zuströmt." Quoted in Strich, *Goethe und die Weltliteratur*, 370.

5. Pizer, *Idea of World Literature*, 6.

6. Mufti highlights this aspect of *Weltliteratur* with a specific eye toward the Herderian underpinnings of the term in Goethe's thought. Mufti, *Forget English!*, 78.

7. "Ein Gesammtbild des Dichterischen Schaffens sämmtlicher Kulturvölker alter und neuer Zeit, welche wirklich eine Literatur besaßen oder besitzen." Scherr, *Bildersaal*, 6.

8. Across three volumes and one thousand pages, Scherr devotes exactly two pages to Turkish literature: namely, to the great poets of the divan tradition, Necâti and Bâkî.

9. Dirlik, "Chinese History," 388.

10. Mithat, *Sid'in Hülasası*, 4–6.

11. Tanpınar, *XIX. Asır*, 42–43.

12. Hilmi Ziya Ülken repeatedly uses the rhetoric of transfer (*nakil, nakletmek*) in reference to the process of translating Western European source texts into Turkish. Ülken, *Uyanış Devirlerinde*, 357–85.

13. "Batıyı çevirmek." Karadağ, "Batı'nın Çevrilmesi Üzerine," 313.

14. Elif Daldeniz describes translation as "the importation of structures and models," and as a mode of "import[ing] and export[ing] cultural, commercial and technical commodities." Daldeniz, "Translation, Modernity and Its Dissidents," 129.

15. Fabian, *Time and the Other*, 144.

16. Ibid., 29–32, 149–50.

17. Mitchell, "Stage of Modernity," 23.

18. Ibid., 1.

19. Eruz, *Çokkültürlülük ve Çeviri*.

20. Incidentally, an Armenian translation also appeared in 1859. Strauss, "Who Read What," 49–50.

21. Ibid., 53.

22. Charrière, "Translating Communities," 179.

23. Kendall, "Between Politics and Literature," 331. Many book-length translations also appeared in journals in serialized format, as, for example, did Victor Hugo's *Les Misérables*, which was serialized in 1862 in the journal *Ceride-i Havadis*. Ibid., 332.

24. Mithat, *Ahbar-ı Asara*, 83–84.

25. It is further notable that *terceme* was only one of many terms used to describe translational practices in the late nineteenth century. Celal Demircioğlu's dissertation investigates a variety of diverse Ottoman terms and concepts related to that of *terceme*, such as *taklid* (imitation), *iktibas* (borrowing), *imtisal* (modeling), *tanzir* (emulation), *ahz* (taking), *idhal* (importing). See Demircioğlu, "From Discourse to Practice."

26. Paker, "Translation as *Terceme* and *Nazire*," 129.

27. Paker, "Terceme, Te'lîf ve Özgünlük Meselesi," 57.

28. Ibid., 59–60.

29. Ibid., 59.

30. Heather Sullivan also discusses the novel's ending in terms of rupture. She reads the rupture of Werther's body in suicide together with the narrative rupture staged in the novel as "the annihilation of the narrative form that claims unmediated immersion into 'nature.'" Sullivan, "Dangerous Quest," 2.

31. For a detailed discussion of this problematic, see Eldridge, *Literature, Life, and Modernity*.

32. Berman, *All That Is Solid*.

33. Kaplan, *Klâsikler Tartışması*, 88.

34. Goethe, "'Verter' 13 Mayıs Tarihli Mektup," 74. (All English translations and transliterations from Ottoman Turkish are my own.)

35. Goethe, *Verter*, 11.

36. Graham, *Goethe*, 15.

37. Goethe, "'Verter' 13 Mayıs Tarihli Mektup," 74.

38. Consider, for example, the following omitted passage: "O meine Freunde! warum der Strom des Genies so selten ausbricht, so selten in hohen Fluten hereinbraust und eure staunende Seele erschüttert?—Liebe Freunde, da wohnen die gelassenen Herren auf beiden Seiten des Ufers, denen ihre Gartenhäuschen, Tulpenbeete und Krautfelder zugrunde gehen würden, die daher in Zeiten mit Dämmen und Ableiten der künftig drohenden Gefahr abzuwehren wissen." Goethe, *Die Leiden*, 19.

39. Ibid., 8.

40. Goethe, "'Verter' 10 Mayıs Tarihli Mektup," 90.

41. Kaplan, *Klâsikler Tartışması*, 50–51.

42. Ibid., 40–41. These remarks, of course, closely mirror Goethe's depiction of a classic in "Literary Sansculottism."

43. Ibid., 36.

44. Saliha Paker has also shown how Necib Asım's contributions to the Classics Debate point toward an understanding of translation based on fidelity and completeness, thus serving to delimit the otherwise wide-ranging connotations of the *terceme* tradition. Paker, "Ottoman Conceptions," 339–41.

45. This move toward anthologization went hand in hand with the increased availability and affordability of books and thus the subsequent commercialization of world literature. With the establishment of a series such as the Reclam Universal-Bibliothek in 1867, world literature became more specifically associated with a middle-class education. Yet these developments occurred simultaneously with rising nationalist sentiment in the periods leading up to and following the establishment of the German nation-state in 1871. In this political climate, world literature was also dubbed overly cosmopolitan and associated with the German-Jewish minority in a pejorative fashion. Mani, *Recoding*, 94–95.

46. See, for example, Moretti, "Conjectures." See also Casanova, *World Republic of Letters*.

47. Even-Zohar, "Laws of Literary Interference," 56.

48. Jauss, *Literaturgeschichte als Provokation*, 49.

49. Goethe, *West-östlicher Divan*, 361.

CHAPTER 3

1. "Bizim yeğenin 'neşr-i medeniyyet' vazifesi imiş." Müftüoğlu, "Yeğenim," 239.

2. "Tahsilini tamamlamak içün." Quoted in Tevetoğlu, *Ahmed Hikmet Müftüoğlu*, 176.

3. "Dilsizdir," "vatansızdır," "O, ne Avrupa'da bir Frenk, ne Türkiye'de bir Türkdür." Quoted in ibid., 177.

4. Hanioğlu, *Young Turks in Opposition*, 8.

5. Mühürcüoğlu, "*Alla Franca* Dandy," 4.

6. Mühürcüoğlu borrows these terms from Marshall Berman's depiction of the modern individual in *All That Is Solid Melts into Air*. Ibid., 5.

7. Mardin, "Super Westernization," 414.

8. See, for example, the first representation of a dandy in Ottoman Turkish literature in Ahmet Mithat's *Felâtun Bey ile Râkım Efendi* (1960). The novel was first published in 1876.

9. Gürbilek, "Dandies and Originals," 615.

10. Ibid., 622.

11. "Bu vakadan tam beş sene sonra, o şampanya gibi kabına sığmayan yeğenim, Zonguldak'tan avdet ettiği zaman, ayran gibi sakin ve rakid, apışmış kalmıştı." Müftüoğlu, "Yeğenim," 242.

12. While Müftüoğlu was an important author for the development of a Turkish national literature, he was also well educated in French and served as a diplomat in both France and Hungary, as well as in the Caucasus.

13. Holbrook, *Unreadable Shores*, 15.

14. The development of Turkology in Hungary, particularly via the scholarship of Ármin Vámbéry, drew connections between Hungarian and Turkic peoples, leading to the establishment of Turanist societies in Hungary. Friedrich Wilhelm Radloff (1837–1918) was an important figure for the development of Russian Turkology via his work on the history, languages, and cultures of Turkic peoples living in Siberia and Turkistan, including the Kazan Tatars and the Bashkurt. Toward the turn of the century, two events in particular were foundational for the modern field of Turkology in Germany: During the 1890s, scholars succeeded in deciphering inscriptions that were discovered along the Orkhon and Yenisei rivers in Mongolia, and between 1902 and 1914, expeditions to Turfan, in the eastern Chinese province of Xinjiang, led to the discovery of thousands of Turkic handwritten manuscripts from the pre-Islamic period. Led by Albert Grünwedel (1856–1935) and Albert August von Le Coq (1860–1930), the Turfan expeditions revived the legacy of the linguist, historian, Orientalist, and explorer Julius Klaproth (1783–1835). Klaproth was well versed in numerous languages, including Chinese, Manchu, Mongolian, Sanskrit, Turkish, Arabic, Persian, and several Caucasian languages, and his work was central to the historical reconfiguration of Turkology in Central Asia. Karakaş, *Türk Ulusçuluğunun İnşası*, 96–97.

15. Heyd, *Foundations of Turkish Nationalism*, 105; Kuran, "Impact," 112–13.

16. "İstanbul'a geldiğim zaman ilk aldığım kitap Leon Cahun'un tarihi olmuştu. Bu kitap adeta Pantürkizm mefkuresini teşvik etmek üzere yazılmış gibidir." Gökalp, *Türkçülüğün Esasları*, 14.

17. Oba, *Türk Milliyetçiliğinin Doğuşu*, 124.

18. Kuran, "Impact," 114.

19. Andrews, "Ottoman Lyrics," 7.

20. Gibb, *History of Ottoman Poetry*, v.

21. Andrews, "Ottoman Lyrics," 7.

22. See ibid., 8. See also Holbrook, *Unreadable Shores*, 14, 22, 23, 31.

23. Schrader completed a translation of the Karmapradīpa for his doctoral thesis. Schubert, "Baron A. von Staël-Holstein," 227.

24. Pischel, "Nachrichten," xxvi.

25. "[Es] fehlte ihnen in der Literatur das originelle Schöpfergenie." Schrader, "Das geistige Leben," 549.

26. "Ein brauchbares Mitglied der europäischen Völkerfamilie." Ibid., 555.

27. "Das litterarische Leben in der Türkei glüht gewissermaßen unter der Asche." Schrader, "Neutürkisches Schrifttum," 1690.

28. "Das Werkzeug war geschaffen; aus einem ungefügen papiernem Jargon, zu dessen Lektüre das Wörterbuch auch für den geborenen Türken nöthig war, hatte sich das Hochtürkische in eine moderne, ausdrucksfähige Sprache verwandelt. . . . Wissenschaftliche Werke konnten nun aus europäischen Sprachen ins Türkische übersezt werden; das Vehikel für die einzuführende Kultur war vorhanden." Schrader, "Das geistige Leben," 551.

29. "Die türkische Moderne allein passt aber nicht mehr nach Asien, sondern nur nach Europa." Horn, *Geschichte*, 1.

30. I use the term "literary modernity" in my translation of this title to connote the double meaning of *Moderne* as both modern (in reference to the field of Turkish literature) and modernity.

31. *Die Litteraturen des Ostens in Einzeldarstellungen* was published by C. F. Amelangs Verlag in Leipzig. This seventeen-volume series covered Polish, Russian, Hungarian, Romanian, Byzantine and modern Greek, Southern Slavic, Czech, Persian, Arabic, ancient Hebrew, Chinese, Indian, and Japanese literatures, as well as Christian literatures of the Orient.

32. Horn, *Geschichte*, 1.

33. Ibid., 4.

34. Mani, *Recoding*, 17.

35. Ibid., 19.

36. Undertaken by Dr. Otto Müller-Kolshorn in 1918, the *sefâret-nâme* in particular includes a concise and readable introductory history of Prussian-Ottoman diplomatic relations from the first initiation of an *Orientpolitik* under Frederick the Great through the end of the eighteenth century. This suggests that the Turkish Library was on some level also invested in German-Ottoman political relations.

37. Jacob, "Vorwort," vii.

38. Venuti, *Contra Instrumentalism*, 5–6.

39. "Ganz objektiv türkische Texte selbst reden zu lassen." Jacob, "Vorwort des Herausgebers," v.

40. While Tevfik originally intended to devote one section of this book to each month of the Islamic calendar year, he only ever produced five sections, all of which were translated by Theodor Menzel for the Turkish Library series. These are: *Tandırbaşı, Helva Sohbeti, Kağıthane, Ramazan Geceleri*, and *Meyhane Yahut İstanbul Akşamcıları*.

41. "Die alten Sitten und Unterhaltungen sind verschwunden und jede deutliche Erinnerung an sie mit ihnen." Menzel, "Einleitung," 7.

42. Ibid., 7.

43. Said, *Orientalism*, 7.

44. "In diesen Vorträgen offenbart sich der ureigenste Charakter des von keiner europäischen Bildung verdorbenen Türken aus dem Volke am

schönsten. Sein trockener Humor, seine dramatische belebte Erzählungskunst erscheinen darin im hellsten Lichte. Es kam dem Herausgeber offenbar darauf an, den der europäischen Kultur möglichst fernstehenden Türken aus dem Volke mit seinen von den Urvätern überkommenen Sitten und Anschauungen darzustellen, bevor eine nivellierende Zeit ihn der großen europäischen Kulturmasse stärker ausgleicht." Schrader, "Türkische Bibliothek."

45. Rosaldo, "Imperialist Nostalgia," 107–8.

46. Ibid., 108.

47. Comprising Müftüoğlu's earliest literary output, this collection was written between 1894 and 1900; the stories were published primarily in the literary journal *Servet-i Fünûn* before appearing in book format in 1901. Schrader translated three stories for the Turkish Library: "Lullaby," "Salha's Sin," and "Aunt Nakiye." Notably, Schrader first undertook these translations seven years prior, the same year the collection first appeared in book format.

48. "Atmet." Schrader, "Einleitung: Ahmet Hikmet,„ 8–9.

49. Müftüoğlu's family hailed from the Morea but migrated to Istanbul amid the 1821 Peloponnesian Revolt, during which his grandfather was killed. This revolt, which initiated the Greek War of Independence (1821–30), was an important factor in Müftüoğlu's family history and his later commitment to Turkism. For information on Müftüoğlu's family background, see Türker Tekin, "Giriş," 11.

50. Kuran, "Impact," 115.

51. "Urteilslosen Nachbetern und Nachahmern des Westens zu werden."

Schrader, "Einleitung: Ahmet Hikmet," 9.

52. "Diese Geschichte enthält persönliche Erlebnisse des Autors. Es ist mit Ausnahme eines Teiles eine Wiedergabe von Tatsachen, ein »document humain« im wahren Sinne des Wortes." Ibid., 31.

53. Schrader's translation reads, "Muster echttürkischer Natur, türkischer Erziehung, türkischer Gesinnung und türkischen Mutes." Schrader, "Naqijje Xala," 46.

54. Schrader's translation reads, "[Die] dasass mit ihrem spitzenberänderten Kopftuch (*jemeni*), mit den hennagefärbten Harren, dem *Tschibuq* aus Jasminholz, mit dem reinen *Halali*hemd, das die hagere Brust halb bedeckte, den schwarzen absatzlosen Schuhen (*mest*), deren Spitzen sichtbar wurden, denn sie hatte die Beine nach türkischer Art gekreuzt—ein Gegenbild zu dem Opfermute der beiden Männer." Ibid., 46.

55. "Der Realismus beruht auf dem Drang nach Wahrheit." Schrader, "Einleitung: Ahmet Hikmet," 2.

56. "Eine recht bittere Satire, eine Kritik in Fleisch und Blut an einem absurden durch die Zeit geheiligten Brauch." Ibid., 5.

57. I take this definition from Ian Watts: "Formal realism is only a mode of presentation, and it is therefore ethically neutral." Watts, *Rise of the Novel*, 117. In Schrader's words, "[Müftüoğlu] weiss . . . durch die leichte spielende Form und den schönen Fluss seiner Erzählung in das rechte Licht zu setzen, ohne dass er jemals doktrinär würde und die Tendenz allzu sehr unterstriche." Schrader, "Einleitung: Ahmet Hikmet," 2.

58. Finkel, *Osman's Dream*, 474–84.

59. Farah, *Die deutsche Pressepolitik*, 96.

60. Ibid., 112.

61. Hamann, *Prekäre koloniale Ordnung*, 230–31.

62. The word "colony" was used to denote the entirety of citizens or wards of a given consul. Fuhrmann, *Der Traum*, 271. This community resided predominantly in Pera, a historically cosmopolitan neighborhood where French, Venetian, and British diplomats had lived since the sixteenth century, together with diverse non-Muslim minorities of the empire. While Germans had resided in Constantinople since the early nineteenth century, the community grew significantly in size following the ascension of Wilhelm II to the throne in 1888 and the new era of German-Ottoman relations he initiated. Dietrich, *Deutschsein in Istanbul*, 78. The use of the word "colony" to describe Germans in the Ottoman Empire was nevertheless not unique to Constantinople; German communities in the Aegean cities of Smyrna and Thessaloniki had also described themselves as colonies from the early eighteenth century onward. However, the term took on new ideological weight following the establishment of the German nation-state under Chancellor Otto von Bismarck in 1871. Fuhrman, *Der Traum*, 142.

63. Ibid., 144–45. With the ultimate goal of maintaining a stable Orient, Bismarck sought, above all, to minimize conflict between major European powers with territorial interests in the Ottoman Empire. Accordingly, he did not undertake sustained economic or military intervention in the empire.

64. Gottschlich, *Beihilfe*, 48–50.

65. Dietrich, *Deutschsein in Istanbul*, 128.

66. This policy was otherwise referred to as *pénétration pacifique*. Fuhrmann, *Der Traum*, 156.

67. Ibid., 56, 78, 80, 128.

68. Farah, *Die deutsche Pressepolitik*, 92. In 1888, the Deutsche Bank founded the subsidiary company Chemins de Fer Ottomans d'Anatolie, which would operate the Anatolian Railway; lines connecting Istanbul, Ankara, and Konya were constructed throughout the 1890s. With the backing of the Deutsche Bank, an additional railway line connecting Thessaloniki to Monastir was also up and running by 1894.

69. "La conquesta!—Sie ist im vollen Gange. Da stolzieren sie in unsren Gassen herum, die Vorkämpfer der Weltmacht, die blonden Konquistadoren mit den Baby-Schnurrbärten, die den Orient unterwerfen wollen. . . . Von unwiderstehlichem Bedürfnis getrieben, kommen die edlen Deutschen . . . dem bedrängten Kulturvolke der Türken . . . herrischer zu Hilfe. Deutsches Kapital, deutsche Waren und deutsche Mord-waffen, alle diese Segnungen ergießen sich in Fülle über die Türkei.—Es ist natürlich die Pflicht jedes Türken, durch diese Beweise aufrichtiger Freundschaft auf das heftigste gerührt zu sein." Schrader, "Vom goldenen Horn," 414.

70. "Es ist ein hartes Schicksal für eine junge Literatur, mit solchen Schwierigkeiten kämpfen zu müssen. Die deutschen offiziösen Blätter nennen China ein Land der Barbarei. Die Barbarei ist in viel schlimmerem Grade in der Türkei vorhanden, als Produkt einer Regierung, die mit der Deutschen einen beständigen Austausch von Zärtlichkeiten vornimmt." Schrader, "Das geistige Leben," 555.

71. Gottschlich, *Beihilfe*, 54.

72. Percy Ernst Schramm, Walter Schlesinger, and Karl Bosl assert that the term first arose in nineteenth-century Slavic discourse; Gerard Labuda traces the genesis of the term more specifically to the work of Polish historian Karol Szajnocha and the Slovak publicist Ľudovít Štúr, who wrote of an "Andrang des Germanenthums." Hans Lemberg argues that the term first arose in the German context and was only later taken up by the Slavs. For a detailed analysis of the genesis of this term, see Wippermann, *Der "deutsche Drang,"* 12–46.

73. "Anreizung, innerer Trieb, Impetus, Impulsus." Grimm and Grimm, *Deutsches Wörterbuch*, 1333.

74. Wippermann, *Der "deutsche Drang,"* 4.

75. Ibid., vii.

76. "Das Deutschtum verfolgt ganz andere Ziele als diejenigen, welche man ihm in übelwollender Absicht untergeschoben hat. Sein interesse für den Osten entspringt lediglich dem Wunsche, auch hier an der Kulturarbeit, zu der alle Völker Europas aufgerufen sind, in friedlichem Wettbewerb mit diesen teilzunehmen und seinen Fleiß, seine Arbeitsmethoden, seine Gründlichkeit in den dienst der großen Aufgabe zu stellen, welche die neue Türkei übernommen hat. Das echte Deutschtum hat keine Tendenz zur Ausschließlichkeit und zur Monopolisierung, es ist kosmopolitisch und bringt fremdem Volkstum, besonders dem türkischen, die weitesten Sympathien entgegen. Möge die Zeit kommen, wo die türkische Presse das einsieht." Schrader, "Der Drang nach Osten."

77. Reviews are too numerous to list in their entirety. See, for example,

Schrader, "Literatur zur jüngsten Geschichte"; "Vom Büchertisch" (1910); "Neue Orient Literatur."

78. Examples are too numerous to list in their entirety. See, for example, Schrader, "Das türkische Theater"; "Das Geschenk des Lebens"; "Türkische Dichtung"; "Die osmanische Miniaturkunst"; "Namık Kemal Bey als Erzähler."

79. These essays appeared in the feuilleton section of the *Ottoman Lloyd*. They were later published as a collection in Schrader, *Konstantinopel*.

80. See, for example, Schrader, "Tante Naqijje"; "Eine Mutter"; "Die Bezauberung des Aga."

81. See, for example, the conclusion of Schrader's review of the Turkish Library for the *Ottoman Lloyd*, where he states, "Der türkischen Bibliothek muß man im Interesse ihres Gedeihens viele Freunde wünschen. Besonders unsere Landsleute in der Türkei sollten an dieser Quelle ihre Kenntnisse des türkischen Lebens und türkischen Volkscharakters zu bereichern suchen." Schrader, "Türkische Bibliothek."

82. And, *Meşrutiyet Döneminde*, 125. The event was advertised and reviewed in the *Ottoman Lloyd*. See "Armenische Schillervorstellung."

83. See, for example, the review of Schrader's talk on Sultan Selim I, "Vortragsabend im Ausflugsverein."

84. For a summary of the commission's activities, see Schrader, "Die Kunstdenkmäler Konstantinopels," 352–54.

85. The Ottoman Turkish reads, "Bu vakadan tam beş sene sonra, o şampanya gibi kabına sığmayan yeğenim, Zonguldak'tan avdet ettiği zaman, ayran gibi sâkin ve râkid, apışmış kalmıştı." Müftüoğlu, "Yeğenim," 242.

86. Schrader, "Der Kulturträger," 2.

87. My translation. The Ottoman Turkish reads, "Bunlar o diyâr-ı irfânda beş senelik geceli gündüzlü . . . bir tahsil-i mütemâdinin semeresi imiş! [. . .] Beş seneden sonra, Napolyonkâri bir vaziyet, Hümbertkâri bir saç, Wilhelmkâri bir bıyık. . . . İşte bu kadar! . . . Yeni kafa olmak için bu kadarı kâfi imiş." Müftüoğlu, "Yeğenim," 238–39.

88. "Bizim yeğenin 'neşr-i medeni-yyet' vazifesi imiş." Müftüoğlu, "Yeğenim," 239.

89. Journals include *Türk Yurdu*, *Resimli Kitap*, *Yeni İnci*, *Yeni Mecmua*, *Tasvir-i Efkâr*, and *Türk Derneği*. For more on Müftüoğlu's publishing history, see Taşdelen, *Literature as a Mirror of History*, 161–62.

90. Müftüoğlu translated a scientific work on potatoes by Antoine-Augustin Parmentier and a book on the beauty routine of the Baronne Staffe. Tevetoğlu, *Ahmed Hikmet Müftüoğlu*, 27–28.

91. *Sivilisasyon* was also in use as a direct transliteration from French during the 1840s; *temeddün*, which is derived from the same Arabic root as *medeniyyet* (m-d-n), was also in use at this time. *Temeddün* signifies the process of becoming refined or civilized and thus hints at a concept of progress.

92. Görgün, "Medeniyet," 298–301.

93. Vogt, "*Civilisation* and *Kultur*," 129–37.

CHAPTER 4

1. Adıvar, *House with Wisteria*, 19.

2. Ibid., 17–24. Halide Edip describes her school, Greek funerals, the clothing of other children, diverse culinary traditions, and Christian ceremonies.

3. Arat, "Nation Building and Feminism," 41.

4. The Turkish version of part one of Halide Edip's memoirs was first published in serialized form in 1955 and later in book form in 1963 as *Mor Salkımlı Ev*. The second section of her memoirs, entitled *The Turkish Ordeal, Being the Further Memoirs of Halide Edip*, was first published in London in 1928. The Turkish version was serialized between 1959 and 1960 and published in book form in 1962 as *Türk'ün Ateşle İmtihanı*.

5. Durakbaşa, *Halide Edip*, 142.

6. Seyhan, "Is Orientalism in Retreat?," 215.

7. Timuroğlu, "Women's Nation," 446.

8. Arnakis, "Turanism," 20–23.

9. Gözütok, "Yeni Turan'da," 413.

10. Adıvar, *Yeni Turan*, 34.

11. Gözütok, "Yeni Turan'da," 427.

12. "*Yeni Tûran* baştan aşağıya kadar Tânzîmat'ın netîcesi bir teceddüdden başka bir şey değil." Kemal, "Yeni Tûran," 171.

13. First formed in Geneva in 1910, this organization was also important for the development of Turanism, due largely to the presence of Russian Turks among its most prominent members.

14. Adıvar, *House with Wisteria*, 264.

15. Ibid., 273.

16. Ibid., 273–74.

17. Schrader, "Einleitung des Über-setzers," ix.

18. "Erwachen des Rassenbewußt-seins." Ibid., vii.

19. "[Turanismus] will es dem türki-schen Volk ermöglichen, nach der Weise der europäischen Völker auf der Grund-lage des eigenen Wesens seinen Fortschritt zu bewerkstelligen." Ibid., xi.

20. Roshwald, *Ethnic Nationalism*, 5.

21. "Zivilisatorischen Instinkt." Schrader, "Einleitung des Übersetzers," ix.

22. For an elaboration on these core components of ethnicity, see Smith, *Ethnic Origins of Nations*, 23–31.

23. "Avrupan'nın açık gözlerinden." Adıvar, *Yeni Turan*, 43.

24. Adıvar, *House with Wisteria*, 273.

25. Ibid., 242.

26. Ibid., 242.

27. Gözütok, "Yeni Turan'da," 429.

28. The remaining volumes were dedicated to Islam (see volumes 1, 8, and 11), German political and economic influence in the Ottoman Empire (see volumes 17 and 18), and other pressing historical and political issues in the Middle East, such as the development of Jewish colonies in Palestine, British political domination of Egypt, and Napoleon's *Orientpolitik* (see volumes 9, 10, and 16, respectively).

29. See volume 7.

30. See volumes 13, 15, and 20, respectively.

31. See volume 2, Tekinalp, *Türkismus und Pantürkismus*; volume 3, *Vom asiatischen Reich der Türkei*; and Volume 6, Schrader, *Das Neue Turan*.

32. Tekinalp, *Türkismus und Pantürkismus*, 55. Overall, Tekinalp believed that Germany and the Ottoman Empire completed one another. While the Ottoman Empire needed German technology, he argued, Germany also needed a market for the exportation of its goods.

33. "Die Türken haben verstanden, daß sie, um zu leben, sich türkisieren, nationalisieren, dass sie wieder sie selbst werden müssen." Tekinalp, *Türkismus und Pantürkismus*, 16.

34. "Ihre Rede ist ganz Bewegung, ganz Enthusiasmus, und dabei vollendete Musik." Schrader, "Einleitung des Übersetzers," xi.

35. Venuti, *Contra Instrumentalism*, 5–6. See also my discussion of the Turkish Library in chapter 3.

36. Hachtmann, *Die türkische Literatur*, 7.

37. Ibid., 7–8:

Die ungeheuren politischen und seelischen Erschütterungen des Balkankrieges und des Weltkrieges haben . . . auf dem Gebiete der Literatur zu einer Erneuerung geführt. Es ist eine wahre Freude, diese geistige Wiedergeburt mitzuerleben! Die türkische Literatur ist durch die Eisenkur des Krieges ihre Bleichsucht losgeworden. Kraftbewußt und helläugig wie ein junger, schlanker Pfadfinder schaut sie in das Morgenrot einer herrlichen Zukunft. In Männern und Frauen schwillt ein ganz neuer, begeisterungsvoller Schaffensdrang: Selbstzucht, Reinheit und Kraft sind die allgemeinen Ideale geworden. . . . Es ist die erwartungsvolle Stimmung vor Sonnenaufgang: ein leuchtendes Morgenrot steht am Himmel der Türkei, die sich so lange mit einem trübseligen Abendrot begnügen mußte. Bald wird die Sonne des neuen Türkentums aufgehen. Hoffen wir, daß ihre warmen Strahlen das erwachende Leben zur Blüte und Reife fördern!

38. "Halbtürken." Ibid., 9.

39. "Für sie ist die Alternative nicht etwa: Franzosentum oder Deutschtum?, sondern: Europäertum oder Türkentum?" Ibid., 9.

40. Schrader, "Einleitung des Übersetzers," x.

41. Adıvar, *Edebiyatta Tercümenin Rolü*, 272.

42. Ibid., 272.

43. Parla, "Object of Comparison," 124.

44. "Literarische Gefangenschaft." Hachtmann, *Die türkische Literatur*, 8. Notably, Halide Edip echoes this rhetoric of enslavement in her 1943 speech. In her depiction of Ottoman divan literature, she argues that the majority of Turkish authors did not simply adapt Persian models but rather wrote in a specifically Persian mode. As a result, she writes, divan poetry remained imprisoned in a foreign spirit and personality. Adıvar, "Edebiyatta Tercümenin Rolü," 266–67.

45. Ironically, Halide Edip's narrator, Asım, expresses exactly the opposite in the opening pages of the novel: "Maksadım, politikamızın esas ve esbab-ı mucibesinden ziyade politikayla karışan bir kalp hikâyesini . . . zapt etmek" ("My aim is to write about a politically influenced love story rather than about the principles and reasons of our politics"). Adıvar, *Yeni Turan*, 1.

46. "Rauen, stammelden Gedichten der Turanier." Schrader, "Die türkische Kultur," 272.

47. Gust, *Armenian Genocide*, 48.

48. "Wir dürfen auch im Ausland nicht, wie wir bisher getan haben, stets zu der Partei halten, die es auf Vergewaltigung wichtiger Kulturelemente zugunsten der eigenen nationalen Vorherrschaft abgesehen hat. Das wird sich stets rächen, wie es sich in der Türkei gerächt hat. Wir hätten nicht türkischer sein dürfen als der Türke." Schrader, *Eine Flüchtlingsreise*, 112–13.

49. Richter, "Deutsche Dichtungen," 2.

50. "Ist nicht das französische Schrifttum, dass eine so tiefe Wirkung auf die türkischen gebildeten Klassen ausgeübt hat, auch aus der Rennaissance hervorgegangen?" "Nochmals deutsche Dichtungen," 2.

51. Mann, "Origins of Humanism," 2.

52. Ibid., 1–2.

53. Ibid., 1.

54. Quoted in Schrader, "Die türkische Kultur," 271.

55. Goethe, *West-East Divan*, 80.1–4.

56. "Antiker Form und Norm." Richter, "Deutsche Dichtungen," 2.

57. Homer used the term *barbarophonoi* to describe those who spoke unintelligible "bar-bar," meaning a language other than Greek. Bisaha, *Creating East and West*, 45.

58. More than half of fifth-century Athenian tragedies employed this trope of the barbarian other. Ibid., 45.

59. Note that the Turks are cast as Asians here, despite the fact that they controlled the Balkans. Ibid., 84.

60. Hay, *Europe*, 83–87.

61. Bisaha, *Creating East and West*, 86.

62. Ibid., 96.

63. Ibid., 133.

64. "Das große Lager aber draußen vor der Stadtmauer schwamm in einem wohlberechtigten Freudensrausch. Gewaltig war die Beute an goldenen und silbernen Gefaßen, Schmucksachen und an wertvollen Stoffen." Schrader, *Konstantinopel*, 111.

65. "Die politischen Verhältnisse haben sich zwar geändert, aber auf dem Wege des Handels ist Byzanz-Stambul noch immer mit den Ländern verbunden, die einst in ihm voll stolzer Bewunderung ihre Hauptstadt sahen." Ibid., 41.

66. Fletcher, *Moorish Spain*, 164–69. Following previously tolerant treaties that guaranteed freedom of religion,

Muslims in Spain were forced to convert to Christianity or face exile in the early sixteenth century. Islam was officially prohibited in Spain from 1525 on. The term "Morisco" designates a Muslim minority that initially remained in Spain and converted to Christianity but maintained allegiance to their Islamic faith in secret. Ibid., 167.

67. Rotter, "Maslama b. ʿAbd-al-Malik b. Marwān," 740.

68. Ames, *Righteous Persecution*, 6.

69. "Aus solchen Werken redet eine uralte, künsterlische Kultur, deren Immoralität selbst für die Höhe der ästhetischen Inspiration spricht.... [Ü]-berall findet man in ihr [die türkische Lyrik] den Sensualismus, der uns an die Antike und an die Renaissance erinnert, eine reife Frucht der Sonne des Südens und der Helligkeit des Mittelmeergestades." Schrader, "Die türkishe Kultur," 270.

70. "Mittelmeerkultur." Ibid., 271. "Mittelmeerzivilisation," Ibid., 273.

71. "Wir Deutsche." Ibid., 272.

72. Schrader, *Konstantinopel*, 1–2.

73. Ibid., 17.

74. Rosaldo, "Imperialist Nostalgia," 107–8.

75. Schrader, *Konstantinopel*, 127.

76. "Zeugen einer andern Welt." Ibid., 12.

77. Ibid., 13.

78. *Commedia dell'arte* was a popular form of comedy in Italian theaters of the sixteenth to eighteenth centuries.

79. Schrader, *Konstantinopel*, 141–42.

CHAPTER 5

1. "Hudâ-yı dâ'im ül vucûd ve vâcib üs-sücûda hamd-i bî nihâyeden sonra bu seyâhatnâme-i mutavvelenin sebeb-i tahririnin beyânına şürû' edildi." Ali, "Mufassal Cermenistân Seyâhatnâmesi," 111.

2. Five scholarships were granted for Germany, France, and England, respectively.

3. Dickinson and Seviner, "Translators' Introduction," 98. Evliya Çelebi's travels throughout Anatolia, parts of Mesopotamia, Transylvania, Central Asia, North Africa, and Eastern Europe are documented across ten volumes.

4. Ibid., 99.

5. Ali, "Mufassal Cermenistân Seyâhatnâmesi," 116.

6. For more on the prohibition of the old script—even for religious books—see Shaw and Shaw, *Reform, Revolution, and Republic*, 386.

7. Seviner, "Between Languages," 84.

8. Ibid., 86.

9. For a concise summary of the history of reforms and their culmination in the 1920s, see Aytürk, "Script Charisma," 119–20.

10. The three vowels of Arabic—which are roughly equivalent to *a*, *e*, and *i*—each have a short and long form. The vowels of Turkish are *a, e, i, ı, o, ö, u,* and *ü*. For a detailed discussion of the applicability of the Perso-Arabic script to Ottoman Turkish, see chapter 3 of Geoffrey Lewis, *Turkish Language Reform*.

11. Ertürk, *Grammatology*, 90.

12. Ibid., 91–93.

13. Aytürk, "Script Charisma," 124.

14. Ertürk, *Grammatology*, 92.

15. State institutions, banks, societies, and corporations were further required to conduct all of their correspondence in the new script by January 1, 1929.

16. Ali, "Comprehensive Germanistan Travelogue," 107. "Potsdam kelimesi, iştikâkıyyûn-ı zamândan Hayrullah

Molla Beyin tefsîri üzere 'Put', 'sedd', 'ümm' kelimelerinden mürekkeb olup, 'Put', ma'lûm olduğu üzere kenâ'is-î Küffârda mevcûd Hıristos tasâvîri ile heyâkil makûlesi esnâmdır; 'sedd', kapamak, örtmek, setr eylemek; 'Ümm', vâlide, burada Meryem Ana mânasındadır. Cümlesi toplu olarak, kübizm üzere, 'Meryem Vâlide, esnâmı setr eyle!' demek olur." Ali, "Mufassal Cermenistân Seyâhatnâmesi," 114.

17. Husserl, *Ideas*, 166.

18. Schutz and Luckmann, *Structure of the Life-World*, 36.

19. Dickinson and Seviner, "Translator's Introduction," 99.

20. Ali, "Comprehensive Germanistan Travelogue," 105. "Lisân-ı sâde isti'mâline gayret olunmuştur." Ali, "Mufassal Cermenistân Seyâhatnâmesi," 112.

21. Ali, "Comprehensive Germanistan Travelogue," 106. "Macar hududunda Avrupa'da olduğumuzu tamamiyle idrâk edüp etrafımızdaki âsâr-ı umrâna hayran olurduk." Ali, "Mufassal Cermenistân Seyâhatnâmesi," 113.

22. Dickinson and Seviner, "Translator's Introduction," 100.

23. Ali, "Comprehensive Germanistan Travelogue," 107. "Ve raksın ismine muvâfık olarak 'pat' diye yere yuvarlandıkları halde 'nâz' etmeyerek kalkup tekrar bir istikâmet-i mechûleye şitâb etmektedirler." Ali, "Mufassal Cermenistân Seyâhatnâmesi," 114.

24. For an insightful discussion of ice-skating in the late Ottoman Empire, see chapter 7 of Brummett, *Image and Imperialism*.

25. Holbrook, *Unreadable Shores*, 22–23. The history of Turkish language reform cannot be explained only through the history of Orientalism.

Nergis Ertürk, for example, describes the trajectory of language reform from the late nineteenth through the mid-twentieth centuries as a form of radical self-surgery. She reads the drive toward linguistic rationalization not simply vis-à-vis a European counterpart but also into the context of new print technologies of the nineteenth century. Ertürk, *Grammatology*, x–xi.

26. The only earlier use of a term for "world literature" in modern or Ottoman Turkish that I have identified thus far is Mehmet Ali Aynî's 1901 translation of Frédéric Loliée's *A History of Comaprative Literature from Its Origins to the Twentieth Century* (*Histoire des littératures comparées des origines au vingtième siècle*) as *Tarih'i Edebî'i Âlem* (*History of the Literature of the World*). WorldCat lists the publication date of Loliée's *History* as 1903; the French National Library has it catalogued as 1904. Together with the fact that Aynî's translation already appeared in 1901, this indicates a cataloguing mistake in the original date of publication.

27. This World Literature series is no longer in print and is not housed in its entirety at any single library, which has made it difficult to track down every single volume. To date, I have located volumes 1, 3, 5, 8, 10, 11, 16, 17, 19, 21, 22, 28, 29, and 31, none of which contain a translation from an "Eastern" literary source.

28. I maintain the slightly awkward literal translation "ways of seeing" here as a gesture toward Özgü's use of the term *görüş yolları*. The current term for point of view is *görüş açısı*; I assume that Özgü's use of *görüş yolları* is the result of linguistic experimentation at a time when the Turkish language was still very much in flux.

29. "Bu noktanın cihan edebiyatındaki mevkii de onun cihan edebiyatındaki şahsiyetini verecektir." Özgü, "Göte'nin Cihan Edebiyatındaki Şahsiyeti," 7.

30. "Şiir bir halk verimi olmakla beraber, ayni [sic] zamanda bir cihan verimidir de, yani kökleri bir milletin toprağındadır, fakat zirvesi yükselebilir, hem o kadar yükselir ki, bulunduğu saha nihayetsiz bir surette genişler, edebî ve umum insanlık sahasına girer. İşte bundan dolayı şiir bütün milletler tarafından anlaşılan bir lisandır. İster Homer, ister Dante, Şekspir, Servantes, Rasin, Dostojevski, yahut ta İbsen olsun; damarlarında akan kan, Yunan, İtalyan, İngiliz, İspanyol, Fransız, Rus, yahut ta şimal kanı olsun, şiirin sesini alan, yani insan olan herkes, onların her birinde kendi ruhundan bir parça duyar." Ibid., 17–18.

31. Ülken, *Uyanış Devirlerinde*, 11–12.

32. Alongside Ottoman, Ülken also cites ancient Chinese and Indian civilizations. Ibid., 16.

33. "Bir kelime ile, *uyanış devirlerinde yaratıcılık kudretini veren tercümedir*" (emphasis in original). Ibid., 18.

34. "Garp medeniyetinin en mühim karakteri, tarih kültürü üzerine kurulmuş olması, kendinden önce doğup kaybolan bütün medeni hamleler kapısını açabilmek için bir çok perspektivlerden bakmağa çalışmasıdır." Ibid., 16.

35. "Tercüme, bütün bir medeniyeti nakletmektir." Ibid., 383.

36. The series published literature in translation and secondary scholarship. Ülken's monograph appeared as volume 26.

37. "Dağınık," "gelişigüzel." Ibid., 383.

38. "*Şuurlu, teşkilatlı ve tam bir tercüme*" (emphasis in the original),

"bugünün büyük fikir ve san'at eserleri yanında bütün san'at ve felsefe klasikleri." Ibid., 384. Ahmet Hamdi Tanpınar described the selection of texts to be translated during the late nineteenth century in similar terms; he uses, for example, the term *tesadüfîlik*, meaning random, accidental, or fortuitous. Tanpınar, *XIX. Asır*, 264.

39. Gürçağlar compares Ülken's conception of the West in *The Role of Translation in Periods of National Awakening* to that of Yaşar Nabi Nayır, who described the West as a "mentality" or a "spirit." Gürçağlar, *Politics and Poetics*, 62–63.

40. "Bu manada Garplılaşmak demek, kapalı medeniyetten açık medeniyete geçmek demektir. Biz Garplı'yız veya Garplı olacağız demek, rasyonel ve üniversal dünya medeniyetine katıldık ve katılacağız demektir." Ülken, *Millet ve Tarih Şuuru*, 13.

41. For more information on the concept of *bütüncü*, see Tunaya, *Türkiye'nin Siyasi Hayatında*, 151–73. For information on the concept of *kısmi'ci*, see ibid., 174–96. For the distinction between civilization (*medeniyet*) and culture (*hars*), see Gökalp, *Türkçülüğün Esasları*, 32–33. For a clear statement on Ülken's belief that the realms of civilization and culture cannot be separated, see also Ülken, *Millet ve Tarih Şuuru*, 29.

42. Oruç, "Rewriting," 340.

43. There is no indication that *cihan* posed an ideological counterpoint to *dünya* in the 1930s and 1940s but rather aligned closely with it. Nowhere is this more apparent than in Fehmi Yahya Tuna's *Dünya Edebiyatı Tarihi*. In the opening sentence of his preface, Tuna self-references his own book as "*Cihan Edebiyatına Toplu Bir Bakış*" ("A Comprehensive View of World

Literature," my emphasis), suggesting the relative unimportance of a systematic term to describe world literature for his larger project.

44. Yücel stepped down as director in 1946, after which the number of books published per year declined. The series also began to publish scholarly works after 1947. Gürçağlar, *Politics and Poetics*, 71. In its later phases, the series also published significantly more works from Eastern literatures. The official bibliography lists sixty-six Eastern/Islamic classics, seven Chinese classics, three Indian classics, and two Iranian classics. Ötüken et al., *Dünya Edebiyatından Tercümeler*, ix–xi.

45. The bureau published ten translated plays in its first year and thirteen books in 1941. Numbers increased steadily in the following years, with twenty-seven books in 1942, sixty-eight books in 1943, ninety-seven books in 1944, 110 books in 1945, and 143 books in 1946. Ibid., 71.

46. While this was the tendency for the majority of translation initiatives at the time, at least one private translation series included reference to the East in its title: Selected Works from the East and the West (Şarktan-Garptan Seçme Eserler) was published by Ahmet Halit Publishing House throughout the 1940s. The series produced translations of *Kalila wa Dimna*, Sa'dī's *Bustan* and *Gulistān*, Niẓāmī Ganjavī's rendition of *Khosrow and Shirin*, Rabindranath Tagore's *The Home and the World*, the *Ramayana*, and Kahlil Gibran's *The Prophet*.

47. İlhan Selçuk also describes Remzi Publishing House in general as having taken the first steps toward translating

"world classics" (*dünya klasikleri*). Selçuk, "Remzi ve Kitab Evi," 86.

48. *Remzi Bengi'ye Saygı*, 219.

49. English translation quoted in Gürçağlar, *Politics and Poetics*, 64. "Bugün hakikî mânâsı ile Rönesans yapıyoruz. Dünya kervanına yeniden katılıyoruz. Bu yolda kendimizi tekrar bulmak için garb metodları bize rehberlik edecektir." Ülken, "Maksad," 2.

50. "Her milletin edebiyatı, diğer milletlerin edebiyatından örnekler alarak zenginleşti. Şimdi bizde de, edebiyatımıza yeni bir istikamet vermek bahis mevzuudur. Bu işte muvaffak olmanın başlıca şartlarından biri, garbın en güzel, en meşhur eserlerini dilimize çevirmektir." *Dünya Muharrirlerinden Tercümeler Serisi Kataloğu*, n.p.

51. "En esaslı gayelerinden biri ucuz ve güzel bir tercüme kütüphanesi yaratmaktır." I understand the word "güzel" in this quote to indicate well done in the sense of quality. Ibid., n.p.

52. Sevük, *Avrupa Edebiyatı ve Biz*, vii. Notably, such rhetorical emphasis on completeness was directed not only at selection processes but also manifested itself in translation practices of the 1930s. While adaptations, as well as abridged and summary translations, had been popular in the late nineteenth and early twentieth centuries, Saliha Paker identifies a growing tendency to produce "full" translations in the republican era in her examination of diverse translations from Greek. Paker, "Changing Norms," 417.

53. "'Avrupalı millet' demek 'Avrupa coğrafyasında bulunan' demek değil. Avrupalı millet evvelâ bütün 'Antiquité'yi, yâni Yunan ve Lâtin'in bütün bellibaşlı eserlerini, sonra diğer Avrupa milletlerinin de yine bellibaşlı

kitaplarını kendi diline nakledendir."
Sevük, *Avrupa Edebiyatı ve Biz*, vi.

54. Spivak, "Aesthetic Education,"
459.

CHAPTER 6

1. This translation of the title is my
own. Auerbach, "Philology," 7–8.
"Schicksalsvollen Zusammenwachsens."
"Überfülle des Materials, der Methoden
und der Anschauungsweisen." Auerbach, "Philologie," 42–43.

2. Auerbach, "Philology," 16. "Er soll
aus ihm herausgewachsen sein, ein
Stück von ihm selbst." "Die Dinge selbst
sollen zur Sprache kommen." Auerbach,
"Philologie," 49.

3. Auerbach, "Philology," 14; "Hand-
habe." Auerbach, "Philologie," 47.

4. Auerbach, "Philology," 15;
"Strahlkraft." Auerbach, "Philologie," 47.

5. Ali's translation of *Verlobung* was
included in the collection *Üç Romantik
Hikâye* (Three Romantic Stories), which
appeared in 1943. This collection also
included Ali's translations of Adelbert
von Chamisso's "Peter Schlemihls
Wundersame Geschichte," translated as
Peter Schlemihl'in Acayip Sergüzeşti, and
E. T. A. Hoffmann's "Doge und Doga-
resse," translated as *Duka ile Karısı*.
Sabahattin Ali, *Üç Romantik Hikâye:
Kleist, Chamisso, Hoffmann* (Ankara:
Maarif Matbaası, 1943).

6. This number includes reprints;
973 of these were first editions.
Gürçağlar, *Politics and Poetics*, 71.

7. Konuk, *East West Mimesis*, 54.

8. The conservatory was founded in
1941. English translation quoted in Berk,
Translation and Westernisation, 154–55.
Yücel, "3 Temmuz 1941," 3–4:

Bir gün bizim gibi bütün insanlığın
idrak edeceğine inanmış bulun-
duğumuz TÜRK HUMANIZMASININ
yepyeni bir safhası, Devlet Konservatuvarının bağrından
doğmaktadır. Türk hümanizması,
beşer eserine istisnasız kıymet
veren, ona zamanda ve mekânda
hudut tanımıyan hür bir anlayış ve
duyuştur. Hangi milletten olursa
olsun insanlığa yeni bir düşünüş,
yeni bir duyuş getiren her esere
bizim yüreklerimizin besliyeceği
his, ancak saygı ve hayranlıktır. Biz
bu saygı ve hayranlık duygumuzu
nazari bir bakışla değil, yaparak ve
yaşıyarak, kendimizin kılarak ifade
ediyoruz. Müellif bizden olmıy-
abilir, bestekâr başka milletten
olabilir. Fakat o sözleri ve sesleri
anlıyan ve canlandıran biziz. Onun
için Devlet Konservatuvarının
temsil ettiği piyesler, oynadığı oper-
alar bizimdir, Türktür ve millidir.

9. During the 1940–41 season, opera
performances included *Tosca* and
Madama Butterfly by Puccini, *Fidelio* by
Ludwig von Beethoven, *The Bartered
Bride* by Bedrich Smetana, and *Le Nozze
di Figaro* by Wolfgang Amadeus Mozart.
Of the nineteen plays performed during
1941–47, only one was Turkish; the
others were translations of European
dramatic texts. Berk, *Translation and
Westernisation*, 121.

10. The Darülfünun offered its first
public lectures in 1863.

11. Not all of the academics who took
positions in Turkey during World War II
were Jewish; others were political
dissenters who had similarly been forced
into exile.

12. Seyhan, "German Academic
Exiles," 277–78.

13. Said describes Auerbach's exile in Istanbul as a "deeply resonating and intense form of exile from Europe," and writes that *Mimesis* "owed its existence to the very fact of Oriental, non-Occidental exile and homelessness." Said, *World*, 6, 8.

14. Apter, "Global *Translatio*," 258, 280.

15. Konuk, *East West Mimesis*, 13.

16. Ibid., 16.

17. Ertürk, "Modernity and Its Fallen Languages" 42. This observation in no way diminishes Kader Konuk's extensive investigation of Turkish humanist reforms. Yet if anything, her reading of *Mimesis* amplifies the myriad ways in which the Turkish side of this history has been largely elided in scholarship.

18. Oruç, "Rewriting," 345; Apter, "Global Translatio," 263.

19. Ibid., 347.

20. Ibid., 347–48.

21. Consider, for example, the following statement: "Ben Doğu ve Batı diye bir ayrılık görmüyorum. İnsan eseri, insan ruhunun iştiyakları, kayguları, korkuları zamana ve zemine göre değişse de özünde bir ayrılık varsa o, tutulan yol ve usuldendir." Quoted in Çıkar, *Hasan-Âli Yücel*, 62.

22. "Bizim kanaatimizce kaynağı ve pınarı eski Yunan'la da tahdit etmeyip daha arkalara ve başka diyarlara gitmek, nerede insan ruhunun kendine göre mana taşıyan bir izi ve eseri varsa, onları da içine alarak en geniş kavramıyla hümanizmayı bütün insanlığı kucaklayan bir anlayış halinde görmek lazımdır. Klasikler yayınını Milli Eğitim Bakanlığı'na işte bu anlayışla yaptırdık. Eflatun'un 'Diyaloglar'ı yanında Konfuçyüs'ların, Mevlâna'ların, Sadi'lerin eserleri bu anlayışla ve beraberce

Türk şuuruna doğdular." Yücel, *İyi Vatandaş*, 145.

23. Yücel uses the terms *terceme seferberliği* and *medeni dünya*. He also states, "Garp kültür ve tefekkür camiasının seçkin bir uzvu olmak." *Birinci Türk Neşriyat Kongresi*, 12.

24. Ahmet Ağaoğlu was one critical voice who argued against a form of culture planning, which he believed would lead to a standardization of the diverse individual thoughts and feelings that make up an aggregate culture: "Ben doğrusu bu maddeden ürktüm. Burnuma, nasıl diyeyim, 'devletleştirme,' 'plânlama,' vesaire gibi ta—sıkılıyorum söylemeğe—'standardize'ye kadar kokular geldi!" Ibid., 187. ("To tell the truth, I was irked by these matters. All of this nationalization, planning, and the like smells a little to me, how should I put it—I am embarrassed to even say it—like standardization!")

25. Holbrook, *Unreadable Shores*, 20.

26. Oruç, "Rewriting," 339–40.

27. For an insightful discussion of the concept of translatability as it relates to architectural projects in the early republican period, see Akcan, *Architecture in Translation*, 9–30.

28. Other categories were: (1) printing, publishing, and sales, (2) petitions, (3) copyright for literary works, (4) children's and youth literature, (5) prizes and propaganda, and (6) a publishing program.

29. In addition to chairman Ethem Menemencioğlu and reporter Mustafa Nihat Özön, the translation committee consisted of the following members: Abdülhak Şinasi Hisar, Ali Kami Akyüz, Bedrettin Tuncel, Burhan Belge, Cemil Bilsel, Fazıl Ahmet Aykaç, Fikret Adil, Galip Bahtiyar Göker, Halil Nihat Boztepe, Halit Fahri Ozansoy, İzzet

Melih Devrim, Nasuhi Baydar, Nurettin Artam, Nurullah Ataç, Orhan Şaik Gökyay, Rıdvan Nafiz Ergüder, Sabahattin Rahmi Eyüboğlu, Sabahattin Ali, Sabri Esat Siyavuşgil, Selami İzzet Sedes, Suut Kemal Yetkin, Şinasi Boran, Yusuf Şerif Kılıçel, Yaşar Nabi Nayır, and Zühtü Uray. *Birinci Türk Nesriyat Kongresi*, 35.

30. The committee's final report furthermore called for the publication of a comprehensive dictionary of modern Turkish, the formation of a state-sponsored translation bureau (*tercüme bürosu*), and the establishment of a translation journal (*tercüme mecmuası*) that would publish diverse translations alongside original texts, together with critical articles on methods of translation and existing translations in Turkish. Ibid., 125–27.

31. Texts by "Eastern authors" (*şark muharrirleri*) included in the list are Rūmī's *Masnavī*, Saʿdī's *Gulistān*, Ferdowsi's *Shahnameh*, Niẓāmī Ganjavī's *Khamsa*, selected texts by Ḥāfeẓ and Omar Khayyam, and selections from *One Thousand and One Nights*. For the full list of proposed works to be translated, see "Türkçeye Tercüme Edilmesi Tercüme İşleri Komisyonunca Teklif Edilen Eserler." Ibid., 277–85.

32. Gürçağlar, *Politics and Poetics*, 123.

33. Additional board members included Bedrettin Tuncel, Enver Ziya Karal, Nusret Hızır, Sabahattin Eyüboğlu and Saffer Pala Ali. Çıkar, *Hasan Âli Yücel*, 82.

34. Gürçağlar, "Translation Bureau Revisited," 121.

35. Ali, *Hep Genç Kalacağım*, 424.

36. "O zamana kadar da kalemimle geçinmeye çalışacağım." Ibid., 429.

37. David Gramling and Martina Schwalm also underscore the importance of reading *Madonna* as an early theorization of world literature in the era prior to decolonization. While also emphasizing the centrality of translation to *Madonna*, Gramling and Schwalm engage in a close reading of its frame narrative, in order to exemplify the novel's refusal to adhere to the tenets of cultural nationalism at the time. Gramling and Schwalm, "World Literature (Already) Wrote Back," 31.

38. Among the authors Ali translated throughout the 1930s are: Max Kemmerich, Fyodor Mikhailovich Dostoevsky, Heinrich Heine, Friedrich von Stendhal, and Gottfried Keller.

39. "Hümanizma ruhunun ilk anlayış ve duyuş merhalesi insan varlığının en müşahhas şekilde ifadesi olan sanat eserlerinin benimsenmesiyle başlar. Sanat şubeleri içinde edebiyat, bu ifadenin zihin unsurları en zengin olanıdır. Bunun içindir ki bir milletin, diğer milletler edebiyatını kendi dilinde, daha doğrusu kendi idrakinde tekrar etmesi; zekâ ve anlama kudretini o eserler nispetinde artırması, canlandırması ve yeniden yaratmasıdır. . . . Hangi milletin kütüpanesi [*sic*] bu yönden zenginse o millet, medeniyet âleminde daha yüksek bir idrak seviyesinde demektir. Bu itibarla tercüme hareketini sistemli ve dikkatli bir surette idare etmek, Türk irfanının en önemli bir cephesini kuvvetlendirmek, onun genişlemesine, ilerlemesine hizmet etmektir." Ali, *Üç Romantik Hikâye*, n.p. This introduction appeared as the preface to every book published in the Translations from World Literature series.

40. Fischer, "Introduction," 4.

41. Helmut Schneider goes so far as to read Kleist's entire textual production

as an ongoing challenge to the project of Enlightenment humanism. Schneider, "Facts of Life," 141–63.

42. Texts by Kleist included in the original translation list were: the complete short stories, *Der zerbrochene Krug, Hermanns Schlacht* [*sic*], and *Prinz Friedrich von Homburg. Birinci Neşriyat Kongresi*, 278. Texts actually translated include: *Die Verlobung in St. Domingo* (trans. Sabahattin Ali in 1943), *Michael Kohlhaas* (trans. Necip Üçok in 1944), *Der zerbrochene Krug* (trans. Hayrullah Örs in 1945, reprinted in 1964), *Die Marquise von O . . .* (trans. Melahat Togar in 1952), *Die Familie Schroffenstein* and *Prinz Friedrich von Homburg* (trans. Burhanettin Batıman in 1955), *Penthesilea, Das Käthchen von Heilbronn*, and *Die Hermannsschlacht* (trans. unknown). *Dünya Edebiyatından Tercüme Listesi* (Ankara: Maarif Basımevi, 1959), 73. See also Ötüken et al., *Dünya Edebiyatından Tercümeler*, 3–32.

43. Buck-Morss, "Hegel and Haiti," 827.

44. Ibid., 832.

45. Ibid., 821.

46. Ibid., 827. The colony of Saint-Domingue produced more than sixty-three thousand tons of sugar in 1787.

47. Ibid., 833.

48. Ibid., 835.

49. For a discussion of the "betrothal" as a moment that hides histories of violence and rape, which themselves led to racist classificatory terms such as "Mestize" and "Mulattinn," see Haverkamp, "Schwarz / Weiß," 400–402.

50. The verb he uses here is "yok etmek." Ali, *Üç Romantik Hikâye*, 3.

51. Ali uses the word "melez" to translate "Mestize." "Çok fena muamele görüyorlardı." Ibid., 4.

52. Ibid., 4.

53. Ibid., 5.

54. "Entrissen." Kleist, *Die Verlobung*, 8. Ali uses the same word, *zulüm*, in his translation of this scene from the novella.

55. Gilman, "Aesthetics of Blackness," 665–67.

56. Ibid., 672.

57. Byrd, "Family," 225.

58. Ibid., 231–32.

59. Ibid., 244.

60. Todd Kontje discusses the figure of Gustav in terms of "passing," which he uses to mean an act that "complicates identity politics by highlighting the tension between cultural constructs and biological essence, between convention and nature. The figure who crosses borders between fixed sexual, racial, or national identities provokes what Marjorie Garber has termed a 'category crisis.'" Kontje, "Passing for German," 68–69.

61. Konuk, *East West Mimesis*, 59.

62. Gökalp, "Maarif Meselesi," 111–12.

63. Doris Bachmann-Medick succinctly describes cultural translation as "an anti-essentialist and anti-holistic metaphor that aims to uncover . . . heterogeneous discursive spaces within a society." Bachmann-Medick, "Meanings of Translation," 37.

64. For an insightful discussion of the concept of smooth translatability as it relates to architectural projects in the early republican period, see Akcan, *Architecture in Translation*, 1–26.

65. For an insightful discussion of the hierarchies of racialized and gendered power between Congo Hoango and Babekan, and Babekan and Toni, see Byrd, "Family," 235.

66. Kleist, *Die Verlobung*, 43.

67. Ali, *Üç Romantik Hikâye*, 31.

68. The contemporary word for subtext is *altmetin*. In my research, I have not located the term *altmetin* or *alt tarafı* in dictionaries or reference books from the 1940s.

69. Ali, *Üç Romantik Hikâye*, 31.

70. "Sanat eserinin dili, diğer yazılı eserlerden farklı olarak, canlı bir mevcudiyettir. . . . Tercüme esnasında, mütercim kelimelerin manâlarını nakil ile kanaat ettiği müddetçe, bu hayat yok olur, ortada sadece birtakım ölü kelimeler silsilesi kalır. Asıl mütercim, bu cansız malzemeye, naklettiği dilde yeni bir hayat vermesini bilen kimsedir." Ali, *Markopaşa Yazıları*, 104. "Mütercimin hem eserini tercüme ettiği muharrire, hem de bu eseri arz ettiği insan kütlesine karşı büyük bir vicdan borcu olduğunu ve ağır bir mesuliyet altına girdiğini asla unutmaması lâzımdır." Ibid., 111. Ali originally composed these remarks for the article "İkinci Dilden Tercüme Meselesi ve Bir Misal," which appeared in *Tercüme* on March 19, 1941.

71. Sevük, *Avrupa Edebiyatı ve Biz*, vii.

72. Gailus, "Language Unmoored," 34 (my emphasis).

73. Ali, *Madonna in a Fur*, 147–49.

74. This does not imply that Kleist's characters lack complexity or serve merely symbolic functions. According to Ray Fleming, "Kleist allows action rather than psychological analysis to present us with the key to understanding the complexity of his black characters and their world. One might object that this is but another example in Western canonical literature of the marginalization of the Other as represented by Congo Hoango, Babekan, and Toni, but if this were so the black characters would, typically, only have a symbolic role in the literary work . . .

rather than a structurally and thematically essential role." Fleming, "Race and the Difference It Makes," 309.

75. Ali, *Kürk Mantolu Madonna*, 43.

76. Ali, *Madonna in a Fur*, 2. "Kendilerine göre bir iç âlemleri olacağını hiç aklımıza getirmeyiz. Bu âlemin tezahürlerini dışarı vermediklerine bakıp onların mânen yaşamadıklarına hükmedecek yerde, en basit bir beşer tecessüsü ile, bu meçhul âlemi merak etsek, belki hiç ummadığımız şeyler görmemiz, beklemediğimiz zenginliklerle karşılaşmamız mümkün olur." Ali, *Kürk Mantolu Madonna*, 11.

77. Ibid., 23.

78. Ibid., 25.

79. Ibid., 37.

80. Bozdoğan, *Modernism and Nation Building*, 67–68.

81. Ali, *Kürk Mantolu Madonna*, 24.

82. Ali, *Madonna in a Fur*, 56. "İşte Avrupa! Ne var burada sanki?" Ali, *Kürk Mantolu Madonna*, 52–53.

83. Ali, *Madonna in a Fur*, 54. "Burası da en nihayet bir şehirdi. Sokakları biraz daha geniş, çok daha temiz, insanları daha sarışın bir şehir. Fakat ortada insanı hayretinden düşüp bayılmaya sevk edecek bir şey de yoktu. Benim hayalimdeki Avrupa'nın nasıl bir şey olduğunu ve şimdi içinde yaşadığım şehrin buna nazaran ne noksanları bulunduğunu kendim de bilmiyordum. . . . Hayatta hiçbir zaman kafamızdaki kadar harikulade şeyler olmayacağını henüz idrak etmemiştim." Ali, *Kürk Mantolu Madonna*, 51.

84. I borrow the term "textual substructure" from Roswitha Burwick, who argues that the substructures of *Verlobung* "mirror the unsolved social, political and racial problems" it addresses. Burwick, "Issues of Language," 321.

85. Hermans, "Cross-Cultural Translation," 386–87.

86. Ibid., 123.

87. Ali, *Madonna in a Fur*, 140. "Ömrünün sonuna kadar beni unutamayacağını, kendimi kanla hatırasına bağladığımı anlayacaktı." Ali, *Kürk Mantolu Madonna*, 125.

88. Ibid., 91–92.

89. Ali, *Madonna in a Fur*, 130. "Halis Alman kanında bir Protestan." Ali, *Kürk Mantolu Madonna*, 110.

90. "Zayıf," "durgun," "sessiz." Ibid., 156.

91. "Müstemleke tüccarı." Ibid., 152.

92. Ali, *Madonna in a Fur*, 186. "Kocamın sıcak memleket mahsulleri üzerinde ihtisası var." Ali, *Kürk Mantolu Madonna*, 152.

EPILOGUE

1. There is no evidence that the Robert Bosch Foundation drew inspiration from the earlier Turkish Library translation project. The contemporary Turkish Library (Türkische Bibliothek) follows two other "libraries" funded by the Robert Bosch Foundation: the Polish Library (Polnische Bibliothek, 1982–2000; 50 volumes) and the Czech Library (Tschechische Bibliothek, 1999–2007; 33 volumes).

2. Dikici, *Die Rezeption*, 108.

3. By 2011 the Turkish Library had sold thirty thousand books. Ibid., 152.

4. While Glassen and Laut made final decisions regarding the selection of texts and translators, they worked with a team of individuals, including Bettina Berns from the Robert Bosch Stiftung; publisher Lucien Leitess and editor Alice Grünfelder from Unionsverlag; and an expert advisory board consisting of Tayfun Demir, Börte Sagaster, and Tevfik Turan. Glassen, "Der rote Faden."

5. Laut, "Geleitwort," 12.

6. Dikici, *Die Rezeption*, 108–9.

7. "Die Türkische Bibliothek präsentiert Meilensteine der türkischen Literatur von 1900 bis in die unmittelbare Gegenwart. Sie soll der deutschsprachigen Leserschaft helfen, tiefer in die geistige Welt der heutigen Türkei einzudringen." "Die Türkische Bibliothek," Unionsverlag, http://www.unionsverlag.com/info/text.asp?text_id=2953.

8. Glassen, "Der Stellenwert," 297.

9. Turkey joined the Council of Europe in 1949 and the European Economic Community in 1987; it was later recognized as a candidate for full membership in the European Union in 1999. Negotiations for full membership began on October 3, 2005.

10. "Der Abkehr von der eigenen östlichen Tradition" and "der Prozess einer permanenten Verwestlichung." Glassen, "Der rote Faden."

11. Ibid.

12. Glassen, "Der Stellenwert," 292. *Gesamtüberblick* could alternately be translated as "comprehensive overview." I have translated this term as "complete picture" in order to underscore the literal meaning of "gesamt" as total, entire, or complete.

13. Glassen, "Der rote Faden."

14. Ibid.

15. "Kulturelle Wurzeln" and "ursprüngliche Heimat." Glassen, "Der Stellenwert," 297.

16. For detailed discussion of the so-called guest worker programs, see Chin, *Guest Worker Question*. According to a sample census, approximately 2.9 million persons of Turkish descent were living in Germany in 2015. At the time,

1.5 million of these persons held Turkish citizenship. Schührer, "Türkeistämmige Personen in Deutschland," 5. In addition to labor recruitment, people have migrated to Germany for other diverse reasons. In particular, communists, leftist intellectuals, ethnic minorities, and other persecuted individuals have historically sought asylum in Germany.

17. "Ein einzigartiger Fundus der türkischen Kunst . . . wie es ihn noch nie in Deutschland gab." Arend, "Zum Abschluss."

18. "Ein literarischer Reisebegleiter durch die Vielfalt von Völkerschaften, Lebensformen und Landschaften." "Von Istanbul nach Hakkâri," Unionsverlag, http://www.unionsverlag.com/info/title.asp?title_id=2347.

19. Akcan, *Architecture in Translation*, 14.

Bibliography

Adıvar, Halide Edip. *Edebiyatta Tercümenin Rolü*. Istanbul: Kenan Matbaası, 1943.

———. *House with Wisteria: Memoirs of Turkey Old and New*. New York: Routledge, 2017.

———. *Mor Salkımlı Ev*. Istanbul: 1963.

———. *Das neue Turan: Ein türkisches Frauenschicksal*. Translated by Friedrich Schrader. Weimar: Gustav Kiepenheuer, 1916.

———. *The Turkish Ordeal, Being the Further Memoirs of Halide Edip*. New York: Century, 1928.

———. *Türk'ün Ateşle İmtihanı: İstiklâl Şavaşı Hâtıraları*. Istanbul: Can Yayınları, 1962.

———. *Yeni Turan*. Istanbul: Can Yayınları, 2014.

Ahmed, Sara. "Orientations: Toward a Queer Phenomenology." *GLQ: A Journal of Lesbian and Gay Studies* 12, no. 4 (2006): 543–74.

———. *Queer Phenomenology: Orientations, Objects, Others*. Durham: Duke University Press, 2006.

Akcan, Esra. *Architecture in Translation: Germany, Turkey, and the Modern House*. Durham: Duke University Press, 2012.

Ali, Filiz, Atilla Özkırımlı, and Sevengül Sönmez, eds. *Sabahattin Ali: Anılar, İncelemeler, Eleştiriler*. Istanbul: Yapı Kredi Yayınları, 2014.

Ali, Sabahattin. "The Comprehensive Germanistan Travelogue." Translated by Kristin Dickinson and Zeynep Seviner. *Türkisch-deutsche Studien: Jahrbuch* 8 (2017): 103–10.

———. *Hep Genç Kalacağım: Bütün Yapıtları; Mektup*. Edited by Sevengül Sönmez. Istanbul: Yapı Kredi Yayınları, 2008.

———. "İkinci Dilden Tercüme Meselesi ve Bir Misal." In *Markopaşa Yazıları ve Ötekiler*, edited by Hikmet Altınkaynak and Sevengül Sönmez, 104–11. Istanbul: Yapı Kredi Yayınları, 2009.

———. *Kürk Mantolu Madonna*. Istanbul: Yapı Kredi Yayınları, 2008.

———. *Die Madonna im Pelzmantel*. Translated by Ute Birgi-Knellessen. Zurich: Dörlemann, 2008.

———. *The Madonna in the Fur Coat*. Translated by David Gramling and İlker Hepkaner. Unpublished manuscript, 2014.

———. *Mahkemelerde: Belgeler*. Edited by Nüket Esen and Nezihe Seyhan. Istanbul: Yapı Kredi Yayınları, 2004.

———. *Markopaşa Yazıları ve Ötekiler*. Edited by Hikmet Altınkaynak and Sevengül Sönmez. Istanbul: Yapı Kredi Yayınları, 1998.

———. "Mufassal Cermenistân Seyâhatnâmesi." *Türkisch-deutsche Studien: Jahrbuch* 8 (2017): 111–18.

Almond, Ian. *History of Islam in German Thought from Leibniz to Nietzsche*. New York: Routledge, 2010.

Ames, Christine Caldwell. *Righteous Persecution: Inquisition,*

Dominicans, and Christianity in the Middle Ages. Philadelphia: University of Pennsylvania Press, 2008.

And, Metin. *Meşrutiyet Döneminde Türk Tiyatrosu, 1908–1923*. Ankara: Türkiye İş Bankası Kültür Yayınları, 1971.

Andrews, Walter G. "Ottoman Lyrics: Introductory Essay." In *Ottoman Lyric Poetry: An Anthology*, edited and translated by Walter G. Andrews, Nejaat Black, and Mehmet Kalpaklı, 3–24. Austin: University of Texas Press, 2006.

———. "Starting Over Again: Some Suggestions for Rethinking Ottoman Divan Poetry in the Context of Translation and Transmission." In *Translations: (Re)shaping of Literature and Culture*, edited by Saliha Paker, 15–40. Istanbul: Boğaziçi University Press, 2002.

Apter, Emily. *Against World Literature: On the Politics of Untranslatability*. New York: Verso, 2013.

———. "Global *Translatio*: The 'Invention' of Comparative Literature, Istanbul, 1933." *Critical Inquiry* 29, no. 2 (Winter 2003): 253–81.

Arat, Yeşim. "Nation Building and Feminism in Early Republican Turkey." In *Turkey's Engagement with Modernity: Conflict and Change in the Twentieth Century*, edited by Celia Kerslake, Kerem Öktem, and Philip Robins, 38–51. London: Palgrave Macmillan, 2010.

Arend, Ingo. "Zum Abschluss der 'Türkischen Bibliothek' im Unionsverlag." Deutschlandfunk, January 27, 2011. https://www.deut schlandfunk.de/zum-abschluss-der -tuerkischen-bibliothek-im-union sverlag.700.de.html?dram:article _id=84927.

"Armenische Schillervorstellung." *Osmanischer Lloyd* 278 (November 27, 1909).

Arnakis, George G. "Turanism: An Aspect of Turkish Nationalism." *Balkan Studies* 1 (1960): 19–32.

Auerbach, Erich. "Philologie der Weltliteratur." In *Weltliteratur: Festgabe für Fritz Strich zum 70. Geburtstag*, edited by Walter Muschg and Emil Staiger, 39–50. Bern: Francke Verlag, 1952.

———. "Philology and *Weltliteratur*." Translated by Maire Said and Edward Said. *Centennial Review* 13, no. 1 (Winter 1969): 1–17.

Aytürk, İlker. "Script Charisma in Hebrew and Turkish: A Comparative Framework for Explaining Success and Failure of Romanization." *Journal of World History* 21, no. 1 (March 2010): 97–130.

Babinger, Franz. "Ein orientalischer Berater Goethes: Heinrich Friedrich von Diez." *Goethe-Jahrbuch* 34, no. 28 (1913): 83–100.

Bachmann-Medick, Doris. "Meanings of Translation in Cultural Anthropology." In *Translating Others*, edited by Theo Hermans, 1:33–42. Manchester: St. Jerome, 2006.

Balcke, Curt. "Heinrich Friedrich von Diez und sein Vermächtnis in der Preußischen Staatsbibliothek." In *Von Büchern und Bibliotheken*, edited by Gustav Abb, 187–200. Berlin: Verlag von Struppe & Winckler, 1928.

Berk, Özlem. *Translation and Westernisation in Turkey from the 1840s to the 1980s*. Istanbul: Ege Yayınları, 2004.

Berk Albachten, Özlem. "The Turkish Language Reform and Intralingual Translation." In *Tradition, Tension and Translation in Turkey*, edited by Şehnaz Tahir Gürçağlar, Saliha

Paker, and John Milton, 165–80. Amsterdam: John Benjamins, 2015.

Berman, Antoine. *The Experience of the Foreign: Culture and Translation in Romantic Germany*. Translated by S. Heyvaert. Albany: SUNY Press, 1992.

Berman, Marshall. *All That Is Solid Melts into Air: The Experience of Modernity*. New York: Viking Penguin, 1988.

Berman, Nina. "Was Dokumentiert die Literatur? Praxistheorie und vergleichende Literaturwissenschaft zum deutsch-türkischen Kulturkontakt im 18. und 20. Jahrhundert." *Türkisch-deutsche Studien: Jahrbuch* 1 (2010): 157–68.

Bett, Richard. "Pyrrhonian Skepticism." In *The Routledge Companion to Epistemology*, edited by Sven Bernecker and Duncan Pritchard, 403–13. New York: Routledge, 2011.

Beyatlı, Yahya Kemal. "Yeni Tûran." In *Edebiyata Dair*, 167–71. Istanbul: Baha Matbaası, 1971.

Bhambra, Gurminder K. "Postcolonial Europe, or Understanding Europe in the Times of the Postcolonial." In *The SAGE Handbook of European Studies*, edited by Chris Rumford, 69–85. Los Angeles: SAGE, 2009.

Bhatti, Anil. "Der Orient als Experimentierfeld. Goethes 'Divan' und der Aneignungsprozess kolonialen Wissens." *Goethe-Jahrbuch* 126 (2009): 115–28.

Birinci Türk Neşriyat Kongresi: Raporlar, Teklifler, Müzakere Zabıtları. Ankara: Maarif Vekilliği ve Neşriyat Müdürlüğü, 1939.

Birus, Hendrik. "Weltliteratur." In *Reallexikon der deutschen Literaturwissenschaft*, edited by Georg Braungart, 3:825–27. Berlin: Walter de Gruyter, 2007.

Bisaha, Nancy. *Creating East and West: Renaissance Humanists and the Ottoman Turks*. Philadelphia: University of Pennsylvania Press, 2004.

Bobzin, Hartmut. "Friedrich Rückert (1788–1866) und die türkische Sprache und Literatur." In *Germano-Turcica: Zur Geschichte des Türkisch-Lernens in den deutschsprachigen Ländern*, edited by Klaus Kreiser, 69–78. Bamberg: Universitätsbibliothek, 1987.

Bosse, Anke. *Meine Schatzkammer füllt sich täglich: Die Nachlassstücke zu Goethes "West-östlichem Divan."* Göttingen: Wallstein Verlag, 1999.

Bozdoğan, Sibel. *Modernism and Nation Building: Turkish Architectural Culture in the Early Republic*. Seattle: University of Washington Press, 2001.

Brummett, Palmira. *Image and Imperialism in the Ottoman Revolutionary Press, 1908–1911*. Albany: SUNY Press, 2000.

Buck-Morss, Susan. "Hegel and Haiti." *Critical Inquiry* 26, no. 4 (Summer 2000): 821–65.

Burwick, Roswitha. "Issues of Language and Communication: Kleist's 'Die Verlobung in St. Domingo.'" *German Quarterly* 65, no. 3/4 (Autumn 1992): 318–27.

Byrd, Vance. "Family, Intercategorical Complexity, and Kleist's *Die Verlobung in St. Domingo*." *Germanic Review* 92, no. 3 (2017): 223–44.

Casanova, Pascale. *The World Republic of Letters*. Translated by M. B. DeBevoise. Cambridge: Harvard University Press, 2004.

Çelebi, Evliya. *An Ottoman Traveller: Selections from the Book of Travels of Evliya Celebi*. Translated by

Robert Dankoff and Sooyong Kim. London: Eland Books, 2011.

Charrière, Etienne E. "Translating Communities: Reading Foreign Fiction Across Communal Boundaries in the Tanzimat Period." In *Ottoman Culture and the Project of Modernity: Reform and Translation in the Tanzimat Novel*, edited by Etienne E. Charrière and Monika M. Ringer, 177–92. London: Bloomsbury, 2020.

Charrière, Etienne E., and Monika M. Ringer. Introduction to *Ottoman Culture and the Project of Modernity: Reform and Translation in the Tanzimat Novel*, edited by Etienne E. Charrière and Monika M. Ringer, 1–17. London: Bloomsbury, 2020.

Cheah, Pheng. "Grounds of Comparison: Around the Work of Benedict Anderson." *Diacritics* 29, no. 4 (Winter 1999): 2–18.

———. *What Is a World? On Postcolonial Literature as World Literature.* Durham: Duke University Press, 2016.

Chin, Rita. *The Guest Worker Question in Postwar Germany.* New York: Cambridge University Press, 2007.

Çıkar, Mustafa. *Hasan-Âli Yücel ve Türk Kültür Reformu.* Ankara: Türkiye İş Bankası Kültür Yayınları, 1997.

Corneille, Pierre. *Sid'in Hülasa'sı.* Translated by Ahmet Mithat. Istanbul: Tercüman-ı Hakikat Matbaası, 1891.

Daldeniz, Elif. "Introduction: Translation, Modernity and Its Dissidents: Turkey as a 'Republic of Translation.'" *Translation Studies* 3, no. 2 (2010): 129–31.

Damrosch, David. *What Is World Literature?* Princeton: Princeton University Press, 2003.

Davison, Roderic H. *Reform in the Ottoman Empire, 1856–1876.* New York: Gordian Press, 1973.

Delanty, Gerard. *Inventing Europe: Idea, Identity, Reality.* Hampshire: Macmillan, 1995.

Demircioğlu, Celal. "From Discourse to Practice: Rethinking 'Translation' (Terceme) and Related Practices of Text Production in the Late Ottoman Literary Tradition." PhD diss., Boğaziçi Üniversitesi, 2005.

D'haen, Theo. "Mapping World Literature." In *The Routledge Companion to World Literature*, edited by Theo D'haen, David Damrosch, and Djelal Kadir, 413–22. New York: Routledge, 2011.

Dickinson, Kristin, and Zeynep Seviner. "Translators' Introduction." *Türkisch-deutsche Studien: Jahrbuch* 8 (2017): 97–102.

Dietrich, Anne. *Deutschsein in Istanbul: Nationalisierung und Orientierung in der deutschsprachigen Community von 1843 bis 1956.* Wiesbaden: VS Verlag für Sozialwissenschaften, 1998.

Diez, Heinrich Friedrich von. *Buch des Kabus oder Lehren des persischen Königs Kjekjawus für seinen Sohn Ghilan Schach.* Berlin: self-published, 1811.

———. *Denkwürdigkeiten von Asien in Künsten und Wissenschaften, Sitten, Gebräuchen und Alterthümern, Religion und Regierungsverfassung.* 2 vols. Berlin: self-published, 1811–15.

Dikici, Christine. *Die Rezeption der türkischen Literatur im deutschen Sprachraum: Unter besonderer Berücksichtigung aktueller Übersetzungsvorhaben.* Frankfurt am Main: Peter Lang, 2017.

Dirlik, Arif. "Chinese History and the Question of Orientalism." In

Genealogies of Orientalism: History, Theory, Politics, edited by Edmund Burke III and David Prochaska, 384–413. Lincoln: University of Nebraska Press, 2008.

Dizdaroğlu, Hikmet. *Müftüoğlu Ahmed Hikmet*. Ankara: Türk Dil Kurumu Yayınları, 1964.

Dünya Muharrirlerinden Tercümeler Serisi Kataloğu: 1939. Istanbul: Remzi Kitabevi, 1939.

Durakbaşa, Ayşe. *Halide Edip: Türk Modernleşmesi ve Feminizm*. Istanbul: İletişim, 2000.

Eckermann, Johann Peter. *Gespräche mit Goethe*. Edited by Christoph Michel. Berlin: Deutscher Klassiker Verlag, 2011.

Ekrem, Recaizade Mahmut. *Araba Sevdası: Musavver Millî Hikâye*. Istanbul: Alem Matbaası, 1896.

———. *Bütün Eserleri III*. Edited by Ismail Parlatır, Nurullah Çetin, and Hakan Sazyek. Istanbul: Millî Eğitim Basımevi, 1997.

———. *Leidenschaft in Çamlıca*. Translated by Beatrix Caner. Frankfurt am Main: Literaturca, 2014.

Eldridge, Richard. *Literature, Life, and Modernity*. New York: Columbia University Press, 2008.

Emmerich, Karen. *Literary Translation and the Making of Originals*. New York: Bloomsbury, 2017.

Enginün, İnci, ed. *Ahmet Midhat Efendi'nin Tiyatroları*. Istanbul: Edebiyat Fakültesi Basımevi, 1990.

———. *Türkçede Shakespeare*. Istanbul: Dergâh Yayınları, 2008.

Ertürk, Nergis. *Grammatology and Literary Modernity in Turkey*. Oxford: Oxford University Press, 2011.

———. "Modernity and Its Fallen Languages: Tanpınar's 'Hasret,' Benjamin's Melancholy." *PMLA* 123, no. 1 (January 2008): 41–56.

Eruz, Sâkine. *Çokkültürlülük ve Çeviri: Osmanlı Devleti'nde Çeviri Etkinliği ve Çevirmenler*. Istanbul: Multilingual, 2010.

Even-Zohar, Itamar. "Laws of Literary Interference." *Poetics Today* 11, no. 1 (Spring 1990): 53–72.

Evin, Ahmet Ö. *Origins and Development of the Turkish Novel*. Minneapolis: Bibliotheca Islamica, 1983.

Fabian, Johannes. *Time and the Other: How Anthropology Makes Its Object*. New York: Columbia University Press, 2002.

Farah, Irmgard. *Die deutsche Pressepolitik und Propagandatätigkeit im osmanischen Reich von 1908–1918 unter besonderer Berücksichtigung des "Osmanischen Lloyd."* Stuttgart: Franz Steiner Verlag, 1993.

Findley, Carter V. *Bureaucratic Reform in the Ottoman Empire: The Sublime Porte, 1789-1922*. Princeton: Princeton University Press, 1980.

Finkel, Caroline. *Osman's Dream: The History of the Ottoman Empire*. London: John Murray, 2005.

Fischer, Bernd. "Introduction: Heinrich von Kleist's Life and Work." In *A Companion to the Works of Heinrich von Kleist*, edited by Bernd Fischer, 1–20. Rochester: Camden House, 2003.

Fleming, Ray. "Race and the Difference It Makes in Kleist's 'Die Verlobung in St. Domingo.'" *German Quarterly* 65, no. 3/4 (Autumn 1992): 306–17.

Fletcher, Richard. *Moorish Spain*. Berkeley: University of California Press, 1992.

Forster, Georg. "Vorrede des Uebersetzers." In *Sakontala oder der entscheidende Ring: Ein indisches Schauspiel von Kalidas*, xxiii–xxx. Translated by Georg Forster.

Heidelberg: Mohr und Winter, 1820.

Fuhrmann, Malte. *Der Traum vom deutschen Orient: Zwei deutsche Kolonien im Osmanischen Reich 1851–1918*. Frankfurt am Main: Campus, 2006.

Gailus, Andreas. "Language Unmoored: On Kleist's *The Betrothal in St. Domingue*." *Germanic Review* 85, no. 1 (2010): 20–43.

Geiger, Ludwig, ed. "Briefwechsel zwischen Goethe und v. Diez," *Goethe Jahrbuch* 11, no. 5 (1890): 24–41.

Gibb, Elias John Wilkinson. *A History of Ottoman Poetry*. Edited by Edward G. Browne. London: Luzac, 1900.

Gibson, Lela. "Changing States: Ottoman Sufism, Orientalism, and German Politics, 1770–1825." PhD diss., University of California, Los Angeles, 2015.

Gilman, Sander L. "The Aesthetics of Blackness in Heinrich Von Kleist's 'Die Verlobung in St. Domingo.'" *MLN* 90, no. 5 (1975): 661–72.

Glassen, Erika. "Der rote Faden der Türkischen Bibliothek." Unionsverlag, October 2010. http://www.unionsverlag.com/info/text.asp?text_id=3103.

———. "Der Stellenwert der Türkischen Bibliothek im Gesamtkomplex der deutschen Übersetzungsliteratur aus dem Türkischen." *Türkisch-deutsche Studien: Jahrbuch* 1 (2010): 291–300.

Göçek, Fatma Müge. *East Encounters West: France and the Ottoman Empire in the Eighteenth Century*. New York: Oxford University Press, 1987.

Goethe, Johann Wolfgang von. *Goethes Werke*. Section 4, *Goethes Briefe*. Vol. 25, 28. *Juli 1814–21. Mai 1815*. Edited by Sophie von Sachsen.

Weimar: Hermann Böhlaus Nachfolger, 1901.

———. *Die Leiden des jungen Werther*. Cologne: Anaconda Verlag, 2005.

———. "Literarischer Sanscülottismus." In *Johann Wolfgang von Goethe: Sämtliche Werke nach Epochen seines Schaffens*, vol. 4/2, edited by Klaus H. Kiefer, Hans J. Becker, Gerhard H. Müller, John Neubauer, and Peter Schmidt, 15–20. Munich: Carl Hanser Verlag, 1998.

———. *The Sorrows of Young Werther*. Translated by Burton Pike. New York: Modern Library, 2004.

———. *Verter*. Translated by Ali Kâmi Akyüz. Istanbul: Matbaa-i Hayriye ve Şürekası, 1329/1911.

———. "'Verter' 10 Mayıs Tarihli Mektup." Translated by Hüseyin Daniş. *Malumat Dergisi* 12 (1310): 101.

———. "'Verter' 13 Mayıs Tarihli Mektup." Translated by Ahmet Rasim. *Gülşen Dergisi* 19 (1302): 8.

———. "'Verter' 26 Mayıs Tarihli Mektup." Translated by Mustafa Fazıl. *Malumat Dergisi* 21 (1310): 169.

———. *West-East Divan: The Poems, with "Notes and Essays"; Goethe's Intercultural Dialogues*. Translated by Martin Bidney and Peter Anton von Arnim. Albany: SUNY Press, 2010.

———. *West-östlicher Divan*. Zürich: Manesse Verlag, 2004.

Gökalp, Ziya. "Maarif Meselesi." In *Millî Terbiye ve Maarif Meselesi*, 111–12. Ankara: İş Matbaacılık, 1972.

———. *Türkçülüğün Esasları*. Istanbul: Varlık Yayınları, 1966.

Göknar, Erdağ. "Ottoman Past and Turkish Future: Ambivalence in A. H. Tanpınar's *Those Outside the Scene*." *South Atlantic Quarterly* 102, no. 2/3 (2003): 647–61.

Görgün, Tahsin. "Medeniyet." In *Türkiye Diyanet Vakfı İslam Ansiklopedisi*, 28:296–303. Ankara: Türkiye Diyanet Vakfı, 2003.

Gottschlich, Jürgen. *Beihilfe zum Völkermord: Deutschlands Rolle bei der Vernichtung der Armenier.* Berlin: Ch. Links Verlag, 2015.

Gould, Rebecca. "Inimitability Versus Translatability: The Structure of Literary Meaning in Arabo-Persian Poetics." *Translator* 19, no. 1 (2013): 81–104.

Gözütok, Türkan. "Yeni Turan'da Millî Kimlik Sorunu." *Turkish Studies* 5, no. 2 (Spring 2010): 410–48.

Graham, Ilse. *Goethe: Portrait of the Artist.* Berlin: Walter de Gruyter, 1977.

Gramling, David, and Martina Schwalm. "World Literature (Already) Wrote Back: Sabahattin Ali After Germany." *Türkisch-deutsche Studien: Jahrbuch* 8 (Spring 2017): 25–44.

Grimm, Jacob, and Wilhelm Grimm. *Deutsches Wörterbuch*, vol. 2. Leipzig: Verlag von S. Hirzel, 1860.

Gronau, W. *Christian Wilhelm von Dohm nach seinem Wollen und Handeln: Ein biographischer Versuch.* Lemgo: Meyersche Hof-Buchhandlung, 1824.

Gürbilek, Nurdan. "Dandies and Originals: Authenticity, Belatedness, and the Turkish Novel." *South Atlantic Quarterly* 102, no. 2/3 (Spring/ Summer 2003): 599–628.

Gust, Wolfgang, ed. *The Armenian Genocide: Evidence from the German Foreign Office Archives, 1915–1916.* New York: Berghahn, 2014.

Hachtmann, Otto. *Die türkische Literatur des zwanzigsten Jahrhunderts.* Leipzig: C. F. Amelang, 1916.

Hamann, Ulrike. *Prekäre koloniale Ordnung: Rassistische Konjunkturen im Widerspruch, deutsches Kolonialregime 1884–1914.* Bielefeld: transcript, 2016.

Hammer-Purgstall, Joseph von. "Vorrede." *Fundgruben des Orients* 1 (1809): i–vi.

———. "Vorrede." *Fundgruben des Orients* 2 (1811): n.p.

Hanioğlu, M. Şükrü. *The Young Turks in Opposition.* New York: Oxford University Press, 1995.

Haque, Kamaal. "From the Desert to the City and Back: Nomads and the Spaces of Goethe's *West-östlicher Divan.*" In *Spatial Turns: Space, Place, and Mobility in German Literary and Visual Culture*, edited by Jaimey Fisher and Barbara Mennel, 233–53. Amsterdam: Rodopi, 2010.

Hartmann, Martin. *Dichter der neuen Türkei.* Berlin: Der Neue Orient, 1919.

———. *Unpolitische Briefe aus der Türkei.* Vol. 3 of *Der islamische Orient: Berichte und Forschungen.* Leipzig: Rudolf Haupt, 1910.

Haverkamp, Anselm. "Schwarz / Weiß. 'Othello' and 'Die Verlobung in St. Domingo.'" *Weimarer Beiträge* 41 (1995): 397–409.

Hay, Denys. *Europe: The Emergence of an Idea.* Edinburgh: Edinburgh University Press, 1957.

Henkel, Arthur. "Bildermodulation: Zur poetischen Verfahrensweise Goethes im 'West-östlichen Divan.'" In *Spiegelungen*, edited by Werner Knopp, 251–77. Mainz: Hase und Koehler, 1986.

Hermans, Theo. "Cross-Cultural Translation Studies as Thick Translation." *Bulletin of the School of Oriental and African Studies* 66, no. 3 (2003): 380–89.

Heyd, Uriel. *Foundations of Turkish Nationalism: The Life and Teachings of Ziya Gökalp.* London: Harvill Press, 1950.

Holbrook, Victoria R. "Concealed Facts, Translation, and the Turkish Literary Past." In *Translations: (Re)shaping of Literature and Culture,* edited by Saliha Paker, 77–107. Istanbul: Boğaziçi University Press, 2002.

———. *Unreadable Shores of Love: Turkish Modernity and Mystic Romance.* Austin: University of Texas Press, 1994.

Horn, Paul. *Geschichte der türkischen Moderne.* Leipzig: C. F. Amelangs Verlag, 1902.

Humboldt, Wilhelm von. "Einleitung." In *Aeschylos Agamemnon metrisch übersetzt,* i–xxxvii. Leipzig: Gerhard Fleischer dem Jüngern, 1816.

Husserl, Edmund. *Ideas Pertaining to a Pure Phenomenology and to a Phenomenological Philosophy; Second Book: Studies in the Phenomenology of Constitution.* Translated by Richard Rojcewicz and André Schuwer. Dordrecht: Kluwer Academic, 1989.

Jacob, Georg. "Vorwort." In *O weh! Türkisches Drama von Ahmed Mithat,* by Ahmet Mithat, translated by Doris Reeck, v–xi. Berlin: Mayer und Müller Verlag, 1913.

———. "Vorwort des Herausgebers." In *Türkische Frauen,* by Ahmet Hikmet Müftüoğlu, translated by Friedrich Schrader, v–viii. Berlin: Mayer und Müller, 1907.

Jauss, Hans Robert. *Literaturgeschichte als Provokation.* Frankfurt am Main: Suhrkamp Verlag, 1974.

Kaplan, Ramazan. *Klâsikler Tartışması (Başlangıç Dönemi).* Ankara: Atatürk Kültür Merkezi Yayınları, 1998.

Kappert, Petra. "Vom Übersetzen türkischer Literatur ins Deutsche: Tendenzen und Auswahl." In *Türkische Sprachen und Literaturen: Materialien der ersten deutschen Turkologen-Konferenz,* edited by Ingeborg Baldauf, Klaus Kreiser, and Semih Tezcan, 213–21. Wiesbaden: Otto Harrassowitz, 1991.

Karadağ, Ayşe Banu. "Batı'nın Çevrilmesi Üzerine: Tanzimat Dönemi/Sonrası Çevirilerini 'Medeniyet' Odağıyla Yeniden Okumak." *Kritik Edebiyat Eleştirisi Dergisi* 2 (2008): 306–24.

Karakaş, Mehmet. *Türk Ulusçuluğunun İnşası.* Ankara: Elips Kitapları, 2007.

Kendall, Elisabeth. "Between Politics and Literature: Journals in Alexandria and Istanbul at the End of the Nineteenth Century." In *Modernity and Culture: From the Mediterranean to the Indian Ocean,* edited by Leila Tarazi Fawaz and C. A. Bayly, 330–43. New York: Columbia University Press, 2002.

Keudell, Elise von. *Goethe als Benutzer der Weimarer Bibliothek: Ein Verzeichnis der von ihm entliehenen Werke.* Weimar: Hermann Böhlaus Nachfolger, 1931.

Kleist, Heinrich von. "San Domingo'da Bir Nişanlanma." In *Üç Romantik Hikâye,* 9–60. Translated by Sabahattin Ali. Ankara: Maarif Matbaası, 1943.

———. "Die Verlobung in St. Domingo." In *Sämtliche Werke: Berliner Ausgabe,* vol. 2/4, edited by Roland Reuß and Peter Staengle, 7–91. Basel: Stroemfeld/Roter Stern, 1988.

Kolcu, Ali İhsan. *Türkçe'de Batı Şiiri: Tanzimat ve Servet-i Fünûn Devirlerinde Batı Edebiyatından*

Yapılan Şiir Tercümeleri Üzerinden Bir Araştırma (1859–1901). Istanbul: Gündoğan Yayınları, 1999.

Kontje, Todd. *German Orientalisms*. Ann Arbor: University of Michigan Press, 2004.

———. "Passing for German: Politics and Patriarchy in Kleist, Körner, and Fischer." *German Studies Review* 22, no. 1 (1999): 67–84.

Konuk, Kader. *East West Mimesis: Auerbach in Turkey*. Stanford: Stanford University Press, 2010.

Kuran, Ercümend. "The Impact of Nationalism on the Turkish Elite in the Nineteenth Century." In *Beginnings of Modernization in the Middle East: The 19th Century*, edited by Richard L. Chambers and William R. Polk, 109–17. Chicago: University of Chicago Press, 1969.

Kuru, Selim S. "The Literature of Rum: The Making of a Literary Tradition (1450–1600)." In *The Cambridge History of Turkey*, vol. 2, *The Ottoman Empire as a World Power, 1453–1603*, edited by Suraiya N. Faroqhi and Kate Fleet, 548–92. Cambridge: Cambridge University Press, 2012.

Latifi, Monla Abdul, and Aşık Hasan Çelebi. *Latifi, oder Biographische Nachrichten von vorzüglichen türkischen Dichtern, nebst einer Blumenlese aus ihren Werken*. Translated by Thomas Chabert. Zürich: Heinrich Gessner, 1800.

Laut, Jens Peter. "Geleitwort." In *Literatur und Gesellschaft: Kleine Schriften von Erika Glassen zur türkischen Literaturgeschichte und zum Kulturwandel in der modernen Türkei*, edited by Jens Peter Laut, 9–14. Würzburg: Ergon Verlag, 2014.

Levend, Agâh Sırrı. *Edebiyat Tarihi Dersleri: Tanzimata Kadar*. Istanbul: Kanaat Kitabevi, 1932.

Levih, Melih. "How Not to Translate: Cultural Authenticity and Translatability in Recaizade Mahmut Ekrem's *Araba Sevdası* and Ahmet Midhat Efendi's *Felatun Bey ile Rakım Efendi*." In *Ottoman Culture and the Project of Modernity: Reform and Translation in the Tanzimat Novel*, edited by Etienne E. Charrière and Monika M. Ringer, 37–51. London: Bloomsbury, 2020.

Lewis, Geoffrey. *The Turkish Language Reform: A Catastrophic Success*. Oxford: Oxford University Press, 2010.

Louth, Charlie. *Hölderlin and the Dynamics of Translation*. Oxford: Legenda, European Humanities Research Centre, 1998.

Mangold-Will, Sabine. *Begrenzte Freundschaft: Deutschland und die Türkei, 1918–1933*. Göttingen: Wallstein Verlag, 2013.

———. *Eine "weltbürgerliche Wissenschaft": Die deutsche Orientalistik im 19. Jahrhundert*. Stuttgart: Franz Steiner Verlag, 2004.

Mani, B. Venkat. *Recoding World Literature: Libraries, Print Culture, and Germany's Pact with Books*. New York: Fordham University Press, 2016.

Mann, Nicholas. "The Origins of Humanism." In *The Cambridge Companion to Renaissance Humanism*, edited by Jill Kraye, 1–19. Cambridge: Cambridge University Press, 1996.

Mannweiler, Caroline. "Goethes 'Weltliteratur': Begriff oder Diskurs?" *Seminar* 54, no. 2 (May 2018): 133–47.

Marchand, Suzanne L. *German Oriental-ism in the Age of Empire: Religion, Race, and Scholarship.* Cambridge: Cambridge University Press, 2010.

Mardin, Şerif. "Super Westernization in Urban Life in the Ottoman Empire in the Last Quarter of the Nine-teenth Century." In *Turkey: Geographic and Social Perspectives,* edited by Peter Benedict, Erol Tümertekin, and Fatma Mansur, 403–46. Leiden: E. J. Brill, 1974.

Margoliouth, D. S. "Turkish Diplomacy in the Eighteenth Century." *Moslem World* 7, no. 1 (January 1, 1917): 36–54.

Mauvillon, Jakob. *Mauvillons' Briefwech-sel: Oder Briefe von verschiedenen Gelehrten an den in Herzogl. Braun-schweigschen Diensten verstorbenen Obristlieutenant Mauvillon.* Edited by F. Mauvillon. Braunschweig, 1801.

Mendicino, Kristina. *Prophecies of Language: The Confusion of Tongues in German Romanticism.* New York: Fordham University Press, 2017.

Menzel, Theodor. "Einleitung: Mehmed Tevfiq und sein Werk." In *Ein Jahr in Konstantinopel: Zweiter Monat, Helva Sohbeti (die Helva-Abendge-sellschaft),* by Mehmet Tevfik, translated by Theodor Menzel, 1–7. Berlin: Mayer und Müller Verlag, 1906.

Mignon, Laurent. "Tanpınar Kadar Yenilikçi Olmak." In *Ana Metne Taşınan Dipnotlar: Türk Edebiyatı ve Kültürlerarasılık Üzerine Yazılar,* 133–49. Istanbul: İletişim Yayınları, 2009.

Mitchell, Timothy. "The Stage of Moder-nity." In *Questions of Modernity,* edited by Timothy Mitchell, 1–34. Minneapolis: University of Minne-sota Press, 2000.

Mithat, Ahmet. *Ahbar-ı Asara Tamim-i Enzar: Edebi Eserlere Genel Bir Bakış.* Istanbul: İletişim, 2003.

———. *Felâtun Bey ile Râkım Efendi.* Istanbul: Yurttaş Kitabevi, 1960.

———. *Menfa—Sürgün Hatıraları.* Istan-bul: Kapı Yayınları, 2013.

———. *Türkisches Highlife: Erzählungen aus der Gesellschaft.* Translated by Ernst Seidel. Leipzig: Hesse & Becker, 1897.

Mommsen, Katharina. *Goethe und die arabische Welt.* Frankfurt am Main: Insel Verlag, 1988.

———. *Goethe und Diez: Quellenunter-suchungen zu Gedichten der Divan-Epoche.* Berlin: Akade-mie-Verlag, 1961.

———. *"Orient und Okzident sind nicht mehr zu trennen": Goethe und die Weltkulturen.* Göttingen: Wallstein Verlag, 2012.

Moran, Berna. *Türk Romanına Eleştirel Bir Bakış,* vol. 2, *Sabaahattin Ali'den Yusuf Atılgan'a.* Istanbul: İletişim Yayınları,1990.

Moretti, Franco. "Conjectures on World Literature." *New Left Review* 1 (January–February 2000): 54–68.

Mufti, Aamir. *Forget English! Oriental-isms and World Literatures.* Cambridge: Harvard University Press, 2016.

Müftüoğlu, Ahmet Hikmet. "Yeğenim." In *Haristan,* 235–42. Istanbul: İkdam Matbaası, 1324/1908.

Mühürcüoğlu, Korhan. "The *Alla Franca* Dandy; Modernity and the Novel in the Late 19th-Century Ottoman Empire." *British Journal of Middle Eastern Studies* (2018): 1–21.

Müller-Sievers, Helmut. *Desorien-tierung: Anatomie und Dichtung bei Georg Büchner.* Göttingen: Wall-stein Verlag, 2003.

Mutman, Mahmut. *"The Carriage Affair,* or the Birth of a National Hero."

Monograf: Edebiyat Eleştirisi Dergisi
11 (2019): 230–89.

Nicholls, Angus. "The 'Goethean' Discourses on *Weltliteratur* and the Origins of Comparative Literature: The Cases of Hugo Meltzl and Hutcheson Macaulay Posnett." *Seminar* 54, no. 2 (May 2018): 167–94.

"Nochmals deutsche Dichtungen in türkischer Sprache." *Osmanischer Lloyd* (December 1, 1917).

Oba, Ali Engin. *Türk Milliyetçiliğinin Doğuşu*. Ankara: İmge Kitabevi Yayınları, 1995.

Oruç, Fırat. "Rewriting the Legacy of the Turkish Exile of Comparative Literature: Philology and Nationalism in Istanbul, 1933–1946." *Journal of World Literature* 3, no. 3 (2018): 334–53.

Ötüken, Adnan, and Millî Kütüphane Bibliyografya Enstitüsü, eds. *Dünya Edebiyatından Tercümeler: Klasikler Bibliyografyası 1940–1966*. Ankara: Ayyıldız Matbaası, 1967.

Özgü, Melahat. *Göte'nin Cihan Edebiyatındaki Şahsiyeti*. Ankara: Cumhuriyet Halk Partisi, 1938.

Özkan, Hakan. "Turkish Literature Translated into German between 1990 and 2010." *Transeuropéennes* (2011): 1–15.

Paker, Saliha. "Changing Norms of the Target System: Turkish Translations of Greek Classics in Historical Perspective." In *Studies in Greek Linguistics: Proceedings of the 7th Linguistics Conference*, 411–26. Thessaloniki: The Aristotelian University of Thessaloniki, 1986.

———. "Ottoman Conceptions of Translation and its Practice: The 1897 'Classics Debate' as a Focus for Examining Change." In *Translating Others*, edited by Theo Hermans, 2:325–48. New York: Routledge, 2006.

———. "Terceme, Te'lîf ve Özgünlük Meselesi." In *Metnin Hâlleri: Osmanlı'da Telif, Tercüme ve Şerh*, edited by Hatice Aynur, Müjgan Çakır, Hanife Koncu, Selim S. Kuru, Ali Emre Özyıldırım, 36–71. Istanbul: Klasik Yayınları 2014.

———. "Translation as *Terceme* and *Nazire*: Culture-Bound Concepts and Their Implications for a Conceptual Framework for Research on Ottoman Translation History." In *Crosscultural Transgressions: Research Models in Translation Studies II; Historical and Ideological Issues*, edited by Theo Hermans, 120–43. Manchester: St. Jerome, 2002.

Parla, Jale. *Babalar ve Oğullar: Tanzimat Romanının Epistemolojik Temelleri*. Istanbul: İletişim 1990.

———. "Car Narratives: A Subgenre in Turkish Novel Writing." *South Atlantic Quarterly* 102, no. 2/3 (2003): 535–50.

———. "A Carriage Affair (Recaizade Mahmut Ekrem, Turkey, 1896)." In *The Novel*, vol. 1, *History, Geography, and Culture*, edited by Franco Moretti, 775–80. Princeton: Princeton University Press, 2006.

———. "The Object of Comparison." *Comparative Literary Studies* 41, no. 1 (2004): 116–25.

Petritsch, Ernst Dieter. "Die Wiener Turkologie vom 16. bis zum 18. Jahrhundert." In *Germano-Turcica: Zur Geschichte des Türkisch-Lernens in den deutschsprachigen Ländern*, edited by Klaus Kreiser, 25–40. Bamberg: Universitätsbibliothek, 1987.

Pınar, Nedret. "1900–1983 Yılları Arasında Türkçe'de Goethe ve Faust Tercümeleri Üzerinde Bir

İnceleme." PhD diss., İstanbul Üniversitesi, 1984.

Pischel, Richard. "Nachrichten über Angelegenheiten der Deutschen Morgenländischen Gesellschaft." *Zeitschrift der Deutschen Morgenländischen Gesellschaft* 46, no. 1 (1892): 1–53.

Pizer, John. *The Idea of World Literature: History and Pedagogical Practice.* Baton Rouge: Louisiana State University Press, 2006.

———. "Johann Wolfgang von Goethe: Origins and Relevance of *Weltliteratur.*" *The Routledge Companion to World Literature*, edited by Theo D'haen, David Damrosch, and Djelal Kadir, 3–11. New York: Routledge, 2011.

Polaschegg, Andrea. *Der andere Orientalismus: Regeln deutsch-morgenländischer Imagination im 19. Jahrhundert.* Berlin: Walter de Gruyter, 2005.

Remzi Bengi'ye Saygı: Elli Yıllık Kültür Emeği. Istanbul: Remzi Kitabevi, 1979.

Richter, Werner. "Deutsche Dichtungen in türkischer Sprache." *Osmanischer Lloyd* (December 1917).

Riemann, Wolfgang. "How Has Turkish Literature Been Received in Germany? Works Translated from Turkish into German in the Recent Years and Nowadays." TEDA, 2011.

Rosaldo, Renato. "Imperialist Nostalgia." *Representations* 26 (Spring 1989): 107–22.

Roshwald, Aviel. *Ethnic Nationalism and the Fall of Empires: Central Europe, Russia, and the Middle East, 1914–1923.* New York: Routledge, 2001.

Rotter, G. "Maslama b. ʿAbd-al-Malik b. Marwān." In *The Encyclopaedia of Islam*, vol. 6, *Mahk–Mid*, edited by C. E. Bosworth, E. van Donzel, B.

Lewis, and C. Pellat, 740. Leiden: E. J. Brill, 1991.

Roxburgh, David J. "Heinrich Friedrich Von Diez and His Eponymous Albums: Mss. Diez a. Fols. 70–74." *Muqarnas* 12 (1995): 112–36.

Said, Edward. *Orientalism.* London: Penguin Books, 2003.

———. *The World, the Text, and the Critic.* Cambridge: Harvard University Press, 1983.

Scherr, Johannes. *Bildersaal der Weltliteratur.* Vol. 1. Stuttgart: Verlag von A. Kröner, 1869.

Schleiermacher, Friedrich. "On the Different Methods of Translating." Translated by Susan Bernofsky. In *The Translation Studies Reader*, edited by Lawrence Venuti, 43–63. New York: Routledge, 2000.

———. "Ueber die verschiedenen Methoden des Uebersezens." In *Friedrich Schleiermacher's sämmtliche Werke, Part 3: Dr. Friedrich Schleiermacher's philosophische und vermischte Schriften*, 2:207–45. Berlin: S. Reimer, 1838.

Schneider, Helmut J. "The Facts of Life: Kleist's Challenge to Enlightenment Humanism (Lessing)." In *A Companion to the Works of Heinrich von Kleist*, edited by Bernd Fischer, 141–63. Rochester: Camden House, 2003.

Schrader, Friedrich. "Die Bezauberung des Aga." *Osmanischer Lloyd* 308 (December 24, 1913).

———. "Der Drang nach Osten." *Osmanischer Lloyd* (November 10, 1908).

———. "Einleitung: Ahmet Hikmet und sein Werk." In *Türkische Frauen*, by Ahmet Hikmet Müftüoğlu, translated by Friedrich Schrader, 1–9. Berlin: Mayer und Müller Verlag, 1907.

———. "Einleitung des Übersetzers." In *Das neue Turan: Ein türkisches*

Frauenschicksal, by Halide Edip Adıvar, translated by Friedrich Schrader, v–xi. Weimar: Gustav Kiepenheuer, 1916.

———. *Eine Flüchtlingsreise durch die Ukraine: Tagebuchblätter von meiner Flucht aus Konstantinopel.* Tübingen: Mohr, 1919.

———. "Das geistige Leben in der Türkei und das jetzige Regime." *Die neue Zeit* 18, no. 2 (1900): 548–55.

———. "Das Geschenk des Lebens: Eine Geschichte aus der alten Türkei." *Osmanischer Lloyd* (December 6, 1916).

———. "Das jungtürkische Lausanner Programm." *Die Neue Zeit* 18, no. 2 (1920): 6–11, 31–35.

———. "Konstantinopeler Meuterei." *März: Halbmonatsschrift für deutsche Kultur.* (April–June 1909): 169–80.

———. *Konstantinopel: Vergangenheit und Gegenwart.* Tübingen: Mohr, 1917.

———. "Der Kulturträger (Mein Neffe)." *Osmanischer Lloyd* (December 25, 1908).

———. "Die Kunstdenkmäler Konstantinopels." *Der neue Orient* 5 (1919): 302–4, 352–54.

———. "Literatur zur jüngsten Geschichte der Türkei." *Osmanischer Lloyd* (June 26, 1909).

———. "Eine Mutter: Türkischer Erzählung." *Osmanischer Lloyd* 306 (December 25, 1912).

———. "Namık Kemal Bey als Erzähler." *Osmanischer Lloyd* (November 1, 1917).

———. "Naqijje Xala." In *Türkische Frauen*, by Ahmet Hikmet Müftüoğlu, translated by Friedrich Schrader, 31-49. Berlin: Mayer und Müller Verlag, 1907.

———. "Neue Orient Literatur." *Osmanischer Lloyd* (December 23, 1916).

———. "Neutürkisches Schrifttum." *Das literarische Echo: Halbmonatsschrift für Literaturfreunde* 3 (1900): 1686–1690.

———. "Die osmanische Miniaturkunst." *Osmanischer Lloyd* (October 11, 1917).

———. "Tante Naqijje." *Osmanischer Lloyd* (December 25, 1908).

———. "Türkische Bibliothek." *Osmanischer Lloyd* (October 8, 1909).

———. "Türkische Dichtung." *Osmanischer Lloyd* (December 24, 1916).

———. "Die türkische Kultur." *Nord und Süd* 44, no. 174 (January–March 1920): 268–73.

———. "Das türkische Theater." *Osmanischer Lloyd* 55 (March 7, 1909).

———. "Vom Büchertisch." *Osmanischer Lloyd* (February 2, 1910).

———. "Vom Büchertisch." *Osmanischer Lloyd* (December 8, 1916).

———. "Vom goldenen Horn." In *Vorwärts* (Spring 1900): 414–16.

Schubert, Johannes. "Baron A. von Staël-Holstein." *Artibus Asiae* 7, no. 1/4 (1937): 227–29.

Schührer, Susanne. "Türkeistämmige Personen in Deutschland: Erkenntnisse aus der Repräsentativuntersuchung 'Ausgewählte Migrantengruppen in Deutschland 2015' (RAM)." Forschungszentrums des Bundesamtes Working Paper 81. Nürnberg: Bundesamt für Migration und Flüchtlinge, 2018.

Schutz, Alfred, and Thomas Luckmann. *The Structure of the Life-World.* Translated by Richard M. Zaner and H. Tristram Engelhardt. London: Heinemann Educational Books, 1974.

Schwarz, Hans-Günther. *Der Orient und die Ästhetik der Moderne.* Munich: Ludicium, 2003.

Seeba, Hinrich C. "'Germany: A Literary Concept': The Myth of National

Literature." *German Studies Review* 17, no. 2 (1994): 353–69.

Selçuk, İlhan. "Remzi ve Kitab Evi." In *Remzi Bengi'ye Saygı: Elli Yıllık Kültür Emeği*, 86–88. Istanbul: Remzi Kitabevi, 1979.

Seviner, Zeynep. "Between Languages: Translative Acts in Sabahattin Ali's *Comprehensive Germanistan Travelogue*." *Türkisch-deutsche Studien: Jahrbuch* 8 (Spring 2017): 81–96.

Sevük, İsmail Habib. *Avrupa Edebiyatı ve Biz: Garpten Tercümeler*. Istanbul: Remzi Kitabevi, 1940.

Seyhan, Azade. "German Academic Exiles in Istanbul: Translation as the *Bildung* of the Other." In *Nation, Language, and the Ethics of Translation*, edited by Sandra Bermann and Michael Wood, 274–88. Princeton: Princeton University Press, 2005.

———. "Is Orientalism in Retreat or in for a New Treat? Halide Edip Adivar and Emine Sevgi Özdamar Write Back." *Seminar* 41, no. 3 (2005): 209–25.

———. "Saved by Translation: German Academic Culture in Turkish Exile." In *Tradition, Tension, and Translation in Turkey*, edited by Şehnaz Tahir Gürçaglar, Saliha Paker, and John Milton, 107–24. Philadelphia: John Benjamins, 2015.

———. *Tales of Crossed Destinies: The Modern Turkish Novel in a Comparative Context*. New York: Modern Language Association of America, 2008.

Shaw, Stanford J. *Between Old and New: The Ottoman Empire under Sultan Selim III 1789–1807*. Cambridge: Harvard University Press, 1971.

Shaw, Stanford J., and Ezel Kural Shaw. *Reform, Revolution, and Republic: The Rise of Modern Turkey, 1808–1975*. Vol. 2 of *History of the Ottoman Empire and Modern Turkey*. Cambridge: Cambridge University Press, 1977.

Simon, Sherry. *Cities in Translation: Intersections of Language and Memory*. New York: Routledge, 2012.

Smith, Anthony D. *The Ethnic Origins of Nations*. Oxford: Blackwell, 1988.

Spivak, Gayatri Chakravorty. *An Aesthetic Education in the Era of Globalization*. Cambridge: Harvard University Press, 2012.

"Statistics TEDA." TEDA. Republic of Turkey Ministry of Culture and Tourism. https://teda.ktb.gov.tr/EN-252217/statistics-teda.html.

Stegmaier, Werner. *Philosophie der Orientierung*. Berlin: Walter de Gruyter, 2008.

Stein, Heidi. "Zur Geschichte türkischer Studien in Leipzig (von 1612 bis ins 20. Jahrhundert)." In *Germano-Turcica: Zur Geschichte des Türkisch-Lernens in den deutschsprachigen Ländern*, edited by Klaus Kreiser, 41–47. Bamberg: Universitätsbibliothek, 1987.

Stephan-Emmrich, Manja, and Philipp Schröder. "Introduction: Mobilities, Boundaries, and Travelling Ideas Beyond Central Asia and the Caucasus; A Translocal Perspective." In *Mobilities, Boundaries, and Travelling Ideas: Rethinking Translocality Beyond Central Asia and the Caucasus*, edited by Manja Stephan-Emmrich and Philipp Schröder, 27–60. Cambridge: Open Book Publishers, 2018.

Strauss, Johann. "Who Read What in the Ottoman Empire (19th-20th Centuries)?" *Middle Eastern Literatures* 6, no. 1 (2003): 39–76.

Strich, Fritz. *Goethe and World Literature*. Translated by C. A. M. Sym.

London: Routledge and Kegan
Paul, 1949.
———. *Goethe und die Weltliteratur*.
Bern: Francke Verlag, 1957.
Sullivan, Heather. "The Dangerous
Quest for Nature Narratives in
Goethe's *Werther*: A Reading of the
Ruptured Monologue and the
Ruptured Body." *Interdisciplinary
Studies in Literature and Environ-
ment* 14, no. 2 (Summer 2007):
1–23.
Taglia, Stefano. *Intellectuals and Reform
in the Ottoman Empire: The Young
Turks on the Challenges of Moder-
nity*. New York: Routledge, 2015.
Tahir Gürçağlar, Şehnaz. *The Politics and
Poetics of Translation in Turkey,
1923–1960*. New York: Rodopi,
2008.
———. "The Translation Bureau Revis-
ited: Translation as Symbol." In
*Apropos of Ideology: Translation
Studies on Ideology—Ideologies in
Translation Studies*, edited by María
Calzada Pérez, 113–29. Manchester:
St. Jerome, 2003.
Tanpınar, Ahmet Hamdi. "Bizde Roman
I." In *Edebiyat Üzerine Makaleler*,
33–37. Istanbul: Millî Eğitim
Basımevi, 1969.
———. "Millî Bir Edebiyata Doğru." In
Edebiyat Üzerine Makaleler, 77–85.
Istanbul: Millî Eğitim Basımevi,
1969.
———. *XIX. Asır Türk Edebiyatı Tarihi*.
Istanbul: Yapı Kredi Yayınları,
2006.
Taşdelen, Esra. "Literature as a Mirror of
History: A Comparative Study of
the Historical Fictions of Ahmet
Hikmet Müftüoğlu (1870–1927) and
Jurji Zaydan (1861–1914)." PhD
diss., University of Chicago, 2014.
Tekinalp, Munis. *Türkismus und
Pantürkismus*. Weimar: Gustav
Kiepenheuer, 1915.

Tevetoğlu, Fethi. *Ahmed Hikmet
Müftüoğlu: Hayatı ve Eserleri*.
Ankara: Kültür ve Turizm Bakan-
lığı Yayınları, 1986.
Timuroğlu, Senem. "Women's Nation
from Ottoman to the New Republic
in Fatma Aliye and Halide Edip
Adıvar's Writing." In *Women Telling
Nations (Women Writers in
History)*, edited by Amelia Sanz,
Francesca Scott, and Suzan van
Dijk, 431–50. New York: Rodopi,
2014.
Tuna, Fehmi Yahya. *Dünya Edebiyatı
Tarihi: Tefekkür Tarihinin Ana
Hatları*. Istanbul: Üçler Basımevi,
1948.
Tunaya, Tarık Z. *Türkiye'nin Siyasi
Hayatında Batılılaşma Hareketleri*.
Istanbul: Yedigün Matbaası, 1960.
Türker Tekin, Nil. "Giriş." In *Peşte
Günleri: Ahmet Hikmet Müftüoğ-
lu'nun Özel Mektupları*, 11–27.
Istanbul: Ege Yayınları, 2011.
"Die Türkische Bibliothek." Unionsver-
lag. http://www.unionsverlag.com
/info/text.asp?text_id=2953.
Tymoczko, Maria. *Translation in a Post-
colonial Context: Early Irish
Literature in English Translation*.
Manchester: St. Jerome, 1999.
Ülken, Hilmi Ziya. "Maksad." *İnsan* 1,
no. 1 (1938): 1–2.
———. "Şark ve Garp." In *Millet ve Tarih
Şuuru*, 11–16. Istanbul: Pulhan
Matbaası 1948.
———. "Tanzimat'a Karşı." In *Millet ve
Tarih Şuuru*, 22–32. Istanbul:
Pulhan Matbaası 1948.
———. *Uyanış Devirlerinde Tercümenin
Rolü*. Istanbul: Vakit, 1935.
Venuti, Lawrence. *Contra Instrumental-
ism: A Translation Polemic*. Lincoln:
University of Nebraska Press, 2019.
———. "Hijacking Translation: How
Comp Lit Continues to Suppress

Translated Texts." *boundary 2* 43, no. 2 (May 2016): 179–204.

———. *The Translator's Invisibility: A History of Translation*. New York: Routledge: 2008.

Vogt, Emily A. "*Civilisation* and *Kultur*: Keywords in the History of French and German Citizenship." *Ecumene* 3, no. 2 (April 1996): 125–45.

"Von Istanbul nach Hakkâri." Unionsverlag. http://www.unionsverlag .com/info/title.asp?title_id=2347.

"Vortragsabend im Ausflugsverein." *Osmanischer Lloyd* 295 (December 17, 1909).

Watts, Ian. *The Rise of the Novel: Studies in Defoe, Richardson and Fielding*. Berkeley: University of California Press, 2001.

Wippermann, Wolfgang. *Der "deutsche Drang nach Osten": Ideologie und Wirklichkeit eines politischen Schlagwortes*. Darmstadt: Wissenschaftliche Buchgesellschaft, 1981.

Yalçın, Hüseyin Cahit. *Edebî Hatıralar*. Istanbul: Akşam Kitaphanesi, 1935.

Yılmaz, Simge. "Under the Shadow of the Turkological Legacy: The Current Profile of Translators and Publishers in Literary Translations from Turkish into German." *World Literature Studies* 1, no. 12 (2020): 67–81.

Yücel, Hasan Ali. "3 Temmuz 1941, Devlet Konservatuvarı İlk Mezunlarını Verirken." *Güzel Sanatlar* 3 (1941): 3–4.

———. *İyi Vatandaş İyi Insan*. Istanbul: İş Bankası Kültür Yayınları, 2011.

Zantop, Susanne. *Colonial Fantasies: Conquest, Family, and Nation in Precolonial Germany, 1770–1780*. Durham: Duke University Press, 1997.

Index